The Role of the European Investment Bank

SHEILA LEWENHAK

CROOM HELM
London & Canberra

© 1982 Sheila Lewenhak
Croom Helm Ltd, 2-10 St John's Road, London SW11

British Library Cataloguing in Publication Data

Lewenhak, Sheila
 The role of the European Investment Bank.
 1. European Investment Bank—History
 I. Title
 332.1'532   HG3881

 ISBN 0-7099-1613-2

Printed and bound in Great Britain by
Biddles Ltd, Guildford and King's Lynn

C O N T E N T S

LIST OF TABLES

LIST OF APPENDICES

LIST OF MAPS

LIST OF FIGURES

ACKNOWLEDGEMENTS

The material for the book has come largely from the EIB's own
Reports, Bulletins and other publications, with additional
information from the Reports of the US Federal Reserve Board,
Bank of International Settlements, IMF, and OECD. I am
grateful to the OECD's Department of the Environment Urban
Affairs Directorate for permitting me to use material on
Noise pollution ahead of publication so that it could be included in the book. EEC Commission Reports and official
publications have been other important sources, as have the
Financial Times, Times, and some other journals. I should
like to thank the Financial Times and the New Africa Magazine
for permission to use two short quotations. All sources are
duly acknowledged in the footnotes and here with thanks.

In addition, this brief survey could not have been written
without help from a number of people whom I would like to
thank.

EUROPEAN INVESTMENT BANK
Herr K.G. Schmidt, Head of Information : Herr W. Thill,
Deputy Manager, Finance & Treasury Department : Signor F.
Barilli, Technical Advisor : Mr. Steven and Mr. Brian
Morris, London Office.

COMMISSION OF THE EUROPEAN COMMUNITIES
Directorate-General II - Economic & Financial Affairs
M. Jean-Claude Morel, Head of Directorate B, Economic
Structure & Development : M. Petit-Laurent.
Directorate-General V - Employment & Social Affairs
Herr Detlef Fehrs, Directorate A, General Social Policy
Guidelines : Mr. Stewart.
Environment & Consumer Protection Service
Mr. Lawrence, Legal Advisor, General Environment & Consumer
Protection : Signor Delbino, Transport : M. Van Caeneghem,
Nuclear Energy : Mr. Marcus, Liaison with EIB.

O E C D
Department of the Environment - Mr. Jim McNeill, Director :
M. Ariel Alexandre, Head of Urban Affairs Directorate :
M. Dorin, Head of Water Directorate.
International Energy Agency - Mr. Mowinckel : Herr Rolf
Gradin, Head of Energy Conservation.
Directorate of Food, Agriculture & Fisheries Division -
M. Simantov, Director.

Valuable help was also received from:

M. Hubert David, Secretary General, European Environmental
Bureau : Maître Dominique Finon, Director, Institut Econo-
mique et Juridique University of Grenoble : Mr. Robin Grove-
White, Director, Council for the Preservation of Rural Eng-
land : Mr. Steven Hahn, Energy Consultant : Mr. Nigel Haigh,
Director, Institute for European Environmental Policy :
Industrial Common Ownership Finance Ltd. : Minheer Jurjen
Kenning, Stichting Natuur en Milieu : Mr. Roger Kohn, Press
Officer, Intergovernmental Maritime Consultative Organisa-
tion, London : Dr. Macrory, Centre for Environmental Tech-
nology, Imperial College, London : Dr. Colin Marsh, Depart-
ment of Engineering, University of Newcastle-upon-Tyne :
Dr. Gerd Michelsen, Öko Institut, Freiburg : Mss. Ursula
Meyer & Sarah Thomas in respect of technical translations :
M. F. Roelants du Vivier, Secretary General, Interenvironne-
ment Wallonie : Friends of the Earth in London, Paris and
West Germany.

My thanks are also due to the staffs of:

Official Publications Department, British Library : Library
of Senate House, University of London : Hillingdon Public
Libraries, particularly to Ms. Mary Jenkins, AFL. : the City
and Business Library : Ms. Emma Hart, Mr. G. Pau and other
members of the Library and Information Service at the European Commission, London : Reference Library, Westminster
City Council : Statistics and Market Intelligence Library,
Department of Trade.

Special thanks are due to Dr. David Hitchcock, Asst. Course
Leader, Senior Lecturer in Hydrology, Central London Polytechnic, for help with the chapter on water supplies and
matters relating to the aquatic environment, and the very
able preparation of Maps and Figures by Ms. Rosemary Glosby,
Dip. Geog., Central London Polytechnic.

I should also like to thank the Sackville Copy Service for
duplicating and photocopying : Christian Andrews, Pat Bolton,
Hilary Boorer, Kim Chisholm, Lynne Kaye-Plight and Heather
Laughton for typing the initial research report : Mrs. Jean
Palmer of the Swift Typing & Duplicating Service, Broadstairs

for her kindness, patience and expertise in preparing the
typescript for the book and for setting out the tables.

The research, on which this book is based, was carried out
from the London office of <u>Earth Resources Research Ltd</u>.   I
should like to express my gratitude to <u>Earth Resources
Research Ltd</u>. and to the <u>European Cultural Foundation</u> for
funding the research and to Minheer Hemmo Muntingh and the
members of the <u>European Parliament Socialist Group</u> and <u>ERR
Ltd</u>. for their help in funding the preparation of the book.
I should also like to thank the members of ERR Ltd.: David
Baldock, Director, for editorial help : Paul Carnell, Barbara
Dinham, Monica Hayman, Colin Hines, Caren Levy, Hugh Miall,
Francois Nectoux, David Olivier and Mark Opperman for advice
and comment.

Finally, I should like to thank my husband, H. K. Lewenhak,
B.Com., for his helpful comments and criticisms of drafts
and for a great deal of other help and support which enabled
me to do the research and write the book.

                                        Sheila Lewenhak.

N O T E:

The European Investment Bank is the European
Economic Community's principal long-term financing
institution.   It is directly under the control of
the governments of member states.   Yet it is one of
the least familiar Community bodies.

This book considers the EIB's borrowing and
lending operations over the twenty-two years, 1958
to 1980, and some of the environmental and social
effects of its lending activities.   Since the Community countries' interests extend to non-EEC states,
many of them former colonies or dependencies, in
Chapters 14 and 15, some consideration has also been
given to the Bank's operations beyond EEC boundaries.
However, because of limitations of space in an outline such as this, it has not been possible to deal
exhaustively with any one of the Bank's operations.

In a summary of financing over a twenty-two
year period, statistics must be interpreted cautiously because of continual fluctuations in the exchange
rates of currencies and because of price movements,
as the EIB itself stresses in its <u>Annual Reports</u>.
Figures given should be regarded merely as indications of trends in financing, rather than complete
financial statements.   As the EIB's activities are
on-going, by the time this book is published, total
amounts of financing will already exceed those shown
here.

It is hoped that this short study may shed some
light on an important EEC institution which deserves
to be better known by those interested in changes in
EEC member states' infrastructure and industry.

Chapter 1

THE ORIGINS, CHARACTER AND STRUCTURE OF THE EUROPEAN INVESTMENT BANK

It is generally agreed that large-scale investment in infra-structure and industry has considerable impact on the environment and on employment. This has been borne out within the European Economic Community countries of west Europe over the last quarter of a century, with the growth of motorways, energy projects, especially nuclear power, water supply schemes and telecommunications. There has been rapid growth in petrochemicals, and a decline in iron and steel production while southern peasant economies have been disrupted. The major investor in infra-structure and large-scale industrial projects for the EEC has been the little-known and little-publicised European Investment Bank. In order to comprehend developments in employment and the environment within the Community and its Associated States, it is essential to understand how the European Investment Bank operates and the policies it has been pursuing.

a) THE ORIGINS OF THE EUROPEAN INVESTMENT BANK

The European Investment Bank is the main long-term financing institution of the European Economic Community. It was established by Articles 3(j) and 129 of the Treaty of Rome which created the Community in 1958. The European Investment Bank is the chief EEC institution channelling into Community countries finance from the world's capital markets.

Besides its role as the Community's major source of loans for public developmental projects in member states, it is also of considerable importance in providing investment for private industrial development since it is mandated to step in with loans when no other source of finance is available on 'reasonable terms'. It has therefore been the

1

TABLE 1a: DEVELOPMENT OF EEC FUNDS AND LENDING FACILITIES
OTHER THAN THOSE FOR AGRICULTURE

1948 Organisation of European Economic Co-operation
set up to administer the European Economic Recovery Programme and to allocate Marshall Aid

1950 European Payments Union/Marshall Aid to UK
suspended

1951 European Coal & Steel Community established[++]

1953 European Productivity Agency (OEEC) specialising in industrial relations, marketing,
farming methods and technical aid to less
developed areas of Europe

1955 European Monetary Agreement supersedes European
Payments Union - OEEC countries agree to make
currencies freely convertible

1956 OEEC countries have considerably surpassed pre-
war levels in most sectors of production

1957 European Nuclear Agency established by OEEC

1958 Becomes Euratom[++]
Currency Convertibility realised
European Development Fund (Extra-Community
Countries)

1959 Spain enters OEEC

1961 OEEC transformed into wider OECD

1962	
1963	
1967	
1971	
1974	
1975	
1976	
1978	
1979	

TREATY OF ROME

EUROPEAN ECONOMIC COMMUNITY SET UP

Commission of the European Economic Community — European Investment Bank

European Social Fund

European Agricultural Guidance and Guarantee Fund established

European Development Fund

[++]ECSC and Euratom brought under Commission of the European Communities

Agreement - Community to have its own financial resources

*Aid for Hydrocarbon Development

*European Regional Development Fund

*Aid for Uranium Prospection in EEC Territory

Loans for Exploiting Alternative Energy Sources

Demonstration Projects for Energy Saving

New Community Instrument for Borrowing and Lending (NCI) or Ortoli Facility

European Monetary System

*Non-repayable grants and subsidies

decisive factor in whether or not certain projects could proceed.

The Treaty of Rome laid down the EIB's complete autonomy from other Community institutions as Table 1a shows, and it was given its own Statute.[1] It is a separate legal entity from the EEC Commission but obviously the two institutions are linked since both are under the control of the EEC countries' governments and they maintain liaison with one another.

As the Bank pointed out in its first Annual Report in 1958, by creating not another fund, but a bank, the six member states:

> set aside more direct financial intervention methods which no doubt would not in the long run have enabled adequate resources to be raised.   They particularly wished the promotion of investments...to be carried out by existing banking houses....

That is, they wished to utilise the commercial world banking system, with the EIB providing 'an additional source of financing which might prove decisive' in creating or furthering projects they wanted realised.

Thus, the European Investment Bank, unlike a number of other EEC funds, is not a 'caisse' wholly dependent on contributions from member states.[2] The distinction is important since the autonomy of the Bank rests partly on the fact that it has to provide most of its own funds.*

b) REASONS FOR CREATING A EUROPEAN INVESTMENT BANK

Article 130 of the Treaty of Rome defined the purpose of the European Investment Bank as:

> To contribute to the balanced and smooth development of the Common Market in the interest of the Community.[3]

The six founding states, The Federal Republic of Germany, France, Italy, Belgium, Holland and Luxembourg, were anxious to provide financial help to the least developed of their regions.   While the

---

* Euratom and the European Coal & Steel Community were also initially independent but both have subsequently been integrated under the EEC (Table 1a).

TABLE 1b: Capital Subscriptions by EEC Member Countries to the European Investment Bank
(in millions of EIB units of account : see Chapter 2 and Appendix 2A)

	INITIAL SUBSCRIPTION 1958			BY DECISION OF BOARD OF GOVERNORS ON 26 APRIL, 1971		ENLARGEMENT OF THE COMMUNITY (1 January, 1973)			BY DECISION OF BOARD OF GOVERNORS ON 10 JULY, 1975		BY DECISION OF BOARD OF GOVERNORS ON 19 JUNE, 1978		BY DECISION OF THE BOARD OF GOVERNORS ON 15 JUNE, 1981 TO TAKE EFFECT FROM 31 DECEMBER, 1981		
	Distribution according to Member States (rounded %)	Subscribed Capital	Paid up Capital	Subscribed Capital	Paid up Capital	Distribution according to Member States (rounded %)	Subscribed Capital	Paid up Capital	Subscribed Capital	Capital paid up and to be paid up	Subscribed Capital	Capital paid up and to be paid up	Subscribed Capital	Capital paid up and to be paid up	Distribution according to Member States (rounded %)
WEST GERMANY	30.0	300.0	75.0	450.0	90.0	22.22	450.0	90.0	787.5	123.75	1,575.000	202.500	3,150.000	320.625	21.875
FRANCE	30.0	300.0	75.0	450.0	90.0	22.22	450.0	90.0	786.5	123.75	1,575.000	202.500	3,150.000	320.625	21.875
UNITED KINGDOM	-	-	-	-	-	22.22	450.0	90.0	787.5	123.75	1,575.000	202.500	3,150.000	320.625	21.875
ITALY	24.0	240.0	60.0	360.0	72.0	17.78	360.0	72.0	630.0	99.0	1,260.000	162.000	2,520.000	256.505	17.50
BELGIUM	8.65	86.5	21.625	129.75	25.95	5.85	118.5	23.7	207.375	32.5875	414.750	53.325	829.500	84.43	5.76
NETHERLANDS	7.15	71.5	17.875	107.25	21.45	5.85	118.5	23.7	207.375	32.5875	414.750	53.325	829.500	84.43	5.76
DENMARK	-	-	-	-	-	2.96	60.0	12.0	105.0	16.5	210.00	27.000	420.000	42.75	2.925
IRELAND	-	-	-	-	-	0.74	15.0	3.0	26.25	4.125	52.500	6.750	105.000	10.6875	0.729
LUXEMBOURG	0.2	2.0	0.5	3.0	0.6	0.15	3.0	0.6	5.25	0.825	10.500	1.350	21.000	2.1375	0.146
GREECE	-	-	-	-	-	-	-	-	-	-	-	-	225.000	22.90	1.563
T O T A L	100.0	1,000.0	250.0	1,500.0	300.0	100.0	2,025.0	405.0	3,543.75	556.875	7,087.500	911.250	14,400.000	1,465.715	100.00

SOURCE: EIB 1958-1978, 63 : EIB 1979 Annual Report, 72.*
EIB Press Release, 15 June, 1981.

*Each member state contributed its share of paid-up capital in its own currency. The contributions are paid in an agreed number of equal instalments over a fixed period of time, e.g. 10% of the 1978 increase to be paid in 8 equal instalments on 30 April and 31 October of the years 1980-83 : 7.5% of the 1981 increase is to be paid in 8 equal half-yearly instalments starting on 30 April, 1984, so that the total will be wholly paid up by October 1988.

NOTE TO TABLE 1b: The original capital subscribed by the six member states in 1958 and the increased subscriptions in 1971 and new subscriptions in 1973 were both expressed in terms of the original gold/US $ value of the EIB's unit of account. The 1975 subscriptions were calculated on the new system of the sum of the fixed amounts of member states' currencies, then still linked through the connection with the IMF's Special Drawing Right to the old gold parity. The 1978 and 1981 subscriptions were entirely on the new Euro system after the gold parity had been dispensed with. The important point is the overall increase in capital subscribed by member states which gave the EIB more funds with which to operate on the international financial markets.

Community was controlled by national governments of the member states, its integration and growth depended on diminishing national concepts and emphasising regional ones. In this way a single political and economic entity, it was said, would emerge in place of a collection of nation states. The founding member countries also wanted to overcome low productivity in various economic sectors, to improve inadequate parts of their communication systems and to increase electrical power in order to promote greater industrial development and higher living standards. Because they wanted to create new economic activities and installations on a supra-national Community scale, big investments would be needed.

The 'six' constituted a part of the world in which banking was highly developed and where the rate of investment was very high. However, during the preparation of the Treaty of Rome it became evident that there was a danger that depressed areas or economic sectors would not be able to find sufficient financial resources through the existing banks in the EEC to achieve improvements. Through the normal commercial mechanisms funds would be attracted to successful rather than deprived or unsuccessful areas and enterprises. As the EIB explained:

> At Community level, and along the line of action of the Community, this bank would be able to examine these new problems of financing in common and help to solve them.[4]

c) THE FUNDS OF THE EUROPEAN INVESTMENT BANK

In order to create the European Investment Bank, the governments of the six original EEC countries, the Federal Republic of Germany, France, Italy, Belgium, the Netherlands and Luxembourg, subscribed its initial capital from their national treasuries (see Table 1b). When Britain, Denmark and Ireland joined the Community in 1973 and Greece in 1981, the allocation of the Bank's subscribed capital was altered because each of these new member states provided further funds.[5] Consequently, each member state paid a smaller percentage of the EIB's total subscribed capital. There will be a similar adjustment when any other country joins the Community.

The Bank's subscribed capital was also increased by existing member states in 1973, 1975, 1978 and 1981 to enable it to maintain or expand its operations on the world's financial markets and to take account of inflation.

Only a proportion of the total amounts of capital subscribed by member states is ever actually paid over. The rest remains in the form of guarantees. While the ratio of paid-up to subscribed capital has fallen progressively from 25 per cent in 1958[6] to 9.8 per cent in 1981, i.e. by well over half, the actual amounts of cash have risen because of increases in the amounts of subscribed capital. The capital, both paid-up and guaranteed, besides being an important resource in itself, helped to establish the credit-worthiness of the EIB in international markets, so that loans it floated to finance Community projects have readily attracted investors. In addition, a reserve fund of up to 10 per cent of the subscribed capital was built up.[7] Meanwhile, the assets, which the guaranteed capital represents, remain at the disposal of member governments and can be used either in financial markets to earn more money through interest, or to buy capital assets.

The Bank has been helped to build up its reserves because the member states charge no interest on the capital they subscribe. In addition, the Bank is non-profit-making. Together with the very high credit standing which the Bank has achieved, these factors have enabled it to keep interest on its loans low. The EIB uses the paid-up portion of the capital mainly to buy interest-bearing stock, thus generating income for itself. The capital subscribed by member states cannot, however, be given as collateral security and is not attachable. The subscribed capital is also the factor limiting the amounts outstanding in loans and guarantees. These amounts must never exceed 250 per cent of the subscribed capital.

In return for subscribed capital, EEC member states and some countries outside the Community obtain low interest loans repayable over a long term of years.

An immediate and obvious difficulty for an institution representing a number of different countries is that each of them has its own currency. Moreover, their individual currencies are not stable but rise and fall in value in terms of the currencies of other states, in this case both inside and outside the EEC. To take account of this, the EIB, like any international bank or multinational company, has adopted the established practice of using a standardised unit of account which provides a

single medium of accounting for financial transactions and for the assets and liabilities of international organisations. It may also be used to
lessen the effects of variations in currency values
on international lenders to the Bank (see Chapter 2).

d) THE BANK'S MANAGEMENT STRUCTURE

Despite 23 years of often frenzied activity,
the European Investment Bank has maintained a simple
structure, as the diagram on page 8 shows. This is
in contrast to the Commission of the European Communities which, as Table la shows, has not only
absorbed existing Community institutions and created
new ones, but has also set up new funds and lending
instruments, together with a wide range of
specialist departments.

i) The Bank's Board of Governors

The European Investment Bank is the only bank
in the western world directly controlled by the
governments of a group of countries. Its Board of
Governors is composed of the Finance Ministers of
the EEC member states. Therefore, when there is a
change of government through an election or there
is a reshuffle of government ministers affecting the
finance minister, there is change in the EIB's
governor representing that state. Consequently,
the Bank's Board of Governors has included some
famous names, for example: Dennis Healey (March
1974-May 1979); Sir Geoffrey Howe (May 1979--);
Franz Josef Strauss (December 1966-October 1969);
Helmut Schmidt, now Chancellor Schmidt, of the
Federal Republic of Germany (July 1972-May 1974);
and Valéry Giscard d'Estaing, who later became
President of France and who was an EIB governor for
two terms (January 1962-January 1966 and June 1969-
May 1974). A member state may appoint more than
one governor.
It is then, the Finance Ministers of the EEC
member states, changing in response to national
political changes, who lay down the lending policies
of the European Investment Bank. Direct governmental control of the EIB is another determinant of
the Bank's autonomy within the Community.
The Board of Governors' functions[8] are to
appoint and remove members of the Board of Directors
and Management Committee and to fix the Directors'
salaries. It is they who lay down credit policy
and priorities for financial aid through the EIB's
low interest loans. The Governors must also "in-
terpret or supplement...the directives laid down at

8 Fig. 1a:

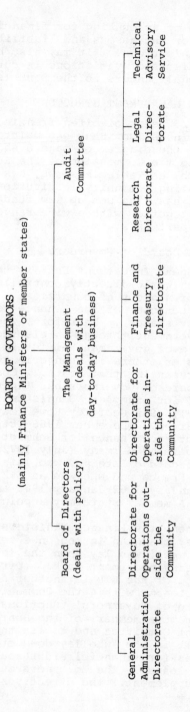

Structure of the European Investment Bank
as at June 1981

BOARD OF GOVERNORS

(mainly Finance Ministers of member states)

Board of Directors
(deals with policy)

The Management
(deals with
day-to-day business)

Audit
Committee

General
Administration
Directorate

Directorate
for
Operations out-
side the
Community

Directorate for
Operations in-
side the
Community

Finance and
Treasury
Directorate

Research
Directorate

Legal
Direc-
torate

Technical
Advisory
Service

SOURCE: EIB, 1980 Annual Report, 6-7.

the request of a member state or of the EEC as a
whole or ex officio.[19]

Tensions may arise on the Board due to differing national policies and between the aims of a
supra-national Community and national interests of
each member state.

To take account of national differences of view
the Board of Governors has a voting procedure.
General decisions are taken by majority vote.   But
in some instances, a 'qualified majority' is called
for, as it is in the EEC Council, when votes of the
member states are 'weighted'.   Originally, weightings were:

West Germany	..	4	Belgium	..	2
France	..	4	Netherlands	..	2
Italy	..	4	Luxembourg	..	1

When the three new members: the UK, Denmark and its
province of Greenland, and Ireland joined in 1973,
followed by Greece in 1981, a similar principle
applied.   The weighting now used is:

West Germany	..	10	Belgium	..	5
France	..	10	Netherlands	..	5
Italy	..	10	Denmark	..	3
U.K.	..	10	Ireland	..	3
Greece	..	5	Luxembourg	..	2

Weightings are determined by size of populations.
It follows that countries with the smallest populations are at the greatest disadvantage when trying
to secure majority support for policies they favour.

ii)   The Board of Directors

The Board of Governors chooses the Board of
Directors from among persons of 'indisputable independence and competence', from Treasury and other
government departments, financial institutions such
as state banks and, more rarely, from industrial
organisations and private banks.   It may remove
them only where they no longer fulfil the conditions
necessary for the exercise of their functions as EIB
Directors, or should it find itself unable to
approve the Directors' Annual Report on the Bank.
In general, Directors from official institutions remain at the EIB over the full term of their appointment, which is five years, and are sometimes re-
appointed, whereas those from more specialist
industrial or financial bodies, who are brought in
at a moment of crisis, do not stay once effective

9

measures have been taken.

The Directors from some countries are assisted by 'Alternates'. The numbers of both were increased when the three new countries joined in 1973 and now are allocated as follows:

	Directors	Alternatives (i.e. Deputies)
Fed. Republic of Germany ..	3	-
France	3	2
Italy	3	2
U.K.	3	2
Belgium	1	-
Denmark	1	1
Netherlands	1	1
Luxembourg	1	1
Ireland	1	-
Greece	1	-
Nominated by EEC Commission	1	1

As in the case of the weighting of votes, the criterion applied in the allocation of numbers of Directors is population size, and not level of financial contributions.

Within the overall policies laid down by the Governors/Finance Ministers, the Bank's Directors have exclusive powers over granting loans and guarantees. They also fix interest rates for the EIB's loans. Their decisions on loan applications are also guided by the detailed assessments made by the Bank's permanent staff. In the matter of raising funds for the Bank, on the other hand, the Directors have complete discretion. They have the sole authority to authorise borrowing operations by the EIB on financial markets. Their initiatives extend to making proposals to the Governors for policy changes concerning the Bank's funds and financial arrangements, for example, increases in member states' subscriptions of capital and methods of funding high risk operations (see Chapters 14 & 15). In respect of raising funds for the EIB, their functions are similar to those of the Commission of the European Communities in submitting proposals for action to Councils of Ministers.

iii) The Management Committee

The permanent staff of the Bank and the Board of Directors are closely linked since the Chairman and Vice-Chairmen also head the EIB's Management Committee as its President and Vice-Presidents. Unlike the other Directors and Alternates, they are employed full-time.

The Management Committee and other full-time staff, like that of any other bank, are responsible for the day-to-day running and control of the EIB, 'preparing decisions for the Board of Directors and then carrying them out.[10]

e) THE CHARACTER OF THE EUROPEAN INVESTMENT BANK

Whatever the differences in interests between member states and between any one of them and the Community, the Bank claims staff owe their first loyalty to it, a supra-national institution. It has specifically stated:

> Whatever national or other commitments they may have, the Directors of the European Investment Bank...are responsible solely to the Bank.... [11]

The extent to which national considerations are in fact subordinated to those of the EEC in the Bank's operations must, for the moment, remain a matter of speculation. Its discreet image has, however, helped to insulate it from public democratic debate. Indeed, many people do not know that it exists.

The people selected to head both the Board of Directors and the EIB's Management Committee have experience in official banks and public authorities. They belong to the 'establishments' of their respective countries, and have generally been of an age to have the requisite experience of traditional economics and banking practice. Changes in the world's economy and economic balance of power, which have occurred with increasing rapidity during the 1970s and early 1980s, have tested their banking expertise and required from them changes in attitudes.

There has been one further strand determining the character and policies of the European Investment Bank, the strong links, built up before 1958, between the United States of America and West European countries, including the six countries that formed the EEC (see Table 1a). This fact is essential to an understanding of EEC monetary policy and the European Investment Bank's operations. [12]

The Organisation of European Economic Cooperation (OEEC), set up in 1948, was a forerunner, not only of the EEC, but also of the wider Organisa-

tion for Economic Co-operation and Development
(OECD). (See Table 1a.) It was in 1959-60 that
representatives of the OEEC countries, which included the initial six members of the Community,
together with the USA, Canada and the Commission of
the European Community, held conferences which
transformed the OEEC into the OECD as from September
1961.[13] So the connection between the Community and
the OECD was very close right from the start.

In addition, the Community decided to maintain
links with colonies and former colonies of member
states (see Chapters 14 and 15). From the outset,
this policy, combined with the EIB's operations on
money markets throughout the world, gave it not
merely an international, but a global character.

f) CONCLUSION

As an international institution, the European
Investment Bank is beginning to approach the scale
of the International Bank for Reconstruction and
Development, known as the World Bank. While the
latter funds only Third World projects and has 134
member countries against the EEC's present total of
10, both organisations borrow in much the same way.
The similarity is not surprising since many of the
EIB's personnel had earlier worked at the International Bank for Reconstruction and Development.

The World Bank is concerned with lending solely
to developing countries, whereas by far the greater
proportion of EIB loans have gone to member states
of the European Community:-

*mills. US $		EIB	World Bank
1980:	Borrowings	3206.8	4363
	Lendings	3378.9	5173

[14]

* 1 Eua = US $1.3

SOURCE: World Bank, 1980 Annual Report, 8. The World
Bank's accounting date is 30 June.
EIB, 1980 Annual Report, pp. 28,38,65. The EIB's
accounting date is 31 December.

The comparison is by no means exact, if only because
the EIB's accounting date is always six months later
than that of the World Bank. The operations of both

institutions fluctuate from year to year in response
to a complex of factors.   In 1979, for example, the
EIB borrowed slightly more than the World Bank.*
Nonetheless, the EIB is of considerable importance
in the world financial market, as above table shows.
      In the EEC, states which have relied most
on EIB loans are most securely linked to the Community.   So that while the EIB assists national
interests, in this and in other respects   it also
fulfils its aim of welding member states together.
      The European Investment Bank's power to influ-
ence and promote national and Community policies
stems from its ability to lend.   It has built up
this potential largely through its success in obtaining funds for Community projects on the international financial markets.   Thus it has fulfilled
the primary purpose for which it was created,
despite the shifts and changes in the global economy
during the past twenty-three years.

NOTES

1. Legally a protocol, annexed to and forming an integral
    part of the Treaty of Rome.

2. EIB Statute, Articles 22 and 24.

3. Treaty of Rome, Article 130.

4. EIB, 1958 Annual Report, 15-16.

5. It was envisaged in the negotiations that began in 1971
    that Norway would also join the EEC and would add
    another 45 mill. units of account to the EIB's subscribed
    capital, but the majority of Norwegians were against EEC
    membership.   EIB Annual Report, 1971, 16-18.

6. The 25% had to be paid in 5 equal instalments not later
    than 2, 9, 16, 23 and 30 months after the Treaty of Rome
    came into force, each payment being: 25% gold; 75% in
    country's national currency.   J. Harrop, National
    Westminster Bank Quarterly Review, May 1978.

7. EIB Statute, Article 24.

8. For the functions of EIB personnel, see EIB Statute,
    Articles 8 and 9 (11-14). See also EIB 1980 Annual
    Report, 4-7.

*US $3,500 as against the World Bank's $3,200. EIB, 1979
Annual Report, 61, Table 7 : World Bank, 1979 Annual Report, 8.

9. EIB Statute, Article 9 (3g): Article 17.

10. EIB _Information_, No.15, Dec, 1978, p.2.

11. Ibid.

12. e.g. Among the first members of the Bank's Board of Directors was M. René Larre, Financial Counsellor at the French Embassy in Washington, who served from January 1958 until October 1961.

13. The Convention agreeing to the change was signed on 14 December, 1960 and ratified by members' legislatures during 1961.
OECD member states:
EEC Countries: Fed. Repub. of Germany, France, Italy, Belgium, Netherlands, Luxembourg, United Kingdom.
Non-EEC Countries: Australia, Austria, Canada, Finland, Iceland, Japan, New Zealand, Norway, Portugal, Spain, Sweden, Switzerland, Turkey, United States of America.

14. The International Bank for Reconstruction & Development, known as the World Bank, and the International Monetary Fund (IMF) (see Chapter 2) were established in New York in 1945 as a result of the 1944 Bretton Woods Agreement. They were followed by the General Agreement on Tariffs & Trade in 1947. The International Finance Corporation (IFC) was also set up to operate along with the World Bank, but it is different in that it deals exclusively with private business and does not require guarantees by governments for its investments; it is an investing rather than a lending institution.

Chapter 2

THE EIB'S BORROWING OPERATIONS AND REACTIONS
TO MARKET CHANGES

The European Investment Bank, like the rest of
the EEC, came into being on 1 January, 1958. Its
first step, obviously, was to invest the capital
subscribed by member states so that the interest on
it generated more funds. Until 1961, the EIB's
loans were not only made from this earned interest
but also from the original capital itself. It
took three years for the Bank to organise itself to
the point where it felt able to approach the international capital market for funds.[1]

a) BORROWING METHODS AND PROCEDURES

In 1961, the EIB launched both its first bond
issue and floated its first public loan. Its borrowing methods have mainly consisted of:

1. The raising of medium-term bank credits (at
   first usually in the form of bond issues)
   which are particularly attractive to foreign
   investors. They prefer bonds floated by big
   official institutions since these are easy to
   resell as the credit of such institutions is
   generally sound.

2. Issues placed with financial institutions,
   including commercial banks.

3. Above all, by conventional bond issues reserved to the general public, which are used
   mainly to obtain large amounts of the world's
   leading currencies.

Considerable amounts of finance have also been
raised by means of private placements (with or without the issue of negotiable certificates) with a
bank or group of banks, i.e. they never appear on
public money markets. Other operations lend themselves to direct negotiations with financial

institutions, e.g. insurance and investment companies, pension funds, savings banks, etc.   As in the case of the International Monetary Fund and the World Bank, shares in EIB loans are sold to third parties on the EIB's own guarantee of repayment. On the international market, the EIB has turned to widespread use of 'purchase funds' where the issuer undertakes, subject to a certain ceiling, to buy up bonds from the market when the rate drops below par.

The EIB's basic strategy has been to borrow in hard currencies so that it could lend in them.   Like any other loan-raising institution, the EIB compares interest rates, currency values, and charges for issuing and handling commissions in order to arrive at the most favourable borrowing terms.   The Bank plays a part in standardising procedures and balancing interest rates when issues are floated, to even out terms and conditions on the market by arbitrage (currency dealings).   It also pays close attention to redemption and optional repayment provisions.[2]

b)   THE EIB'S BORROWING POLICIES DURING
      THE INITIAL EEC BOOM

The Community and the European Investment Bank began operations during an economic boom.   However, at first the Bank experienced difficulty in raising funds on the west European money markets, mainly because, in 1959, the six EEC governments, following an OEEC plan, decided to liberalise capital movements and to return to almost complete convertibility of their currencies for the first time since the 1939-45 war.[3]

The Bank's preference for hard currencies and these financial adjustments in west Europe were additional reasons why it looked chiefly to the United States for raising finance, and not in vain. Its early operations were helped by a large movement of liquid capital out of the United States, which was available for investment in EEC countries. The United States' connection was fostered further by the EIB's association with the International Bank for Reconstruction and Development, which is largely dependent on United States finance and which matched the EIB's contributions in a number of early EEC loan projects (see Chapters 9-15 below).   But the EIB's own investments were heavily dependent on funds from private as well as institutional US investors.

Ultimately, the measures to ease capital flows between west European countries helped the financ-

ing of projects within the EEC.   It led to bigger
and more frequent transactions between financial
markets, to cuts in differences in long-term
interest rates and to agreements between the commercial banks of the EEC countries to finance projects themselves.   Thus a European financial market
gradually developed during the 1960s encouraged by
the growing importance of financial institutions in
the EEC and Scandinavian countries in close collaboration with London and New York.[4] Although the
EIB increasingly used this market, it has persisted
throughout the twenty-three years of its existence
in drawing largely upon United States resources for
its borrowings.
     The early EEC boom was, in part, the result of
heavy public spending required for building infrastructure.   Through their contracts, governments
and public authorities created work and stimulated
consumer demand which, in turn, led to greater private investment, thus stimulating the finance markets and increasing demand for EIB loan issues.   The
level of government investment, however, fluctuates.
A drop in public financing often means a decline in
direct public investment and placings on the financial market.   Very early in the Community's history
the first instance of such a decline occurred,
affecting the EIB through a reduction in government
demands for its loans.[5]   It was, however, only a
minor hesitation.   The level of public spending on
infrastructure, on which the EEC's development depended, soon resumed, and with it calls from public
bodies for EIB finance.

c) EFFECTS OF THE GROWING WEAKNESS OF
   THE US GOVERNMENT'S MONETARY STOCKS

     More ominous for the Bank was the fact that
while there was a great deal of private American
money available for overseas investment, by 1958
the US government's finances were in difficulties.
By the late 1950s, there was a decline in the US net
liquidity balance, although at that time it was not
seen as a secular trend (see Fig. 2a).   In the
1960s, the US economy was further over-extended by
simultaneous commitments to both the space exploration programme, NASA, and to the Vietnam war.
While both enterprises drained public funds, they
generated employment through industrial expansion,
thus boosting consumer demand and creating inflation.
     There was yet another cause of growing weakness
in the US Federal Government's finances.   During
the 1960s, France, one of the EEC states, was

17

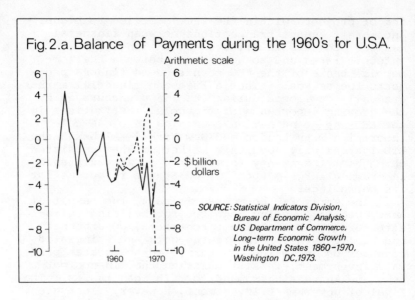

Fig. 2.a. Balance of Payments during the 1960's for U.S.A.

Arithmetic scale

$ billion dollars

SOURCE: Statistical Indicators Division,
Bureau of Economic Analysis,
US Department of Commerce,
Long-term Economic Growth
in the United States 1860-1970,
Washington DC, 1973.

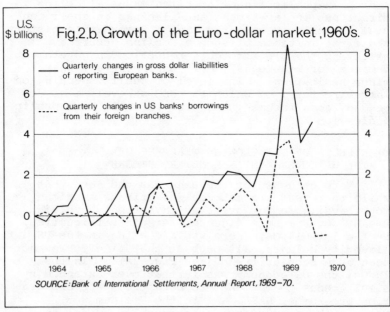

U.S. $ billions   Fig.2.b. Growth of the Euro-dollar market, 1960's.

Quarterly changes in gross dollar liabillities
of reporting European banks.

Quarterly changes in US banks' borrowings
from their foreign branches.

SOURCE: Bank of International Settlements, Annual Report, 1969-70.

refusing to accept paper dollars in payment for its exports to the United States and demanding payment in gold instead. For, under President de Gaulle's leadership, the French claimed that the US was buying up west European industry with paper dollars and, in effect called its bluff. This policy weakened Federal gold reserves steadily from 1962 to 1967. However, the US government retaliated by demanding gold payments for its exports to France and, in 1968, the French desisted.[6]

It was as a result of these pressures that, by 1963, the US government was trying to rectify the growing deficit in its balance of payments. On the one hand, the government discouraged US residents abroad from investing in foreign companies and, on the other, encouraged US companies to bring finance into their country by seeking funds from investors who did not reside in the USA. To this end, in 1963, it imposed the Interest Equalisation Tax which, from 1964, made the huge resources of US institutional investors - big corporations, banks, state governments and other public bodies - virtually inaccessible to borrowers from the Scandinavian countries and the EEC. Clearly, this tax presented the EIB with a considerable problem in the main financial market to which it looked for funds.[7]

The Bank reacted by seeking new ways of tapping the institutional money market within the USA. In 1964, it launched its first bond issue on the dollar market in that country. Thus, in place of attracting US capital to loans the Bank floated outside, the loan was floated inside the USA, creating a formula whereby

> financial institutions in New York and the (EEC) Member Countries are associated in the management of the (loan) syndicate.[8]

This was the Eurobond, floated by a European institution in the USA and denominated in US dollars. The international banking system, therefore, very quickly turned to new techniques for bringing together funds and those who sought them. The Eurobond enabled the EIB to mobilise US dollar savings on EEC financial markets and the Bank's annual rate of borrowing began to rise rapidly from 1964 (Table 3a). The Eurobond-dollar link was fostered by the six EEC governments, especially that of Italy, the heaviest importer of foreign capital, because they encouraged United States companies to set up enterprises in their territories. Hence, there was an increased demand for capital from US companies:

> operating through the intermediary of sub-
> sidiaries especially created for that
> purpose

and established in the EEC and Third World countries.
So while the EIB was borrowing dollars, a number of
United States borrowers were seeking loans from the
EIB for enterprises they were running in the Community.   At the same time there were still a considerable number of US institutional investors who
preferred to keep their funds abroad to escape the
Interest Equalisation Tax.   Their investments were
an important component in the growth of the Euro-
dollar market which assisted the EIB and others
seeking loans[9] (see Fig. 2b).

d) THE EFFECT ON THE EIB OF THE FIRST
EEC CRISIS, 1964-67

As well as surviving the unexpected shortage of
United States institutional funds in the mid-1960s,
the Community and the Bank simultaneously had to
deal with their first internal crisis.   It was
brought on by the very success of the European Economic Community in that high investment and the concomitant high level of employment produced a demand
for goods that outstripped supplies and this, in
turn, caused inflation.   The nature of the crisis
was the same as in the case of the USA, although
the causes of inflation were different.   The very
success of the EEC in achieving a high degree of
economic interdependence between member states
created anxiety.   For now each member was more vulnerable to the effects of economic instability in
the others.   The EEC Commission therefore suggested,
and the member states' governments agreed, that they
should all act together to stop the spread of
'serious inflationary pressures'.   So Medium and
Long-Term Economic Committees of experts were set up
to plan for equilibrium.   Also, in April 1964, the
Council of Finance Ministers, who constituted the
Bank's Board of Governors, drew up a precise series
of recommendations 'tending essentially to limit
public spending and to maintain or reinforce a restrictive credit policy' in order to obtain a better
balance between output capacity and consumer spending.   That is, they adopted the pre-war, pre-
Keynesian policy of cutting public expenditure and
raising interest rates in order to reduce consumer
demand, and so to relieve the upward pressures on
prices. [10]
This deflationary policy was overdone in Italy.

Consequently, in order to restore the economy there, in 1964, three-quarters of the EIB's total lending in the Community went to Italy.[11] In 1966, while economic expansion had been resumed in Italy and France, the Federal Republic of Germany went into recession and pulled the Benelux countries with it. Unemployment increased, but wages continued to rise. The West German government permitted the crisis to deepen until the summer of 1966 when it stepped in to restimulate the economy.[12]

There was a new and growing pressure on loan markets inside and outside the EEC which was helping to make money tight and so driving up interest rates. It was caused by the fact that public authorities were increasingly directly financing infrastructure and other projects, not only from the product of taxation, but also by issuing loans themselves on international finance markets. There they competed with other loan-raising institutions, such as the EIB. Incidentally, this competition for funds constituted another reason for the Finance Ministers' policy of discouraging spending by public bodies.

By 1965, a new European money market had definitely appeared. The EIB was driven by the unexpected difficulties in obtaining United States finance to borrow more from it. Because of the recession, private citizens of Community countries were less inclined to invest in the Community, placing their funds abroad to a greater extent. Consequently, some EEC countries became net exporters of capital. Despite this outflow for the year 1967, about two thirds of the resources the EIB raised came from the money markets inside the Community. Both the growth of the EEC money market and the Bank's borrowings on it were assisted by the growing integration of the economies of EEC countries as well as by the deliberate action of several EEC governments and finance institutions. For they reserved a place on their national financial markets for some issues by Community institutions such as the European Investment Bank, or by borrowers from member countries.[13]

By early 1967, there was an upswing in the economies of EEC countries. Numbers employed rose by 20 per cent, while numbers unemployed dropped by 15 per cent. The trade balances moved back into surplus. By that year, the Bank had established itself in world financial markets. It was confident that, even if the pace of economic evolution of individual member states, or progress towards EEC integration were to slow down, while it would be more difficult for the Bank to act, 'its importance would not diminish'. In a retrospect of the first ten years of its activities, it declared that while it carried out its responsibilities in the Community, it was ready to contribute 'to the solution of the major problems which will arise for the Community in the future.'[14] Its confidence was very shortly tested.

e) THE SECOND CRISIS, 1968-70

The first crisis in the Community countries, allied to growing concern about the use of finite raw materials and about the environment led to the appearance of a new ideology. The student uprisings in Italy and the May 1968 outburst in Paris, which spread throughout France bringing 10 million workers out on strike, challenged, among other things, 'industrialism' and the traditional economic policies on which the early EEC boom was based.

By late 1968, EEC countries were again reported as nearing the limits of their production capacity. As in 1964-66, they were faced with problems caused by their own industrial success. They reintroduced credit restraint and the value of the French franc was forced down.[15] But the Bank steadily channelled finance into infrastructure loans in France. It provided considerable support also, in the late 1960s, for West Germany's energy programme and, when the new decade began, prosperity was once more increasing in the Community countries.

However, the United States Federal Government's difficulties in financing at one and the same time both the Vietnam war and NASA, persisted. In addition, prosperity continued to produce problems, for trade was expanding and, with it, the need to pay for greater quantities of imported commodities and manufactures. Consequently, credit availability in the West became ever tighter and the scarcity of capital drove up interest rates. As a result, the US government had to pay more to finance its mounting balance of payments deficit.

To deal with this new crisis and to try to rescue the US government, in the Spring of 1968, the International Monetary Fund introduced a new method of payment for countries with balance of payments deficits, known as Special Drawing Rights.[16]

Simultaneously, currency problems, mainly the weakness of the US dollar, caused a run on gold and led to a determination, on the part of the EEC and other industrialised countries, to stabilise the gold price.[17] There was, however, another United

States exchange crisis in 1969 as a result of which the values of two of the Community currencies, the Deutschmark and the Dutch guilder, were forced up, and yet another US crisis early in May 1971 when there was a major revaluation of west European currencies.[18]

Inevitably the close economic links between Community countries and the United States involved the former in the USA's monetary problems. At the same time, the crises of the 1960s and early 1970s were not wholly due to the weakness of the US dollar nor to inflation induced by high customer demand. Other reasons became apparent through some of the measures adopted by EEC member states' governments in order to keep up economic growth. For example, they aimed to eliminate unemployment by structural underpinning. To this end they renewed the Social Fund and extended its competence to make grants over a wider range of projects. They proposed a Community Regional Fund to provide resources for sectors other than agriculture. Their purpose in both cases was to ameliorate the effects of a decline in demand for labour due to both the introduction of new labour-saving technologies and to the effects of world competition in established industries (see Chapters 9 & 10). They also acted to prevent competition for finance among the Community's poorer regions which had been a feature in the past.[19] Naturally they looked to the EIB for finance in support of their policies.

Because of the EIB's heavy dependence in its borrowings on the US dollar, the diminishing value of that currency adversely affected the Bank's funds. However, in the early 1970s, there seemed to be no alternative owing to difficulties of raising the amounts required in the EEC's own money markets. So in 1971 and again in 1972, in spite of the dollar's weakness, the EIB had to step up its dollar loan issues. In order to strengthen its ability to support economic expansion in the Community in 1971, the Bank's Board of Governors asked their respective governments to increase the EIB's subscribed capital (see Table 1b).

f) THE EEC BOOM OF THE EARLY 1970s

As in 1964-66, the crisis spurred the EIB into greater activity and growth. In 1969, to raise more funds on international money markets, it began to use the short-term global bearer bond, a special bond issued for a brief period. The entire amount is raised when the loan issue is concluded and it is redeemed from funds coming in some weeks later once an issue of the EIB's longer-term bonds has been fully taken up.

The Bank also pioneered a new type of credit operation, offering institutional investors and banks participation in financing its loans through certificates carrying the EIB guarantee of repayment. By the end of 1972 this method proved to be a new means of drawing in resources by associating a larger number of institutions with the EIB's operations.

The rapid development of Eurobonds from the mid-1960s seems to have been parallelled by a growth in the market for other international credit facilities. Statistics are far from complete due to the rule of banking secrecy, and only some of the most important credits are made public. Nevertheless, from such information as exists, in 1972 international credits were assessed as probably in excess of 6 milliards ua, greater than the Eurobond issues on the international market. This expansion reflected the abundance of resources seeking investment, notably the accumulating funds of Japanese banks. Also, from 1962, the duration of credits offered by banking syndicates was progressively lengthened from 5-7 years to 10-12 years.[20] The international expansion of the EIB's operations was part of a general growth in banking and a part of the post-war economic recovery.

In 1972, the EIB began to borrow outside the old-established financial markets of the USA and west Europe. For the first time, the Bank turned to the banks of the big new industrial power, Japan, in placing its securities.[21]

Despite the crisis in the US government's finance and signs of restiveness among Arab oil-producing countries' governments about declining oil prices, the EIB referred, in 1973, to 'a buoyant world economy'. Not only was the total amount of the EIB's subscribed capital again raised by the accession to the Community, in that year, of three new states, Britain, Denmark and Ireland, there was another absolute increase; for each country's government agreed to subscribe more (Table 1b). In 1973, the EIB's investment income doubled. Economic growth in the Community reached a peak in the summer of that year and, in one of the new member states, Britain, in the first half of 1973, there was an economic recovery greater than for many years.[22]

g) THE EFFECTS OF THE 1970s US DOLLAR CRISIS ON
THE EUROPEAN INVESTMENT BANK'S UNIT OF ACCOUNT
AND OTHER COMMUNITY UNITS OF ACCOUNT

The problems on the exchanges in the early
1970s heralded the onset of world economic depression.
In July 1973, a down-turn began in the
economy of the Community as a whole and in other
western industrialised countries. On top of these
difficulties, the Arab oil-producing states acted
together in October and again in December 1973 to
raise the price of oil on which Western economies
now hinged. The United States in October yet again
devalued the dollar by 10 per cent. The Bank was
once more caught because it had been placing its
loan issues predominantly in US dollars. It suffered
a further net loss in 1974 due to the revaluation
of the unit of account. For the US dollar
crisis forced a change in the EIB and other Community
units of account.

Any unit of account may be an equivalence or
parity expressed in:

(i)   a given quantity of gold;
(ii)   an individual currency;
(iii)   a 'basket' of currencies.

The unit of account first used by the Bank and other
Community institutions was defined by the first of
these methods, that is by reference to a given quantity
of gold. In the Bank's case, the gold parity
of its unit of account was laid down in Article 4 of
its 1958 Statute as precisely the same as that of
the US $, the strongest and most stable of the
world's currencies:

1 ua = 0.8867088 grammes of fine gold = 1 US $

A similar unit of account was adopted by other Community
institutions.[23] As late as 1969, the International
Monetary Fund adopted this same gold parity
for its own Standard Drawing Right.

From August 1971, when President Nixon
announced the suspension of the convertibility of
the dollar into gold, it was allowed to float on the
world currency markets. Its value in terms of gold
fluctuated but was forced downwards. The floating
of the dollar led to floating exchange rates for
other currencies, including the Community's units of
account. This float, in turn, had repercussions on
the EIB's Statute and demonstrated that the cumbersome
provisions of Community law could not keep pace
with events. For the governments of the Community
countries decided to alter the definition of the

EIB and other similar Community units of account.
They decided, on 10 July, 1974, to adopt instead of
the gold parity, the basket of currencies definition.   By this method, the unit of account was declared equal to the sum of fixed amounts of the nine
member states' currencies, i.e. the 'basket'.

DM	...	0.828	Belg. fr	...	3.66
UK £	...	0.885	Lux. fr	...	0.14
F. fr	...	1.15	Dan. kroner	...	0.217
Lire	...	109.0	Irish £	...	0.00759 *
Guilder	...	0.286			

In fact the sum or basket of these currencies still
equalled the EIB unit of account's original gold
value of 0.88867088 grammes of fine gold, and thus
was the equivalent of the IMF's Special Drawing
Right which had adopted this gold parity.   This
gold value has not been altered for either the unit
of account or the SDR.   But because of the decline
in the gold value of the US dollar, the new unit of
account now had a higher dollar value, US $1.20635
in 1974.
     The fixed amounts of the EEC countries' curren-
cies in the basket, however, represent notional and
not their actual values on the financial exchanges.
The practical conversion rates of member states'
currencies on the international exchanges are worked
out daily by the Commission of the European Communities and published in the financial press and the
Official Journal of the European Communities.   The
European Investment Bank, for the purposes of
arranging loans and settling member states' contributions to its own funds, has, since 30 December,
1974, used the international exchange rates as the
bases for its conversion of its unit of account into
other currencies.   The Bank provides operational
statistics for each quarter, using the conversion
rates obtaining on the last working day of the preceding quarter and publishes an annual average of
the exchange values of the member states' currencies
in its annual report.
     Under the new system, if the parity of a
member state's currency on the international exchanges is reduced in relation to the fixed notional amounts of the ua, that state is bound to adjust
loan repayments already paid to the EIB by making a
supplementary payment within two months of the

* In 1981, the Greek drachma was added, its fixed amount for
purposes of the 'basket' being: Dr ... 61.2587.

change.   On amounts still to be repaid, on the
dates when they fall due for payment, member countries must pay any difference due to a drop in the
value of their currencies.   On the other hand,
should the value of a member state's currency, on
the international exchanges, rise, the EIB has to
make an appropriate payment to the state concerned
within the same time limit.[24]
The currency upheavals led to the introduction
of a number of other units of account.   For
instance, the EIB joined with other EEC banks in
pioneering the European Composite Unit or Eurco
which also has a basket of EEC currencies for its
definition, but of a slightly higher value in each
case than the unit of account.   Whereas the Bank
normally issues loans in national currencies, the
Eurco loan issue offers investors a 'mix' of EEC
currencies, thus enabling them

> to spread their investment among all the
> currencies of the European Economic Community
> on a suitably weighted basis.

It thereby provided them, the EIB hoped, with
greater stability for their investments.   The
amounts of each of the component currencies in the
Eurco remains unchanged for the duration of the
loan.[25]
Most of the Bank's transactions and statements
were, however, in the Eua which was gradually
adopted by Community funds and lending instruments.
Although the 1971 monetary crisis slowed down the
establishment of the EEC Economic and Monetary Union,
in March 1972 it was relaunched.   The adoption in 1974
by Community funds and institutions of a common unit of
account was a step in the progress towards a Euro-
currency.   A further step was taken when the name,
'European Unit of Account', was changed to 'European
Currency Unit' or Ecu, resembling more closely the
name of a currency in its own right and not just an
accounting device.   The EIB adopted the change as
from 1 January, 1981.[26]
As important as the actual change in method of
defining the Bank's unit of account was the way in
which it was introduced'and the timing of decisions
by Community bodies.   The Treaty of Rome laid down
that any change in the EIB's Statute required a
further treaty of modification ratified by each member state, a lengthy process.   Whereas the Treaties
establishing the European Coal and Steel Community,
Euratom, the EEC and the provisions for the accession of new member states all provided for Treaty

clauses to be waived, the power of authorisation of these 'derogations' resting largely with the Commission.[27] The timetable of decisions on the adoption of the new method of calculating the unit of account shows that the Bank's Board of Governors made the alteration ahead of the change in the Treaty. The process of ratification of the necessary alteration to Article 4 of the Bank's Statute took over three years, from 10 July, 1974 to 1 October, 1977, and the actual change was made two and a half years before ratification, that is on 18 March, 1975. To avoid a repetition of this experience, the revised Article 4 laid down that

> The Board of Governors, acting unanimously on a proposal from the Board of Directors, may alter the definition of the unit of account.

The justification for setting aside the provisions of the EIB's Statute was the need to react quickly in unforeseen circumstances so as to keep funds flowing via the Bank to Community projects. A precedent had, however, been created that, under pressure, the EEC member states and thus the Bank's Board of Governors were prepared to act ahead of changes in Statute provisions.[28]

h) MANAGEMENT OF LIQUID FUNDS

Mainly through long-term borrowings, the EIB has a certain amount of funds for which there is no immediate demand. Although its own borrowings are kept closely in line with calls on its resources, its funds must be kept flexible to a certain extent in readiness for repayment of its own borrowings, as these become due, and for paying out as progress on projects, which it is financing, warrant. Its Statute prohibits it from engaging in currency dealings (arbitrage) not directly required for its lending operations or for the repayment of loans it has raised or guarantees it has given. But since the whole of its dealings are directed to these ends, the EIB may use arbitrage as one of its methods of raising funds for the Community. Furthermore, elsewhere in its Statute, it is given the right to dispose freely of that part of its capital which is paid up in gold or convertible currency and of any currency borrowed on markets outside the Community.[29] It therefore has cash in hand with which to play the money markets, by buying and selling securities issued both by those who borrow from it, or by any kind of financial operation 'consistent with its

28

function'. In this connection it has set up a comprehensive worldwide network of correspondents which it uses to obtain information, chiefly for placing short and medium term deposits of its funds and also for covering short and medium term liquidity requirements. It has thus gradually built up 'a portfolio' (i.e. a mixed bag) of securities to hold its reserve funds. Its net statutory and supplementary reserves amounted to over 785 million ua at 31 December, 1980. Naturally it buys only those securities which carry 'a first-rate signature', and enjoy access to a large secondary market on which they may always be placed or dealt.

During the development of world recession in the 1970s, and the Community's particular financial difficulties caused by the oil price rise, the EIB continued to show considerable resourcefulness in obtaining funds from financial markets for investment in Community projects, partly by means of the use of its liquid funds. For instance, it recouped its 1974 losses due to devaluation of the US dollar and the revaluation of the unit of account, by placing funds it borrowed in short-term investments which carried very high interest rates. In this way, over the year, the EIB added 50 per cent to its investment income. But in 1975 interest rates fell so that the Bank lost on its short-term investments. This time it made up for its losses by lending at considerably higher interest rates than those at which it borrowed. It also made a profit on the sale to third parties of participation in its loans.[30]

In 1974, the USA rescinded the Interest Equalisation Tax. In 1975 the EIB promptly placed its first bond issue wholly on the US market, amounting to $75 million. In September it floated the largest ever bond issue on the international market in one tranche ($100 million). In 1976, the EIB set a record with its international bonds denominated in US dollars. Its immediate reason for going into US dollars even more deeply was that still, despite the Federal Government's difficulties, the dollar was a more stable currency at that time than any in the EEC.

At the same time, the EIB continued to turn to new Asian markets for its financing. In 1975, it became the first non-Asian borrower on the Asian dollar market, with an issue of US $20 million in Singapore. In 1976, it issued a bond on the Arab market for US $30 million, and a public loan of $50 million placed under the management of an exclusively Arab banking syndicate.[31] A number of loans are now handled by Arab Banks.

Bonds issued by the EIB are not necessarily managed by the Bank itself, but are handed over to other international banking syndicates, that is, major banks in different countries who form a syndicate for the express purpose of managing a particular loan. For example, in the prospectus of 14 October, 1976, for the loan issue of $30 million worth of bonds bearing 8 per cent interest, repayable in 1983, the issue was being managed by:

Morgan Grenfell (Asia) Ltd.
Indosuez Asia Ltd.
DES-DAIWA Securities International Ltd.
Trident International Finance Ltd.
Bancome International Ltd.
The Development Bank of Singapore Ltd.
Jardine Fleming & Company Ltd.
United Overseas Bank Ltd., Singapore.
Wardley Ltd.

and copies of the prospectus were registered by the Registrar of Companies in Singapore and Hong Kong respectively.

i) EFFECTS OF DEEPENING WORLD RECESSION
    ON THE EIB

The increasing calls on the Bank for long-term investment funds by the EEC member states were not only due to the increase in the number of members in 1973 nor to the growth in the number and size of investment projects. They were also the result of inflation and, in the case of some countries, particularly Britain, of the decline in the value of their own currencies on the exchanges.

The EEC countries' governments, as in the mid-1960s, agreed on common action to combat inflation, to achieve greater monetary stability and to expand international trade. At the same time, they met the growing economic crisis by holding to policies of action at three levels (see p.23):

1) aid to resolve specific labour market problems, especially training and employment opportunities for young people and women;

2) a higher level of investment in member states;

3) a halt to economic divergence and promotion of convergence in their economic performance.

They now also proposed, in 1978, concentrated Community action on a greater scale than hitherto in place of their previous policy of leaning towards stimulation of the economies of the strong-currency member states. They believed that this change in emphasis would lead to a general recovery throughout the Community.32

Because of their growing requirements for finance, the member states increased their subscriptions to the EIB's funds in 1975 and yet again in 1978 (Table 1b).

By 1980, however, it was clear that the world economic recession was deepening and, with it, balance of payments difficulties in the Community countries. Between the end of 1978 and mid-1980, crude oil prices rose by nearly 150 per cent. The EIB stated in its 1980 Annual Report:

> The worsening terms of trade of the oil-importing industrialised countries caused a deterioration in their balance of payments on current account.

Of the Community countries, the only one in which there was not a sharp increase in the deficit on balance of payments was the United Kingdom, cushioned by her exploitation of North Sea oil and gas deposits.

At first industrial growth in the Community countries was little affected, mainly because people reduced their rate of saving and so offset the slower rate of growth in real incomes. However, from the middle of 1980, increasingly stringent monetary and credit policies were applied as a means of stemming both current and estimated future inflation. These policies contributed to a reduction in personal consumption and, in most EEC countries, led to economic growth slowing or even stopping. The volume of the Community's aggregate gross domestic product rose by only 1.3 per cent in 1980 compared with 3.4 per cent in 1979. Simultaneously, world trade markedly diminished. Growth in Community countries was sustained mainly through exports to OPEC countries.

Restrictive monetary policies, international political uncertainties and inflation, particularly in the United States where it caused a change in the operation of monetary policy, led to sharp fluctuations in interest rates, on both the Euro-dollar and national capital markets. Because of

TABLE 2a: Statement of EIB's Funded Debt showing changes between 31 December 1979 and 31 December 1980 and currency composition (units of account)

	Borrowings outstanding at 31.12.79	Operations during the financial year			Borrowings outstanding at 31.12.80		
		Borrowings	Redemptions	Exchange Adjustments	Amount	Rate of Interest paid by EIB (weighted averages)	Due dates
EURCO	89 705 945	–	–	391 294–	89 314 651	8.13	1981/1989
DMarks	1 997 098 817	814 057 724	224 510 582	70 143 597–	2 516 502 362	7.69	1981/1999
Ffrs	470 222 816	136 588 933	31 647 444	15 546 830–	562 617 475	11.22	1981/1996
£ Sterling	134 100 268	45 686 400	14 603 756	26 017 394+	191 200 306	11.25	1981/1992
Lire	127 272 790	42 711 314	14 035 774	7 569 212–	148 379 118	8.60	1981/1995
Belg. frs.	384 415 436	–	21 835 652	9 066 668–	353 513 116	8.27	1981/1993
Dutch Florins	772 667 603	226 164 518	26 625 065	15 729 188–	956 477 868	8.86	1981/2004
Lux. frs.	167 621 986	51 680 006	29 347 441	4 562 475–	185 392 076	8.81	1981/1991
US$	3 522 196 345	665 954 997	254 342 200	364 577 425+	4 298 386 567	9.62	1981/2000
Swiss frs.	565 751 165	234 013 773	47 555 662	2 674 765–	749 534 511	5.85	1981/1994
£Lebanese	7 517 354	–	1 025 296	150 778–	6 341 280	7.13	1981/1985
Yen	232 223 980	166 630 216	15 322 702	88 402 236+	471 933 730	8.16	1981/2000
Austrian Schillings	69 913 643	–	–	1 246 661–	68 666 982	7.92	1981/1989
T O T A L	8 540 708 148	2 383 487 881	680 851 574	354 915 587+	10 598 260 042		
Redemption Premiums	6 351 451	–	222 072	228 083–	5 901 296		
G R A N D T O T A L	8 547 059 599	2 383 487 881	681 073 646	354 687 504+	10 604 161 338		

SOURCE: EIB, 1980 Annual Report, p.79.

increased calls by west European countries on
finance markets for loans to cover their budget
deficits, the trend throughout 1980 was for
interest rates to remain high.[33]
There was a net increase in the EIB's borrowings in 1980, but that increase was smaller than in
the previous year:

Increases in EIB borrowings (mills. Euas)

1978	...	...	1,949.7
1979	...	...	2,481.2
1980	...	...	2,466.8

(see Table 3a)

On 31 December, 1980, the outstanding borrowings of
the European Investment Bank, amounting to
10,598,260,042 million units of account were denominated in 13 different currencies, the most
important still being way and ahead the US dollar,
as Table 2a shows, with the Deutschmark in second
place.   However, in 1980 the US dollar accounted
for a smaller proportion of the EIB's borrowings than
in 1979, while borrowings in a number of other
currencies, notably the Deutschmark, the Dutch
florin and the yen, rose.[34]   However, the Bank's
total resources, comprising paid-in capital, reserves and provisions, balance of profit and loss
account and borrowing proceeds rose from 9,882.7
mill.Euas in 1979 to 12,237.6 mills. Euas in 1980.
Until 1980, there is in the EIB's Annual
Reports a sense very nearly of enjoyment in over-
coming crises through the expertise and flair of its
staff.   But, in 1980, a note of doubt was sounded
for the first time at the Annual Meeting of the
Board of Governors by the Managing Director, M.
Yves Le Portz (see Chapter 4).   It was a reaction
not only to demands for higher amounts of loans inside the Community but to other increasing calls
made upon the Bank's staff.   Once more, in 1981,
the Board of Governors decided to increase the subscriptions of their respective governments to the
EIB's capital in order to enlarge its ability to
raise finance by operating on the world's finance
markets.   They raised the Bank's subscribed
capital by 100 per cent, from 7,200 million to
14,400 million units of account (see Table 1b).
This increase is not as high as it sounds in that
member states' governments are to pay in only 7.5
per cent of this amount, or 540,000 units of
account.   This will raise the amount of paid-in
capital from 925,715 million to 1,465,715 units of
account.   As is usual, the payment of this 7.5 per

33

cent is spread, in this instance, over four years, 1984-85 to 1987-88.   In the case of Britain, the payments will amount to about £16 million in each of these four years.   With amounts as small as this there would appear to be no suggestion, therefore, that the member countries are restricting credit in order to bring down inflation by depositing extra large amounts of cash with the EIB, thereby taking it out of circulation.[35]

The increase would appear to signify the con-tinuing belief of member states' governments that the European Investment Bank is an essential insti-tution over and above their own national and commer-cial banks, for bringing into the Community the extra amounts of finance needed for its development. For this reason they have supported the EIB through the initial years while it was establishing itself and latterly through various economic crises.   The Bank's success in raising funds has been due partly to their support as well as to its own expertise.

NOTES

1.   EIB Annual Reports, 1958, pp.16-17; 1961, 25.
     First bond issue launched from Netherlands capital
     market: first public loan launched in March, together
     with second loan issue later in year for total of 21.4
     mill. ua.   The EIB also obtained a loan of 9 mill.
     Swiss frs.

2.   EIB, Information, No.15, December, 1978, 3,

3.   EIB, Annual Reports, 1959, 13; 1960, 13-14, 1967, 17-18.
     The First Ten Years of Activity, 1958-1968, 3-4.   The
     first Directive of the EEC Council of Ministers was on
     the liberalisation of capital movements.

4.   The EIB's definition of Euromarket Loans: Loans which do
     not interest subscribers in the country whose currency is
     concerned, due to tax regulations, e.g. non-bond issues
     in US dollars, since US citizens themselves had to pay the
     Interest Equalisation Tax.   Or, bond issues in Deutsch-
     marks, which did not originate in the Federal Republic of
     Germany, since similarly, West German nationals obtained
     better yields from their own domestic market following a
     rise in interest rates.
     Loans reserved for non-resident subscribers, e.g. issued
     by Dutch enterprises in the Netherlands for placement out-
     side that country.
     Loans issued with special monetary clauses, e.g. issues in
     units of account or with a multiple currency clause.
     The EIB excluded from its definition of Euromarket loans:

34

a) Swiss loan issues in Swiss frs. since these were open
to Swiss nationals;
b) Loans expressed in the Dutch, Italian, French or
Belgian currencies, such as those issued by the EIB,
the ECSC, the different portions of the ENEL-Europe
issue other than the DM portion, as these were considered as being floated on the different national
markets.

See EIB 1965 Annual Report, 41-2.

5. Ibid., 40-41.

	1959	1960
Net issue of government securities and bonds	4,560	3,600
Government Share issues	1,410	1,900
		(mill. ua)

EIB, 1960 Annual Report, 16.

6. Bank of International Settlements Annual Reports:

		Total US Gold Sales to Europe	US Gold Sales to France only
1962	...	$ 729	$518
1963	...	921	405
1964	...	1299	884
1965	...	1665	600

By 1969 the US was buying gold from France.
In 1965-66, military expenditures abroad rose by about
$800 million.   By the end of 1968, they were running at
an annual rate of $3.8 billion compared with $2.7 billion
in 1964.   See US Federal Reserve 1966 Report, p.78.

7. EIB, Annual Reports, 1965, 42-3 : 1967, 18-19.

8. Eurobonds originated in the late 1950s and grew rapidly
from 1960, mainly due to governments and official institutions.   Private borrowers, particularly foreign subsidiaries of US companies turned to them following the US
Interest Equalisation Tax.   Eurobond issues maintained
their importance after the lifting of the Tax in 1974.
See Carlos Emmanuel, IMF Exchange & Trade Relations Dept.,
in IMF Survey, Vol.4, No.4, Nov. 1975, 332-34.   The EIB
floated this loan in New York and it was taken up by a
consortium of 3 US banks and 6 EEC banks, one for each of
the member states.
EIB 1965 Annual Report, 43-4/58.

9. US companies, in 1966, took 41% of loan issues, EIB 1966
Annual Report, 35;   there was a flight of capital from
Italy because of high interest rates offered abroad, EIB
1968 Annual Report, 60.

10. In 1963, the EEC trade deficit nearly trebled:

```
                 1962  ..          ..    1.6 US $ milliards
                 1963  ..          ..    3        "
```

EIB 1963 Annual Report, 15.

But overall balance of payments remained in surplus
partly because of a continuing important in-flow of
private capital, and partly because exports from the EEC
rose:

	INCREASES	
	1962	1963
Inter-EEC trade	+14% Value terms	+17%
Exports to non-member countries	+ 1%	+ 5%
Gold & foreign currency reserves	+16.2 milliards	+18.3

Ibid, 16. EIB 1964 Annual Report, p.16 : 1965 Annual
Report, p.21 : Bank of International Settlements, Annual
Reports, 1963-64, 31.

11. EIB 1964 Annual Report, 25, 49. Investment by enterprises in
Italy dropped by about 14% in value compared with 1963,
and about 20% in real terms.   It was claimed that increasing labour costs were not being matched by increasing productivity.   Private investment also declined in
Luxembourg and was stationary in France and Belgium.
See also EIB 1967 Annual Report, 45.

12. EIB 1966 Annual Report, 17, 48 : 1967 Annual Report, 43-5.
Public expenditure and thus calls for finance were cut back
in West Germany.   Liquidity of funds was reduced by a
restrictive credit policy and a balance of payments
deficit.

13. EIB borrowings inside the EEC in 1967:

	mua		mua
Luxembourg ..	1	Fed. Rep. of Germany	68
Belgium ..	43	France	93
Netherlands ..	47	Italy (incl. US Funds)	120

EIB $ issues by 1967 amounted to 180 mua. EIB 1967
Annual Report, 18-19.

In the FRG, non-residents were given incentives to invest
abroad.   However, because of rising interest rates,
people were reluctant to invest in fixed interest securities.   EIB 1966 Annual Report, 19-31.

14. EIB 1967 Annual Report, 42-3.

EEC Balance of Trade - milliard ua			
	1966		1967
Deficit 1.3		Surplus 4	

15. EIB Annual Reports: 1968, 17-18; 1969, 22, 88.
    Bank of International Settlements Annual Reports, 1967-
    68, 44. Even at that time, growth of real output in
    Western Europe was slowing down, due to monetary re-
    straint.

16. The Articles of the International Monetary Fund were
    amended in March 1968 and approved by the IMF's Governors
    on 31 May, 1968. They established Special Drawing Rights
    available to participating countries to meet a balance of
    payments deficit or decline in reserves due to changes in
    the composition of reserves in other countries. Also,
    under voluntary agreements, a country could use any
    amount of SDRs to obtain its own currency held by other
    participants. The IMF Directorship is in the
    hands of West Europeans; the President of the World
    Bank is usually from the USA.

17. At the same time, Western countries agreed on a policy of
    official intervention to hold the price of gold steady at
    about $35 an ounce, as a result of a wave of speculative
    buying. It was known as 'the gold pool'. The seven
    active members were:

EEC	Non-EEC
Belgium	Switzerland
Fed. Rep. of Germany	UK
Netherlands	USA
Italy	

    But in mid-March, 1968, there was another switch into
    gold, due to fears about the weakness of the £ sterling.
    The Bank of England ordered the closure of the London gold
    market. And the governors of the Central Banks of the
    Seven agreed to end sales of gold to private markets but
    reaffirmed adherence to $35 = 1 oz. gold for official
    transactions. Most IMF countries agreed, since with the
    SDR it would no longer be necessary to buy gold from the
    market. In this way a 2-tier system was set up. The
    2-tier system was a step away from dependence on gold.
    The bulk of future additions to international reserves
    were expected to consist of SDRs.

18. The dollar was rendered inconvertible and a 10 per cent
    duty imposed on imports into that country.
    In 1970 the US Economic Stabilisation Act was passed,
    enabling the Federal Government to institute wage and
    price controls. It was extended in 1973. The balance
    of payments deficit trebled, rising from $1 billion in
    1970 to $3 billion in 1971.
    See US Fed. Reserve System Annual Reports , 1963, 8;
    1970, 7; 1971, 51-3, 61; 1972, 29.
    Bank of International Settlements Annual Reports, No.41,
    1968-69, 37; 1970-71, 3,5,46.

EIB Annual Reports, 1967, 72, 75; 1970, 9-14; 1971, 125-26.

19. EIB 1971 Annual Report, 8-11, 13-14.

20. EIB, Les investissements dans la Communauté en 1972 et leur financement, 27.

21. EIB 1972 Annual Report, 43.

22. EIB 1973 Annual Report, 11.

23. EIB Information, No.4, February 1976, p.2; Emile Noël, Sec. Gen. of the Commission of the European Communities, Working Together, the Institutions of the European Community, 1979, p.11, Footnote 1. The practice of finding a common denominator for various currencies originated in the Middle Ages. Most current units of account originated in the 1939-45 war, or just after, e.g. ua of European Payments Union constituted in 1950 for clearing the mutual debts of its 17 member countries. The value could be changed by agreement. There were different EEC units of account relating to agriculture and various other sectors of the Community. The agricultural unit of account has the same gold parity value as the original EIB ua, and the European Monetary Unit of Account, EMUA, also retains the original gold parity value.

24. EIB Statute up-dated, 19 June, 1978, Art.7,1 & 2. Agreed by Board of Governors, in force on 1 October, 1977.

25. EIB 1973 Annual Report, 46-7. Eurco Basket: The EURCO consists of the sum of fixed amounts of the currencies of all the member states of the EEC: 1 Eurco = DM 0.9 + Ffrs 1.22 + £0.075 + Lit 80 + Fl 0.35 + Bfrs 4.5 + Dkr 0.2 + IR£0.005 + Lfrs 0.5. Source: 1980 Ann.Report, p.79.

26. EIB, Annual Reports, 1971, 13-14; 1980, 8.

27. E. Noël, op. cit., 13.

28. Centre des Recherches Européenes, La Banque Européene d'Investissement, Lausanne, 1977, 92. EIB Statute updated, 19 June, 1978, 7-8.

29. EIB Statute, Articles 22, 23, 25.

30. EIB, Annual Reports, 1973, 49-50; 1974, 45; 1976, 55: Receipts for interest on cash lent by EIB up by 94.2 mua; interest on charges for cash borrowed by EIB up by only 74.2 mua:L Anell & B Nygren,The Developing Countries and the World Economic Order, 1980, 99ff, oil price rises.

31. EIB, 1975 Annual Report, 47.

32. EIB, Annual Reports, 1977, 15-16; 1978, 9.

33. EIB, 1980 Annual Report, 9-10, 12-13.

34. EIB, Information, No.26, July 1981, 2; No.22, July 1980, 2.

35. Ibid. Hansard 30 June, 1981, Column 330, p.165. Written Answers, Sir Geoffrey Howe.

Chapter 3

THE LENDING MECHANISMS AND POLICIES OF
THE EUROPEAN INVESTMENT BANK

a)   THE EIB'S MANDATE

The Treaty of Rome, in Article 130, laid down the task of the European Investment Bank as:

> to contribute, by having recourse to the capital market and by using its own resources, to the balanced and steady development of the common market in the interest of the Community.[1]

It specified three principal kinds of projects which the EIB was to support through loans and guarantees:

i)   developing less developed regions;

ii)   modernising and converting undertakings or developing fresh undertakings called for by the progressive establishment of the common market, where these projects are of such a size or nature that they cannot be entirely financed by the various means available in the individual member states;

iii)   projects of common interest to several member states which are of such a size or nature that they cannot be entirely financed by the various means available in the individual member states.[2]

The Bank's Board of Governors was charged with issuing its own directives concerning the granting of loans to:

1.   Member states;

2.   Public or private enterprises for projects in the European territories of member states to the extent that they cannot obtain these FROM OTHER SOURCES ON REASONABLE TERMS:

TABLE 3a: Scale of European Investment Bank's Fund Raising & Lending Operations, 1959-80 (Mills. Ua)

Year	Funds Raised by EIB	% Change + or -	Lending from own Resources	% Change + or -	Lending from EIB & other EEC Funds for which EIB acts as Agent	% Change + or -
1959	-	-	34.1	-	-	-
1960	-	-	25.5	-25	-	-
1961	21.4	-	86.5	+339	-	-
1962	32.3	+51	66.4	-23	-	-
1963	35.2	+9.3	56.2	-15.4	71.2	+11
1964	66.8	+90	112.4	+100	120.4	+69
1965	65.0	-3	88.1	-21.6	109.1	-9
1966	138.5	+131	104.2	+18	197.0	+81
1967	194.5	+40	148.2	+42	212.6	+8
1968	212.5	+9.3	172.5	+16.4	214.0	+7
1969	146.0	-31	247.9	+44	321.8	+50
1970	168.9	+15.7	282.6	+14	354.4	+11
1971**	412.9	+44	432.1	+53	502.2	+42
1972	479.5	+16	488.7	+13.1	526.8	+5
1973**	612.3	+28	696.8	+43	815.8	+55
1974	825.5	+35	849.7	+22	996.4	+22
1975**	830.7	+1	917.5	+8	1,006.5	+10
1976	748.9	-10	967.9	+6	1,273.3	+27
1977	1,161.5	+55	1,401.3	+45	1,571.5	+23
1978**	1,949.7	+68	1,966.5	+40	2,188.3	+39
1979	2,481.2	+27	2,281.2	+12	3,071.1	+40
1980	2,466.8	-0.6	2,753.0	+20.2	3,498.5	+14

Annotations alongside years: First EEC crisis — 1964; US government & world monetary crisis — 1969-1971; 2nd EEC crisis & OPEC oil price rise — 1973-1975; 2nd OPEC Oil price rise — 1979.

Notes: ** Years in which EEC member states increased their subsidies to the European Investment Bank

SOURCE: EIB 1980 Annual Report, p.87, Table 9 : p.65, Table 7; EIB Information, No.26, July 1981, 1.

3. Exceptionally (it was thought at the time) they were to authorise unanimously, on a proposal of the Board of Directors, loans for projects 'in whole or in part outside the European territories of member states.'3

The Bank had to carry out the policies laid down for it in the Treaty of Rome without giving any one area too much of a competitive edge, hence it showed some preference for projects shared by EEC member countries.

b) THE EIB'S LENDING POLICIES

Within the general policies laid down by the Treaty of Rome and by the Bank's Board of Governors, decisions to grant loans rest, to a large extent, with the Bank's Management Committee and permanent staff. For it is on their assessments of the economic viability of projects that they recommend to the Board of Directors whether or not to lend. Although the Directors may disagree with the Management Committee's recommendations, the financial and technical assessments made by the Bank's staff are of cardinal importance. The Bank's own criteria governing choice of projects are:

i)   their economic utility;

ii) their financial profitability;

iii) interpenetration of enterprises between member states and those outside the Community.[4]

The EIB is never the only Bank or other source of funds involved in financing the whole of a project. When it began operations, the Bank fixed a ceiling for each of its loans of 80 million ua, but it now lends considerably in excess of this amount.   Its policy generally has been never to lend more than 50 per cent of the fixed capital cost of a project.[5] It also sets a lower limit on loans, preferring them to be of not less than 1 million ua. Recent inflation and economic crises have led to the Bank increasing the proportion it would fund of the total cost of a project.   It raised the upper limits of its loans in 1973 and again in 1977, with the result that, in 1978, its loans averaged 28.1 per cent of the capital cost of projects as compared with 23.4 per cent over the years 1973-77.[6]

Article 20, 1(a) of the Bank's Statute lays down the condition that in the case of loan projects

TABLE 3b: Breakdown of the European Investment Bank's
            loans outstanding at 31 December, 1980
            by principal form of guarantee*

            Loans for projects within the Community
            (and related loans**)

	ua
Loans granted to, or guaranteed by, member states	8 617 219 783
Loans granted to, or guaranteed by, public institutions in the Community	1 410 758 693
Loans granted to, or guaranteed by, financial institutions (banks, long-term credit institutions, insurance companies)	469 961 365
Loans guaranteed by companies outside the financial sector under majority control of member states or public institutions in the Community	215 297 809
Loans secured by fixed charge on real estate	70 280 014
Loans guaranteed by non-bank companies in the private sector	292 308 020
Loans secured by fixed charge on assets other than real estate or other security	259 167 506
	11 334 993 190

*   Certain loans are covered by several types of guarantee or
    security.

** Loans for operations involving non-EEC countries.

SOURCE: EIB, 1980 Annual Report, p.78.

42

in the production sector, interest and amortisation payments are to be covered out of borrowers' operating profits, or, in other sectors, by a commitment by the state in which the project is carried out or by some other means. The EIB harmonises loan amortisation with industrial amortisation, that is loans have to be paid off in step with the depreciation of plant and equipment. Therefore, there is usually an interval of 3-4 years between the date on which a loan contract with the EIB is actually signed and the date at which repayments of the loan start. Loans are usually repaid in equal six-monthly instalments of both principal and interest.[7]

The average length of the EIB's loans varies considerably but tends to be shorter for industrial than for infrastructure projects. At one time, in the 1970s, they were averaging 7-12 years, but as Table 2a shows, the EIB now lends in the Community for anything from 8 to 20 years.[8]

It is, however, neither the length of its loans nor the proportion of total costs which its loans cover that make the EIB important as a lending institution for private industrial schemes. It is rather the fact that the Bank is charged with stepping in to finance projects when the outstanding borrowing requirement cannot be met on what are considered reasonable terms from any other source. The Bank's role as a make-weight gives it considerable power in determining which schemes may go ahead.

c) SOURCE OF CONFLICT IN EIB LENDING POLICIES

The European Investment Bank is not a policy-making body within the Community. It is an instrument for promoting policies of the Community as a whole and also those of individual member states. Hence, the Bank operates within the dual constraints of the law and policies of both the Community and its component countries. It is the national laws and policies of the EEC states, however, which are paramount.[9] Therefore, despite the EIB's assertions that its permanent staff are required to put their national sentiments aside as servants of a supra-national institution, there has been inevitably a dichotomy in the Bank's lending policies because it can grant a loan only with the agreement of the government of the member state in which the loan project is situated. Although its Board of Governors, the Finance Ministers, of the member governments might agree on certain Community policies, each might well have an objection to a particular policy, or be unable to introduce the necessary

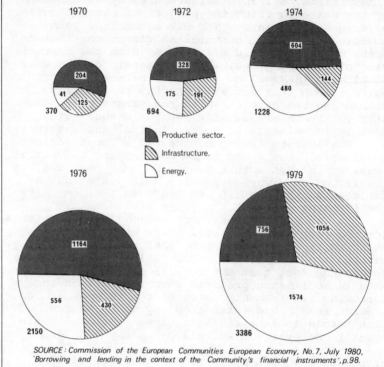

Fig.3.a. Sectoral trend in lending activities of European Community instruments, at current prices, (EIB, ECSC, Euratom, NCI), in millions European Composite Unit (EURCO).

1970

204

41

125

370

1972

328

175   191

694

1974

604

480   144

1228

Productive sector.

Infrastructure.

Energy.

1976

1164

556   430

2150

1979

756   1056

1574

3386

SOURCE: Commission of the European Communities European Economy, No.7, July 1980, 'Borrowing and lending in the context of the Community's financial instruments', p.98.

legislation, so there might be a delay in the implementation of agreed Community Directives. In the
vast majority of EIB loan projects no conflicts have
arisen, but in a few they would appear to have done so.

The national control of the EIB also operates at
the actual level of financing, for the Bank lends
only in accordance with the nature of the financial
institutions in the member countries. It is through
them that loans are channelled to specific projects,
both directly from the EIB's own resources and from
other funding bodies which the EIB may have been
able to associate with a loan.

d) LOANS FOR REGIONAL DEVELOPMENT

The Bank has often operated not with the mere
agreement, but at the positive behest of member
states in the promotion of particular policies.
There has been less call for EIB loans from the
Federal Republic of Germany, the Netherlands and
Luxembourg because of the relatively low national
interest rates prevalent in those countries[10] (see
Table 2a). Belgium has progressively increased her
requests for finance because of the decline in her
steel and textile industries. France's calls for
infrastructure loans enormously increased in the
1970s, especially for telecommunications and nuclear
energy so that she has received the third largest
amount of total EIB lending over the 22 years, 1958-
80. The two countries which received most from the
EIB's own resources were Britain with 27.7 per cent
and, first and foremost, Italy with 37.0 per cent. EIB
help for Italy to assist an on-going government programme of development for the whole of the south was
laid down in a Special Protocol forming Article 239
of the Treaty of Rome.

Broadly speaking, the Common Market countries
contain two distinct types of area: urban-
industrialised and rural-peasant. Some large industries are, however, situated in or near small
towns as in the east of Belgium and west of Luxembourg. Besides the south of Italy, in 1958, rural-
peasant economies still prevailed in north Holland,
parts of the Federal Republic of Germany, especially
on its borders with the German Democratic Republic,
and in large areas of France. The centuries-old
migration of the young able-bodied, particularly men,
to the industrialised centres and to cities where
there was a growing demand for services, was proceeding. One role of the Bank was to assist the
establishment of industries in these rural areas in
order to lessen the flow of migrants, and to create

TABLE 3c: Totals of EIB Loans and Guarantees
to EEC Member States

	1968-72	1973-80
Belgium	67.2	318.5
Federal Republic of Germany	353.6	547.4
France	570.5	1,739.7
Italy	1,412.3	4,530.0
Luxembourg	9.0	-
Netherlands	42.9	62.3
Denmark		288.9
Ireland		948.5
United Kingdom		3,316.1

SOURCE: EIB, Annual Reports, 1972, 68, Table 12.
1980, 88, Table 10.

a demand for services through a greater local prosperity. In the south of Italy, the largest of the rural-peasant regions in the Community, the product per head of the population, measured in the conventional terms of Gross Domestic Product, was, on average, only one third of the EEC average. As a result of increased investments, from 1958, the rate of growth rose. In the south of Italy, by 1962 it was higher than in the other more prosperous parts of the country, and France and Italy were showing the highest rises in Gross National Product in the Community.[11] But many of the big firms receiving EIB loans were in other EEC countries with prosperous industrial sectors, or even based in the United States of America.

In the less developed regions of the member states the EIB is required to intervene 'even if other means of financing are available' and these regions 'are entitled to reinforced aid from the Bank when unforeseen difficulties of financing complicate the execution of projects.' In 1970, there was just such a situation with a considerable rise in numbers of calls made on the Bank, those from Italy being 'particularly copious'. But the Bank was bound to meet

> the surfeit of requests addressed to it when the projects were in conformity with the conditions laid down in its Statute.

Capital was generally short and interest rates therefore high and the EIB congratulated itself on meeting the increased demands. To relieve the pressure on its own funds it did not lend, but merely guaranteed loans from some West German financial institutions for projects which it had itself investigated in Italy and France.[12]

Beneficiaries from EIB loans inside the Community have included not only public authorities and private industry from large multinationals to very small businesses, but also another large Community institution, the European Coal and Steel Community.

As shown in Chapter 2, the Bank makes short-term loans of liquid funds not immediately required for Community projects which, through the interest they earn, add to the Bank's funds. Non-EEC borrowers of such resources have included international syndicates: for example, in North America and Japan.[13]

e) THE PROVISION OF JOBS

In the Treaty, there was, moreover, an implicit threat to employment in traditionally industrialised areas. Article 130 b) set out the EIB's role in facilitating the financing of projects for modernising and converting enterprises. Modernisation and conversion frequently involve the closure of old plants and the introduction of labour-saving technologies. By the late 1950s, in the EEC, new, speeded-up production methods were being introduced in various kinds of work at an increasingly rapid rate and were reducing the demand for labour. A similar sort of industrial development was, moreover, occurring in an ever-increasing number of areas throughout the world.

For a time the Bank occasionally cushioned the effects of the decline in traditional kinds of work by making loans available to enterprises which provided jobs for the redundant workforce. Mass unemployment was generally regarded by the Community as undesirable. Increasing emphasis has been given to maintaining employment and reducing unemployment throughout the 1970s, both by the Community as a whole and by the European Investment Bank (see pp. 23, 30).[14]

The extent to which the Bank's investments were effective was inevitably increasingly circumscribed by the recession. The number of jobs it claimed had been created as a result of its investments, rose year by year. However, because of the EIB's emphasis on loans for construction work, especially in infrastructure, the vast majority of these jobs are short rather than long-term.

Any job-creating activity has, of course, been welcome. The widening gap between available work and the numbers seeking it could only have been lessened by more fundamental structural changes than were contemplated (see pp. 163-165). The need for investment in research, in order to develop new labour-intensive kinds of work less threatened by overseas competition was apparently not realised.

f) LOAN APPLICATION PROCEDURES

All applicants for European Investment Bank loans have to provide the usual information required by banks, that is:

1) the most recent annual reports with balance sheets;

2) operating accounts;

3) profit and loss accounts;

4) a description of the investment project to be financed;

5) nature and cost of the project, including requirements of working capital;

6) programme of production or utilisation;

7) expected markets;

8) prospects of profitability on the project;

9) specifications of the financing plan envisaged.

When the European Investment Bank lends, like any institution operating with borrowed funds, it must be strict in demanding security. The Bank obviously checks loan applications carefully to ensure that they are technically valid. As well as the financial standing of the would-be borrower, it also checks that the marketing of the products which result and utilisation prospects are satisfactory.

Where the Bank gives guarantees on loans other than for a member state, it covers these by further guarantees. By the terms of its Statute, when it lends for projects located in states that are not EEC members, it must obtain a guarantee from the country in whose territory the project is situated or some other appropriate security, for example, from a public authority, major bank or industrial or financial group with a first class credit standing which is itself associated with the project.[15]

All applications for loans or guarantees, whether they come to the Bank directly or through the Commission or a member state's government, are considered by all three bodies. While a member government can veto an application without reference to the Commission or the EIB, the Bank's Board of Directors can overrule both the Commission and the advice of their own Management Committee providing their decision is unanimous. The Directors must, however, accept an unfavourable opinion if it comes from both the Management Committee and the Commission.

Like other stages of the EIB's investigations, its check-ups on would-be borrowers are 'covered by the strict rules of banking secrecy'. The strongest power of decisions on loan applications, therefore,

rests with member governments, and after them, with
the Bank's Board of Directors.

However, governments of member states and their
public authorities and departments, like any other
lenders, are closely scrutinised by the Bank.   It
keeps a careful check on the economies of member
states.   For the usefulness of the EIB to governments of member states, to the Community institutions and to private borrowers depends absolutely
upon the maintenance of its complete reliability.
Its high standing in the world of finance rests as
much on its trustworthiness as on its expertise in
accumulating funds.

Applications for loans are submitted to the
Board of Directors, which meets at intervals of one
or two months.   If the Directors decide to grant
the loan, a financing contract is concluded between
the borrower and the Bank.

At the negotiating stage, the Bank steps in
particularly to:

1)   align settlement procedures;

2)   co-ordinate the activities of security-
     clearing systems.

In order to attract investors for its loan
issues, the Bank has to choose loan projects likely
to find favour on the world's capital markets.   The
more highly regarded the projects which it funds
are, the more highly regarded is the Bank's portfolio.   The EIB's choice of loan projects also
affects the interest rates which the Bank has to pay
on its own borrowings and so, in a circular process,
ultimately the EIB's portfolio is one of the factors
enabling it to hold down its interest charges.

g) CURRENCY ARRANGEMENTS FOR EIB LOANS

Because the European Investment Bank holds resources in different currencies and receive applications for loans from people of different nationali-
ties, it offers clients a choice of currencies when
arranging payment of loans,[16] currently as follows:

1)   loans paid over in a single non-Community
     currency, mainly the US dollar, Swiss franc
     and yen, or, for major financing operat-
     tions, equal amounts of these and of Com-
     munity or other currencies;

2)   loans paid in several currencies made up in
     varying mixes, according to the preferences

of the borrower and depending on the different currencies available to the Bank;

3) loans paid in several currencies made up of
standard mixes, with make-up, term and
interest rate all fixed in advance.[17]

Borrowers have to bear any adverse changes in the
exchange rates. In the 1970s, as British borrowers
were particularly vulnerable because of the decline
in the value of sterling, the British Treasury, in
return for a small charge, guaranteed all public
enterprises, particularly those repaying long-term
loans, against exchange fluctuations arising from
loans from the European Investment Bank. At the
end of 1977, the Treasury extended this guarantee to
the private sector (see p.74).[18]

h) INTEREST RATES ON EIB LOANS

The EIB's interest rates are set no higher for
risky projects, nor for borrowers with a low credit
rating than for safe projects, since it covers itself by guarantees from third parties.[19]
Because of the differences in the exchange
values of the currencies which the Bank borrows, the
interest rates on its own loans are also determined
by the mix of currencies in a loan. For example,
interest rates on the third type of loan the Bank is
now offering (i.e. a loan paid in several currencies
made up of standard mixes with make-up, term and
interest rates all fixed in advance), as at 10 July,
1979, were:

	8 years	10 years	12 years	15 years	20 years
Composition	50% US $	40% US $	40% US $	50% US $	60% US $
	30% DM	30% DM	30% DM	25% DM	25% DM
	20% Sch	20% Fl	20% Bfrs	15% Fl	15% Fl
	-	10% Yen	10% Yen	10% Yen	-
Interest rate	9.20%	9.35%	9.50%	9.65%	9.85%

SOURCE: EIB, Information, July 1979, p.8.[20]

One of the great attractions of an EIB loan is that
the interest rate is fixed for the term of the loan
and does not fluctuate with base lending rates.[21]
Otherwise, the attraction of EIB loans depends on
whether the interest rates it offers are significantly lower than those offered by a country's own
national banks. This has been less the case in the

Federal Republic of Germany and the Benelux countries because their own bank interest rates have
been low.   In 1979-80, for example, for British
borrowers interest rates on EIB loans were very advantageous.   The base lending rate at the end of
March 1979 was 13 per cent.   By November, it had
risen to 17 per cent and it only started to come
down in July 1980 when it dropped to 16 per cent.
By 31 March, 1981, it was still 12 per cent.   French
banks, in the autumn of 1979 and spring of 1980,
were asking 18 per cent interest on certain loans.

i) DIFFERENCES BETWEEN THE EIB'S LOAN
   CRITERIA AND COMMUNITY LAW

    Differences between the Bank's lending policies
and those of the Community were few so long as the
Community's economic development proceeded on lines
foreseen when it was established.   But, in the
1970s, deteriorating economic circumstances and
radical changes in attitudes to industrial exploitation and development have occasionally revealed
such differences.   Problems arise largely because
of the extreme slowness of the process whereby Community law is adopted as the law of the member
states since it is always the latter which has precedence in determining whether or not the EIB will
lend.
    One main instrument of Community law is the
Directive generally proposed by the Commission of
the European Communities and agreed by the appropriate national ministers for energy, industry,
finance, social and regional development, etc.,
meeting as the Community's Council of Ministers.
Once agreed, a Directive is binding on member
states.   Since the Community countries are democracies, EEC Directives only pass into law when they
have been voted through by their respective national
legislatures.
    Usually member governments are given a period
of grace, generally 2 years, in which to make
arrangements for the enforcement of Directives.   The
Treaty of Rome lays down a procedure for bringing
countries that are lagging into line, which adds at
least another 6 months to the 2 year implementation
period.   During the period between the passing of
a Directive and its final passage into national law,
strictly speaking the existing law of member states,
not the new proposed law prevails.[22]

j) THE CASE OF ENVIRONMENTAL PROTECTION

    One of the prime examples of an unforeseen and

abrupt rethinking of Community policies during the 1970s has been in the matter of the protection of the environment.   There was nothing definite in the Treaty of Rome in general, nor in the Bank's Statute in particular, in the way of a commitment to safeguard natural resources or the environment. Neither the EIB nor the EEC Commission could have been expected to take these matters into account during the first 8-10 years of their existence since there was little concern about them anywhere.   In the 'sixties, however, consciousness was gradually awakened by concern over nuclear installations, the effects of the increasing use of pesticides and fertilisers in the USA and of chemical pollution, particularly in Japan [23] (see Appendix 3A).

The Treaty of Rome did, however, give scope for Community action to improve the quality of life. From 1967, under this head, member governments began to take decisions conjointly in the Community on consumer protection.   The following year, the EEC Commission set up a Special Service for Consumers under its Directorate of Competition.

The year of key developments in environmental protection was 1972.   In line with the United Nations' Stockholm Conference on the Human Environment and the Club of Rome's study, The Limits to Growth, the OECD, of which the EEC countries were members, issued its Declaration of Environmental Policies.   In response to this growing concern, the EEC Commission upgraded its Special Service for Consumers, making it the Environment and Consumer Protection Service.   On 21 October, 1972, a Conference of EEC Heads of Governments in Paris issued a declaration:

> underlining the importance of a Community
> policy on the environment and called upon
> the (Community) Institutions to draw up a
> programme of action, together with a pre-
> cise timetable before 31 July, 1973. [24]

This declaration is now generally held to be the official start of the Community's efforts to protect the environment.   The view of Community countries, as enunciated in an Information Agreement of 5 March, 1973, was:

> ....that Western Man, as he moves freely from
> country to country within the framework of the
> Common Market, has the right to expect broadly
> similar environmental conditions at least as
> far as his own health is concerned.[25]

It was the first step towards trying to establish a
uniform level of environmental protection in all
member countries, especially with a view to bringing
the most backward up to a set standard. Here then
was an entirely new field which the Bank's Technical
Staff would have to take into account in their
assessments of loan projects.

The European Investment Bank claims to have required borrowers to satisfy new standards of consumer and environmental protection as these were laid
down by the Council of Ministers of the EEC from
1967 onwards, in order to ensure that working and
living environments were safeguarded and limited
natural resources used wisely. It has stated quite
clearly its policy on these matters in a letter to
the author in which it also points out (para.2) the
limitations on the extent to which it can protect
the environment:

1) In its technical appraisal of projects the
   EIB includes careful consideration of the
   possible impact on the environment, e.g.
   gaseous emissions, liquid effluents, solid
   wastes, noise level, landscape, working environment. A minimum condition for Bank
   lending is the satisfactory fulfilment of
   all laws and regulations in force
   (regional, national and, where such exist,
   Community directives or regulations formulated in International Conventions).

2) The EIB is not a regulatory agency, and has
   no power to be, and does not establish any
   'environmental code' of its own.

   However, the Bank's concern for environmental protection is not of a passive
   nature, i.e. only ensuring formal compliance with existing rules: the EIB takes
   into account in its appraisals the evolution of environmental standards which in
   due course could modify existing regulations or lead to new regulations.

   In less developed countries, where environmental directives are often missing or in-
   complete, it is normally required that
   adequate criteria based on the typical
   standards of the corresponding technologies
   in European countries be adopted.

3) When studying the sectoral and regional
   economy involved, the Bank indeed considers

any potential environmental impact and the
need to avoid what you,(i.e. the author)
term as "unnecessary expense to the
Community".*

The Bank subsequently publicised these views in its
quarterly Information in July 1980, where it claimed
that within 'a full appraisal' of the viability of
a project

the possible impact on the environment is one
aspect....and one which has been given increasing importance within recent years. The Bank
takes into account not only physical effects
such as gaseous emissions, liquid effluents,
solid wastes, etc., but also noise levels,
effect on the landscape and working environment.

Its list of Environmental Parameters to be taken
into consideration in the evaluation of possible
variants of a project covers:

1) Quality of water: dissolved oxygen; biochemic demand for oxygen; total organic carbon; biomass; phosphates;
nitrates; salinity; specific toxic elements; temperature;
degrees of alkalinity and acidity (pH); solid matter in suspension; bacteria; viruses; parasites.

2) Quantity of water: supply; seasonal variations;
floods.

3) Pleasure/Leisure: clean water; turbidity; colour/
smell; appearance of surface (dèbris, oily film); extent and
quality of water.

4) Soil quality: erosion; sedimentation; protection
of beaches; elimination of solid wastes; land unrestored
after industrial usage; acidity; separation of substances
(into soluble and non-soluble); alkalinity; fertility.

5) Quality of air: sulphurous oxides; nitrogen oxides;
other volatile substances (hydrocarbons, fluorines); solid
and fine particles; carbon monoxide.

6) Aquatic ecosystems: breeding conditions; migrations;
maintenance of natural and genetic resources particularly
threatened rare species.

* Letter dated 17 March, 1980, AG/No. 03178.
  See also EIB Statute, Article 20, 4.

7) <u>Land ecosystems</u>: breeding conditions; migrations; maintenance of natural and genetic resources, including threatened rare species and systems; introduction of favourable new systems; plant rotation.

8) <u>Undesirable and/or irreversible changes</u>: salinity; poisoning; choking of lakes, water courses, etc., with plant life causing extinction of animal life.

9) <u>Exposure to natural hazards</u>: earthquakes; tidal waves; typhoons; hurricanes; geological anomalies (vulnerability of dams, flood barriers).

10) <u>Aesthetic considerations</u>: disappearance of rare and precious countryside, historic, cultural and archaeological sites.

11) <u>Microclimate</u>: lessening of frost/ice; incidence of mist; lessening of range of registered temperatures; in-increase in humidity.

12) <u>Noise nuisances</u>: building works; industry; power stations; traffic.

But unless member governments insisted or laws decreed that public and private enterprises in member states should also take such parameters into consideration, while the EIB's Technical Staff could assess and point out likely consequences of projects, the Bank could not make its loan contracts conditional upon standards being met.

In some of the member states legislation was ahead of Community action. For example, over a century before 1973, the British Factory Acts were laying down environmental standards in places of work. In some cases, new national laws were passed in advance of Community Directives, such as the United Kingdom's Town and Country Planning Act of 1972, which gives scope for environmental protection measures. The idea of environmental impact analysis spread slowly in the Community countries through this and subsequent measures in Ireland, Luxembourg, France and the Federal Republic of Germany. But it was only in June 1980 that, after years of negotiations, government representatives passed a Community Directive requiring Environmental Impact Assessment Statements from member countries. Even this measure covered only certain major development projects, both public and private. Full implementation is not due until June 1982. Only then, and only in respect of the listed projects, can the EIB begin to insist on environmental impact statements as a 'minimum condition' for granting each of its loans.[26]

In its 1972 environmental protection measures, the OECD enunciated the principle: 'the polluter pays.' It drew the ineluctable conclusion, however, that costs of implementing anti-pollution measures would be passed on to consumers in the form of higher prices. Insistence on optimum standards is indeed tempered by regard to costs by governments, Councils of Ministers, Commission and Bank. The introduction of special plant and methods often necessary to diminish pollution, waste and misuse of resources may entail greater expenditure on the part of manufacturers and other employers. Increasingly various interests in Community countries, including sections of their legislatures, have fought EEC Directives on environmental matters on the grounds that since the Treaty of Rome makes no specific provision for Community Action to protect the environment or consumers, such Directives are <u>ultra vires</u>.[27] (See Chapter 13)

Up to the present, however, the public's views have rarely been included in environmental impact assessments; people have not often been asked to evaluate an improved environment and the reduced social costs derived from pollution control, as against a greater cost for products and services. The thinking tends to have been done and judgments made for them by officials, technicians and politicians.

Over the past quarter of a century, public reaction has been gathering force. There are now powerful environmental and conservation lobbies in the Federal Republic of Germany, the Benelux countries, Denmark, France and Britain, some of them becoming more and more effective. The result of their pressure is that member states' governments have increasingly agreed to the introduction of environmentally protective and conservationist measures both nationally and at Community level. In March 1981, for the first time, an EEC country, the Federal Republic of Germany, has recognised 'environmental criminality' and made it punishable at law.[28] These significant changes in policy are reflected in a considerable increase in the number of environmentally protective and conservationist projects funded by the European Investment Bank (see Chapter 13).

k) CONCLUSIONS

The instance of the implementation of EEC environmental and conservation policies provides one classic example both of the slowness of change in

Community institutions and of the dilemma in practice created for the EIB by the discrepancies between, on the one hand, member states' laws, and
regulations which it is bound to observe and, on the
other, Community Directives, endorsed by member
states' governments.

On the one hand, the EIB has proved a powerful
instrument for Community member governments in the
realisation of their own economic policies as well
as in promoting 'the balanced and steady development of the common market.' Without the financing
provided by and through the European Investment
Bank, the development of energy, transport and water
supply projects, the build-up of certain industries
and the radical alteration of whole regions within
the Community would have occurred more slowly and,
in some instances, might not have occurred at all.
On the other hand, the EIB is almost wholly a
creature of Community governments in that they both
provide subsidies to keep up the levels of the
Bank's operations and also guarantee each of its
loans. Their backing, consisting of the guaranteed
total capital resources of each of the ten Community
states, gives the Bank almost cast-iron credit from
whence has sprung its confidence and verve.

The changes in governments in themselves have
had little impact on the direction of the EIB's
loans because most are long-term and what is agreed
by one administration cannot easily be altered by a
different one elected during the term of realisation
of a project. Also an underlying consensus prevails. However, changes in government policies
may affect the level of a country's demands for EIB
assistance. For instance, because of the contraction of UK public spending, demand for EIB loans declined in 1980. Hence Treasury compensation for
any drop in the value of the £ on the exchanges also
declined. Even private firms were discouraged from
applying to the EIB for loans.

The Bank's financing in 1980 continued, however, to be concentrated in Italy and the United
Kingdom, since these were the countries with the
most acute regional problems, and in France. Together, Italy, Ireland and Britain absorbed 79 per
cent of all the EIB's own lending in 1980, or 79.8
per cent if the New Community Instrument loans,
which the Bank handles, are included (see Chapter 4).
Both Belgium and Denmark were struggling to adapt to
a decline in demand for their traditional products
and both borrowed considerably more from the EIB
than in 1979. But in West Germany, the low domestic interest rates from national banks and other

lending bodies still make the EIB's loans relatively less attractive.[29]

Community governments are democratically elected. Consequently, through powers of lobbying, through selection of candidates to legislatures and through elections, Community citizens can influence the lending policies of the European Investment Bank. This is one aspect of the importance of the example of environmental policy where, by moving governments, people have influenced economic policy in a number of Community countries.

In the EIB's lending policies there are a number of elements involved: member governments, investors in EIB loan issues, private and public persons and bodies seeking EIB loans, the vast mass of citizens who will be affected by the projects the EIB finances and the Bank itself. Finally, there is the Commission of the European Communities, the proposer, administrator and, to some extent, the executor of agreed policies. The European Investment Bank's lending reflects the interplay of all these forces.

NOTES

1. Treaty of Rome, Article 130, given in EIB Statute.

2. Ibid.

3. EIB, 1958 Annual Report, 16-17; Statute, Article 18, 1.

4. Ibid. and pp. 38-9, App. 11. These criteria were laid down by the Board of Governors at a meeting on 4 December, 1958.

5. J. Harrop, The European Investment Bank, The National Westminster Quarterly Review, May 1978, 20.

6. EIB, 1978 Annual Report, 21.

7. EIB, 1959 Annual Report, 15-16, i.e. initial policy only 3-4 years before repayments start.

8. Harrop, op. cit.; EIB, Information, No.18, July 1979, 8; EIB, 1980 Annual Report, 42, Table 4.

9. EIB Statute, Article 20, 6.

10. EIB, 1967, Annual Report, 21; EIB Information, No.4
    February 1976, 2; Harrop op. cit., 21.

11. EIB, 1963 Annual Report, 37.   38% of the Italian popu-
    lation lived in the Mezzogiorno, Sardinia and Sicily.

12. EIB, 1970 Annual Report, 18.

13. EIB, Annual Reports, Balance Sheets, Cash and Bank De-
    posits, Undisbursed Balances of Loans.

14. EIB, Information, No.22, July 1980, 2.

15. EIB, Statute, Art. 21; Information, No.15, Dec. 1978, 4.

16. EIB, 1959 Annual Report, 16.

17. EIB, Information, No. 18, July 1979, 8, for original
    choice offered.
    The EIB also guarantees loans for projects it has
    investigated granted on mandate by and for other banks.
    For instance, in 1970, when credit was tight, it used
    this procedure with West German banks operating in the
    field of municipal credit for projects in Italy and
    France.   EIB, 1970 Annual Report, 19.

18. The Public Sector in Britain borrows from the Treasury
    money supplied by the EIB via the Public Works Loan
    Board.   The Treasury repays the EIB at the agreed rate
    of interest, but it charges the borrower an interest
    rate of 1-2% above that.   The Private Sector is also
    charged at a higher rate of interest than the Treasury
    pays to the EIB.   Enterprises in development areas get
    a preferential rate.   The difference between the
    interest rate paid to the EIB by the Treasury and what it
    charges to borrowers is the price of the exchange risk
    cover.   I am indebted to Mr. Brian Morris, EIB Office,
    London, for this information.
    See also Harrop, op. cit. 20-1.

19. Harrop, op. cit., 20.

20. The rate of interest applying to loans disbursed in
    several currencies is equal to the average of the
    interest rates fixed by the EIB's Board of Directors for
    each of these currencies, weighted according to the
    proportion of each currency in the mix and also, where
    appropriate, the dates at which the loans must be repaid.
    However, the EIB's interest rates move up and down with
    the market rates, i.e. according to how tight capital is:
    e.g. 1970 EIB Annual Report, 20, the EIB raised its
    interest charges on loans for 12 years and under from
    7.5% to 8% on 3 March, 1970, to 8.75% in November 1970.
    The rate would, of course, remain fixed once the loan
    contract was signed.

21.   There is an exception to this EIB rule in respect of
      funds channelled to small borrowers, see Chapter 13.
      I am grateful to the National Westminster Bank Economic
      Intelligence Unit for information on interest rates.

22.   I am grateful to the Legal Section of the Division of
      General Environmental & Consumer Protection Matters,
      EEC Environmental and Consumer Protection Service for
      information on the making and implementation of Com-
      munity Law.

      In the event of a government's failure to take the steps
      at the times set out by a Directive, the procedure is:

      a) unofficial approaches to it by the Commission's En-
         vironmental and Consumer Protection Service;
      b) in the event of no reaction, the issuing of a formal
         notification;
      c) followed by a 'Reasoned Statement'.

      If there is still no response and counter-arguments from
      the recalcitrant government are judged inadequate, the
      Environmental Service must obtain authorisation from
      the European Commissioners to take the case before the
      European Court of Justice.   The carrying out of this
      procedure adds at least another 6 months to the 2-year
      implementation period.

23.   Commission of the European Communities, State of the
      Environment, Second Report, 1979, 27-8 for Japan;
      The Times, 20-1, 23, 26-31 July, and 3-5, 7, 9-12, 18
      August, 1976, for chemical accidents and Appendix 3A.

24.   6th General Report on the Activities of the Community,
      1972; Communiqué of the 1972 Heads of Government Paris
      Conference.

25.   Commission of the European Communities, State of the
      Environment, First Report, 1977, 13.

26.   COM (80), 313 Final, 11.6.1980, OJC 169, 9.7.1980.
      Lee & Wood, Environmental Impact Assessment for Major
      Projects and Physical Plans in the European Community,
      December, 1977;   The Introduction of Environmental
      Impact Statements in the European Community, May 1976.
      Timmermans, Citizen Participation in Decision of Public
      Authorities within the Member States of the European
      Community, February 1979.

27.   The most famous case is the Directive on the Protection
      of Wild Birds, see OJC L103/1, OJC 193, 13.6.1977, Pt.1.

28.   The Times, 21 July, 1981.

29.   EIB, 1980 Annual Report, 25-6.

APPENDIX 3A: Growth of EEC environmental measures in relation to serious polluting accidents and international action to protect the environment

Date	Examples of Types of Accidents	International Action	EEC Action
Dec. 1953	Japan - first case of Minimata disease (due to mercury poison) identified		
1957	Windscale nuclear-processing plant fire		
1959	Cause of Itai-itai disease identified as cadmium discharges into the River Jintsu, Japan: decalcifies bones		
1963	Accident in Philips Duphar chemicals factory, Amersterdam (subsidiary of Philips of Einelhoven) dioxin poisoning	International Commission for Protection of the Rhine established	
1965	Accident at Coalite & Chemical Products Ltd., Bolsover, Derbyshire, England, dioxin poisoning		
1966		Japanese Government required monitoring of all mercury effluents	
1967	Oil tanker, 'Torrey Canyon', spill, off S.W.coast of England		EEC Council of Ministers first Directive on Approximation of Laws, Regulations & Administrative Provisions on the classification & labelling of dangerous substances

Apr. 1968	First meeting of the Club of Rome	Special Service for Consumers set up under the Directorate of Competition Special Service for Consumers transferred to the Directorate General of Industrial Affairs.
1970	OECD Environmental Committee set up/US Environmental Protection Agency set up in December. Publication of the Club of Rome's Limits of Growth.	
1972	UN Stockholm Conference on the Environment: OECD Declaration of Environmental Policies-commitment to promote non-polluting technologies-initiation of the 'polluter pays' principle-start of reduction of pollution in OECD in production of polychlorinated biphenyls, mainly used in making insulators-impregnate workers & cause defects in babies	
1973		Council of Ministers' Agreement on Exchange of Information with a view to harmonisation in the Community of urgent measures.

APPENDIX 3A (cont'd.)

Date	Examples of Types of Accidents	International Action	EEC Action
1973			Council of European Communities Declaration on a Programme of Action on the Environment – 22 Nov: EEC Action Programme published EEC–USA Environmental Co-operation Agreement signed
1974	1 June: Flixborough, Nypro (UK) Ltd., chemical plant explosion 28 killed		
1975	Beek, Netherlands, April: Propylene Explosion – 14 killed, 104 injured	Founding of the European Foundation for the Improvement of Living & Working Conditions – Nov.	
1976	Escape of dioxin vapour from factory of Swiss Hoffman-La Roche at Meda-Seveso – outskirts of Milan, Italy Philips subsidiary: contaminated materials from 1963 dioxin escape finally removed from factory in September: explosion produced cloud of arsenious oxide at petrochemicals plant of ANIC, s.p.a. subsidiary of Ente Nazionale Idrocarburi, at port of Manfredonia, Apulia, S.Italy	Barcelona Convention for Protection of Mediterranean from dumping noxious substances US Standards for Toxic Substances Act 1st meeting of European Foundation for Improvement of Living & Working Conditions	EEC signed Bonn Convention on clean-up & protection of the Rhine and Barcelona Convention on the protection of the Mediterranean
1977		International Labour Organisation Convention 148 on Occupational Hazards of Air Pollution	Publication of EEC Commission's First Report on the State of the Environment

64

		Noise & Vibration	
1977			1st annual seminar of EEC network of Pilot Schools on Environmental Education
			Difficulties over EEC Commission's Proposals on reduction of pollution from oil spills.
			EEC Commission Papers proposing Joint Monitoring Groups on the Paris & Oslo Conventions covering: 1) discharges of mercury; 2) suggesting national networks for monitoring pollution.
1978	March: Amoco 'Cadiz' oil super tanker wrecked off Brittany coast		EEC Naples meeting stressed need for integrated planning of coastline & of protection from oil spills.
			Start of EEC Campaign against noise pollution.
			Acts adopted by the EEC on institution of a Consultative Scientific Committee for Examination of Chemical Toxicity & Eco-Toxicity
			June: start of EEC Action Programme to combat marine pollution
Mar. 1979	Nuclear leak from pressurised water reactor at Three Mile Island, Harrisburg, Pennsylvania, USA Spills from oil tankers off West Indies & in Gulf of Mexico	US Environmental Agency announced suspension of herbicides, 2,4,5-T & 2,4,5-TP containing dioxin	EEC Commission to review member states environmental protection policies: decision to set up high level group on nuclear safety. Proposals to approve UN Economic Commission for Europe Convention on long-range trans-boundary pollution; for measures to prevent major indus-

APPENDIX 3A (cont'd.)

Date	Examples of Types of Accidents	International Action	EEC Action
1979	Mexican offshore oilfield blow-out resulting in worst oil pollution disaster ever recorded		trial accidents, including improvement of storage conditions & through more information to workers Community signed Council of Europe Convention on Conservation of Wild-life and Habitats EEC Agreement on Environmental Impact Assessments
Apr. 1980	Fire & release of liquid effluent into sea from Cap La Hague nuclear waste treatment plant, Cherbourg, Brittany		
July 1980	Chemical tanker leak, Shoreham, Sussex harbour. Town evacuated		

Chapter 4

THE RELATIONS BETWEEN THE EUROPEAN INVESTMENT
BANK AND THE COMMISSION OF THE EUROPEAN
COMMUNITIES

The European Investment Bank is not controlled
by the Commission of the European Communities.
However, the policies of the two institutions are
co-ordinated implicitly since the Commission's
policy and action proposals have to be ratified by
Councils of appropriate Ministers from member states'
governments, so Finance Ministers (EIB Governors) duly deal with financial and economic matters.   The
Bank acknowledged at the outset that it must work
closely with the Commission.[1]

a)   LIAISON BETWEEN THE EIB AND THE COMMISSION
     OF THE EUROPEAN COMMUNITIES

Liaison between the Commission and the European
Investment Bank is through the Commission's single
representative on the Bank's Board of Directors,
usually the Director-General for Economic and Financial Affairs or the Director-General for Regional
Affairs, and their Alternates.   As stated, (p.49),
the Bank informs the Commission of each loan application and the Commission, through its representative,
must give an opinion on it.   If the Commission
opposes a loan, then the EIB's Board of Directors
may only grant it by unanimous decision, the Commission's representative abstaining.[2]   Thus, the
Commission has some control over the projects which
the EIB funds, but its power of veto can be over-
ridden.   Neither institution cares to admit the
number of times or kinds of projects over which conflicts have arisen.   There are daily contacts between the two organisations and meetings between
Commission staff from the appropriate Directorates
and Bank staff to review current and prospective
developments of common concern.   For example, a
member of the Environment and Consumer Service staff
represents the EEC Commission at discussions with

the Bank's Technical Assessment staff on possible
ways in which loan projects may affect the environment, while the Commission's Directorate of Social
Affairs is represented at discussions on possible
effects on employment and social repercussions.

b) LENDING INSTRUMENTS ADMINISTERED BY THE
   COMMISSION OF THE EUROPEAN COMMUNITIES

As well as lending directly itself, the European Investment Bank also acts as an agent for and
on the mandate of either the whole EEC or individual
member states.   This process is particularly connected with loans outside the EEC (see Chapters 14
and 15), but in the late 1970s was increasing within
the Community.   It arises partly from the fact that,
while the Bank has been far and away the most important source of long-term finance in the Community,
it is not the only one.   Other Community instruments
drawing funds from the world capital market are:

i)   the European Coal and Steel Community
      (ECSC)

ii)   Euratom.

iii) European Development Fund (EDF).

iv)   Community borrowings and loans, balance
      of payments.

v)   Loans for exploiting Alternative Energy
      Sources.

vi)   Loans for Demonstration Projects in
      Energy Saving.

vii) the New Community Instrument for Borrow-
      ing and Lending.

viii) 3% interest subsidies for less prosperous
      countries which have joined the European
      Monetary System (Italy and Ireland have
      been designated).[3]

                          (See Table 1a)

The European Development Fund was intended to
assist overseas territories and its relations with
the EIB are dealt with below in Chapters 14 and 15.
    The ECSC was in existence for six years before
the EEC was set up.   When it and Euratom were both
brought under the Commission of the European Communities in 1967, the Commission's Directorate
General for Credit and Investments raised funds for
both bodies through public and private borrowings
on the capital market.
    The European Coal and Steel Community fund is

raised partly also through a levy on coal and steel production in Community countries which is paid to the Commission. Altogether, between 1954 and the end of 1978, the ECSC borrowed and re-lent a total of 5,320 million ua. The arrangement whereby the Bank of International Settlements acts as depositary for ECSC funds continues.[4] The EIB has supported ECSC projects and has lent funds to the ECSC. Euratom carried out only two borrowing operations between 1958 and 1977,[5] which is rather surprising in view of the growth of member countries' nuclear power programmes from 1967 and especially after 1973 (Table 6c). While both the EIB and ECSC have reserves to back up their commitments, Euratom and the EDF do not, debts of defaulters being covered out of the general Community budget.[6]

In 1969, the EEC introduced a system of medium-term monetary credits to supplement the existing EEC system of short-term money supports so that a country with a serious balance of payments problem might receive credits from other Community countries for 2-5 year terms, in line with Article 108 of the Treaty of Rome, an occasion on which the weighted voting system, the 'qualified majority', could be used (see page 9).[7] The Community Balance of Payments Financing was created in 1975 precisely for the same reason, that is to put borrowed capital at the disposal of member states with balance of payments problems due to the rises in prices of petroleum products.

However, the EEC's share of borrowings on the capital markets has so far been small. Like the EIB, the main currency the Community has borrowed has been US dollars. The funds raised in the market are administered by the Community until they are used.

c) THE ENCOURAGEMENT OF REGIONAL DEVELOPMENT IN THE LATE 1970s

Other much more extensive means of putting funds directly at the disposal of the Commission of the European Communities were created in the late 1970s. They largely provide finance for projects which the existing borrowing bodies cover. The Commission gave the following reasons for setting up yet more financing instruments:

All regions of the Community with structural problems that justify and necessitate assistance from the public authorities can now call on more than one Community financial instrument.

Since virtually all regions are affected by the oil price rise and need to develop their transport and telecommunications networks, in effect the whole of the Community is covered by this statement. But they could previously 'call on more than one Community instrument.'

The Commission states that it favours a combination of different types of Community and national assistance for regional developments, that is subsidies as well as loans. To facilitate a combination of two or more financial instruments at the end of 1977, it set up a Task Force for Coordination of the Financial Instruments with one of its staff in charge.[8]

The Commission is also trying to integrate operations by geographical areas, and hence the finance for each of these:

> The idea is to attempt to ascertain the area's essential needs, to look into the various ways in which these can be met at national and Community levels, to fit specific projects into a coherent overall framework and to ensure the appropriate follow-up. These operations must then be kept under continuous close scrutiny and be monitored until significant economic progress has been made.[9]

The reason for setting up new instruments, acknowledged by the Commission in the quotation above, is the efforts to achieve a Community of regions in which national boundaries wither away and the concept of 'European' (meaning EEC) citizenship replaces that of national citizenship. There were, however, three other reasons which are now acknowledged: the effects, firstly, of oil price rises from 1973; secondly, competition from overseas industry to the whole industrial and infrastructure development of the Community countries and, thirdly, a desire to diminish the independence of the EIB.

d) ECONOMIC DIFFICULTIES IN THE LATE 1970s

The discomfiture caused by the oil price rises and by the decline in the steel industry in the Community is, to some extent, reflected in the EIB's borrowing and lending figures (see Table 3a). In 1974, there were considerable increases in both types of operation. But these tailed off in 1975-76, although the Bank received an injection of subscribed capital in 1975. The Community, on the other hand, in 1976 borrowed 1,249 million ua to assist balance of payments financing and the ECSC 956 million ua as against the EIB's total for that year for all projects of 732 million ua.

The disquiet was also reflected in a pronouncement from the European Council of Ministers' Meeting on 25-6 March, 1977, which invited:

> On the one hand, the Commission, in particular by better use of Community instruments, and on the other hand, the Board of Governors of the European Investment Bank to seek ways of improving their activities.[10]

The implication was that neither body had been doing as well as expected. The Commission reacted by proliferating borrowing instruments and by its scheme for integrated regional economic development. The EIB reacted by stepping up its borrowing in 1977 and, in 1978, it was also granted another instalment of subscribed capital.

e) LOANS FOR THE DEVELOPMENT OF RENEWABLE ENERGY SOURCES

A belated Community decision to diversify led to the creation in the 1970s of several new funding and lending instruments. Following the 1973 oil crisis, in 1974 they set up grant-giving bodies for Aid for Hydrocarbon Development and, in 1976, to subsidise Uranium Prospection in EEC territory. In 1975, for the first time, the Council of the Communities decided to encourage research on solar power. By 1978, there had been enough success with this form of energy at a commercial level to lead them to create an instrument for granting loans for exploiting Alternative Energy Sources and another for Demonstration Projects for Energy Saving.[11] It could be said that the two lending bodies, like the two giving grants, were different from other EEC lending instruments in that, at first, they were for research and for projects regarded as experimental. They were not for profitable business enterprises, nor immediately for infrastructure except insofar as all energy is a contribution to infrastructure. Any financial hazards in developing new sources could, however, have been dealt with through the EIB under existing provisions for particularly risky schemes (see Chapter 14). These were instruments of the EEC Commission, not of the Bank.

f) INCREASED EURATOM LOANS

Early in 1977, the EEC Council of Energy Ministers, under the Presidency of Anthony Wedgwood Benn, then British Secretary for Energy, decided to empower the Commission, at its own discretion, to grant Euratom loans to finance nuclear power stations, in order to increase electricity production.[12] On 29 March, 1977, therefore, the Commission was authorised to contract loans in the name of the European Atomic Energy Community to finance investment in industrial-scale generation of electricity from nuclear sources, and for the installation of plant for processing nuclear fuel. The Council of Energy Ministers authorised a first tranche of loan issues so that the Commission might borrow up to 500 million ua, 'provided that the (European Investment) Bank be invited to act as agent in carrying out the lending operation'. Thus, it signified its confidence in the EIB's methods of appraisal of loan applications, of concluding finance contracts, of administering and monitoring projects.

In the following 22 months, these Euratom loans via the Commission were granted to:

Sociétés réunies d'energie du
Bassin de l'Escaut - EBES
(Belgium)   ..   ..   ..   c.   50 mua

Centrale nucléaire européene à
neutrons rapides - NERSA (France)   c.   89 mua

Sté. Luxembourgeoise de centrales
nucleaires ..   ..   ..   c.   111 mua

Ente nazionale per l'energia
ellectrica - ENEL (Italy)   ..   c.   70 mua

By 1979, the initial loan level of 300 million ua, agreed by the Council of Energy Ministers, had been relaxed. The Council therefore agreed that the Commission should have the right to grant Euratom loans up to a total of 1 billion European units of account.[13]

g) THE NEW COMMUNITY INSTRUMENT FOR BORROWING AND LENDING - THE 'ORTOLI FACILITY'

Besides reacting to these economic shocks, as early as the end of 1970, the Commission's officials apparently awoke to the immense power of the autonomous European Investment Bank.

At that time there were a number of plans being

formulated within the Commission to strengthen the Community's economic and monetary union.[14] The control over the EIB's lending by national governments meant that the Bank's loans could be used rather more individualistically by each Community country in pursuit of national aims and less in favour of regional as opposed to national development. The realisation was unwelcome to those wishing to build a supranational Community. Hence, the Commission's emphasis on regional development through its financing. Relations between the two institutions appear to have been difficult for seven years thereafter until, in 1977, there was a change of leadership of the Commission's Directorate of Economic and Social Affairs. M. Francois-Xavier Ortoli then became the Commissioner in charge. As French Economic and Finance Minister in the first Pompidou administration, he had been the French representative on the Bank's Board of Governors from July 1968 until June 1969. He therefore had some first-hand experience of the Bank. According to members of the Commission, relations with the Bank improved from the time of his appointment.

Yet, in the middle of 1977, a new instrument for obtaining and granting loans was proposed by the Commission, on the grounds that it would enable the Community to step up action to tackle unemployment, sluggish investment and lack of progress in levelling out economic performance among member states, and that it would provide additional finance. Thus it would duplicate everything which the European Investment Bank was created to do. On 6 December, 1977, the Council of Finance Ministers declared in favour of creating, on a trial basis, a New Community Borrowing & Lending Instrument, again with the Bank to handle resulting loans. The New Community Instrument for Borrowing & Lending (NCI), known as the Ortoli Facility, was duly authorised in May 1978 and created in 1979. As in the case of the Bank and the other big EEC institutions, the ECSC, Euratom and the European Development Fund, capital is subscribed by member states. Also, in the same way, it operates in the world financial markets.

Thus, through the Ortoli Facility the Commission is empowered by the Council of Finance Ministers to borrow up to 1 billion units of account on the world money markets, including the internal EEC market, in the name of the EEC. The idea of the NCI operating on a trial basis has apparently been forgotten.

The NCI funds are deposited with the European Investment Bank. They are to be used for loans to

further the Community's priority objectives as laid
down by the Council - currently, energy, industry
and infrastructure, with due regard to the regional
impact of the projects concerned and the urgent need
to combat unemployment.   The Commission decides
which projects are eligible for loans in conformity
with these objectives.   The EIB floats issues on
the world financial market to raise funds for the
NCI, assesses applications for loans and makes the
final decision on whether or not a loan is to be
given.   The initiative is with the Commission, not
the Bank, however;   the Bank has only a power of
veto.   This is the reverse of the situation on the
Bank's Board of Directors in respect of its own
financial operations.

The EIB does not itself provide security for
Commission loans.   On 4 August, 1977, the Board of
Governors decided that they would be dealt with
under the Bank's Special Section.   The Special
Section had been set up in 1963 and covered loans to
countries outside the Community and schemes in which
the risks of non-repayment were so great that the
Bank considered them unacceptable (see Chapters 14
and 15)[15]   The Bank had long lived with the problems
of financing in the Mezzogiorno and the comparative
poverty of Ireland was well known when she joined
the Community.   But the economic problems of the
United Kingdom in general and of the chemicals, textiles, metals and metal products industries in the
rest of the Community, which had developed by 1977,
were unforeseen and the Bank was unhappy about the
extra financing required of it by the Community
countries to meet the crisis:

> The expansion of Bank financing in support of
> objectives defined by the European Council,
> i.e. to meet the crisis, could, in certain
> cases, be facilitated greatly by the intro-
> duction, for example, within the framework of
> national aid systems, of measures to provide
> exchange risk cover for industrial borrowers,
> and financial guarantees in favour of econo-
> mically viable projects in sectors in diffi-
> culty.[16]

As we know (Chapter 3), the British Government introduced exchange risk cover.   For the rest, the
Special Section was invoked as from August 1977.

In respect of its own financing, the European
Investment Bank is not required by its Statute to
obtain a government guarantee of repayment for each
loan, but may instead accept either the customary

collateral security asked for by any bank when it
lends money. [17]   Whereas, in the operations brought
under the EIB's Special Section, loan security is
the responsibility of the Community or member countries, [18] and is:

> either supplied directly by the responsible
> authorities or collected (by the EIB) under
> mandate for the account and at the risk of
> member states, the European Economic Commu-
> nity and the European Atomic Energy Communi-
> ty. [19]

The security for the Commission's lending instruments, therefore, is the assets of each of the member states, because the Commission itself, while
administering a vast budget, has only a small reserve fund.

This extension of the EIB's Special Section
permitted a greater and more flexible use of the reserves and assets of Community countries as security
for loans.   The New Community Instrument also provided more flexibility in that Euratom loans could
only be for nuclear energy, while the NCI loans can
provide finance for any kind of power and for other
infrastructure projects.   In addition , the Commission, by preserving control of the selection of loan
projects, raised its own importance in EEC loan
operations vis-a-vis the Bank.   The Bank's stated
view was that its role in these New Community instruments not only assured the use of the Bank's
expertise and its high financial standing, but also
the co-ordination of two new important funds. [20]

After consulting the European Parliament on 14
May, 1979, the Council adopted a Decision, authoris-
ing an initial first tranche of borrowings up to
500 mua for the NCI, the same as in the Commission's
Euratom operations.   The first loans were made the
following September. [21]

h)   THE COMMISSION's CHALLENGE TO EIB AUTONOMY

All big banks raise and manage loans on behalf
of other parties, charging fees for handling such
operations.   The EIB is unusual only in that it charges
no fees for handling such business on behalf of other
Community institutions, despite the greater load due to
the new Commission borrowing and lending instruments.

By the end of 1979, the borrowings and lendings
of the three Commission instruments, the ECSC,
Euratom and the NCI, equalled about half those of
the EIB's borrowing and lending from its own re-

sources.   Moreover, the Commission, with its Euratom loans and the Ortoli Facility putting poten-
tially a total of 2,000 mill. units of account at its
disposal, was then on the way to emulating the total
amount the EIB lent from its own resources which, in
1980 amounted to 2,753 million units of account.[22]

The Ortoli Facility has begun to function, however, at a time of unrest affecting both capital
markets and many currencies.   By the end of September 1979 it was being said that the Ortoli borrowings might be on a fairly modest scale as a result and, indeed, in 1980 they were 79.4 mill. ua
less than the previous year.   The Commission's
plans for launching loans in favour of transport development have been shelved, (p.137).

i)   THE DEVELOPMENT OF EEC ECONOMIC LINKS -
     CURRENCY & INTEREST SUBSIDIES

When a move was made to EEC integration with
the adoption by the European Council, on 4-5 December, 1978, of a decision to take a first step towards the merging of national currencies in a Euro-
currency through the European Monetary System, there
was also a reiteration of the need to strengthen
less prosperous members.   As a result, Community
institutions and the Bank were invited to make
available to them loans of up to 1000 million ua per
year for up to five years.   The Commission promptly
submitted to the European Communities a proposal to
provide a 3 per cent interest subsidy on certain of
the loans made from the Bank's own resources and on
loans from the New Community Instrument for Borrowing and Lending, to Italy and Ireland, both EMS
members.   The NCI loans were to be raised on the
capital markets and made available in five annual
tranches, at a cost of up to 200 mua each.   And
they were only for financing certain infrastructure
projects which would 'neither directly nor indirectly distort the competitiveness of specific industries in member states.'[23] Subsidies had been made
available from the Regional Development Fund to pay
off the interest on EIB loans.[24]   But the Regional
Development Fund is made up of grants whereas the
new EMS subsidies come from the world's capital
markets.

j)   THE STRAIN OF INCREASED BORROWING ON THE EIB

In a 1980 study of the outlook for the Bank, a
working party recruited from the EIB's Board of
Directors concluded that there might, as a result of
the recession, be some limitations on the Bank's

activities.[25] They set out an order of precedence for Bank lendings:

> The upward trend in financing outside the Community should not jeopardise the maintenance and, if possible, the boosting in real terms of the volume of Bank lending in the less prosperous member countries....

> Should the financial market situation leave the Bank temporarily unable to raise the resources it needs to deal with all the applications it receives, it will be constrained selectively to reduce the proportion of its contribution...and apply more restrictively its eligibility criteria, concentrating the resources available in the kind of investment that takes the greatest priority.[26]

It was once more accorded an increase in the total of subscribed capital as we have seen (Table 1b).

k) CONCLUSIONS

A superficial look at relations between the EIB and the Commission of the European Communities might suggest that the Bank is much more an instrument of individual government policies than the Commission. However, the Commission, too, is the creation of member states' governments. It was as a result of their collective invitation that lending by both the Bank and the Commission was increased. To assist member states in the resolution of their economic difficulties, from 1977 the Commission itself was empowered to raise loans against the guarantees of each member country or of them all as a Community. The aim was to increase financing through the world capital markets via the existing channels of the EIB and ECSC, by the use of other EEC bodies.

Thus, the vast national resources of the EEC countries are increasingly used to provide more liquidity and to create credit without necessarily a concomitant increase in their cash base. This, taken together with a new drive to promote regional development and thus the realisation of the Community, would appear to provide sounder reasons for the EEC's creation of lending instruments with an almost rococco abandon during the deepening economic crisis of the late 1970s than a desire to exercise a degree of control over the EIB's activities.

However, the question raised for the ordinary citizen of a member state of the European Economic Community is which of the two institutions, Commission or Bank, is more within reach of democratic control in case the direction of financing may cause anxiety. While the Commission apparently has the welfare of Community persons at heart with its concern for employment and the environment, the profusion and complexity of its financing makes any kind of informed opinion extremely difficult to attain. The publicity of the EIB, on the other hand, like its structure, is commendably clear. Furthermore, although given little publicity by the media and therefore having a rather retiring image, in fact as already pointed out, since it is run directly by the member states' governments, it is susceptible theoretically of a more direct degree of democratic control than the Commission with its ever-changing Councils of Ministers and multifarious consultative bodies. Moreover, any one government can only influence the Community institutions administered by the Commission if it succeeds in persuading a majority of the other member governments of its views and much horse-trading goes on. Unanimity in policies is not always achieved as it was over measures to meet the crisis in 1977.

For the ordinary citizens, the upshot of the activities of both institutions under the direction, to a greater or lesser degree, of successive and politically different governments has been, as shown below, by means of 'modernisation and conversion of enterprises' to reduce employment and by many infrastructure and chemical industry loans to increase the hazards to the environment.

NOTES

1. EIB, 1958 Annual Report, 16.

2. EIB, Statute, Articles 21 (6) & 11 (2).

3. Commission of the European Communites, 'Borrowing and Lending Instruments in the context of the Community's financial instruments from European Economy', No.6, July 1980, 77 ff.

4. E. Noël, Working Together, the Institutions of the European Economic Community, 1979, 11; Bank of International Settlements, 1974 Annual Report, 7, 158.

5. Commission of the European Communities, op. cit., 79, Note 2.

6. Commission of the European Communities, op. cit., 87.

7. EIB 1969 Annual Report, 22.   There was a ceiling on the amounts of credits each country contributed:

    Federal Republic of Germany   ..   600⎫
    France   ..   ..   ..   600⎬   TOTAL:
    Italy   ..   ..   ..   400⎬   2,000 mill. ua.
    Netherlands   ..   ..   200⎬
    Belgium and Luxembourg   ..   200⎭

    It was a step towards the European Monetary System.

8. Commission of the European Communities, 'Borrowing and Lending Instruments in the context of the Community's financial instruments', European Economy, No. 6, July 1980, 87.

9. Ibid. 88

10. EIB, 1977 Annual Report, 15.

11. Commission of the European Communities, Grants and Loans from the European Community, April 1979, 37.

12. The Times, 21.7.78, letter from Nigel Haigh, Vice-President, European Environmental Bureau, Director of the Institute for European Environmental Policy, 19 October, 1978, & Michael Shanks' comments. EIB, 1977 Ann. Rep., 16.

13. EEC OJ No. L 12/28, 17.1.80, amending Decision 77/271 Euratom; OJ No. C 316/13, 17.12.79, answer to written question from Mrs. Lizin, European MP on the First Report on Euratom borrowing and lending activities.

14. EIB 1971 Annual Report, 21-2: the Barre Plan, see Memorandum Special Memorandum from the Commission on the Community's medium-term economic policy, December 1969 and July 1970; Council of the Community Resolution, see Official Gaz. of the European Communities, 27 March, 1971, No. C28: the Third Programme of Medium-term Economic Policy adopted by the Commission on 9 February, 1971.

15. EIB, Annual Reports, 1964, 51-2: 1967, 20-1; Statute, Art.6 (6).

16. EIB, 1977 Annual Report, 15.

17. EIB, 1959 Annual Report, 16.

18. EIB, Annual Reports, 1964, 51; 1980, 51.

19. Ibid, 74, Note 1.

20. EIB 1978 Annual Report, 9.   The recipients of the first Ortoli loans were the United Kingdom, Ireland and Italy.

21. EIB Press Release, 29 January, 1980.

22. EEC Council Decision of 14.5.79, applying Decision 78/870/ EEC (of 16.10.78) empowering the Commission to contract loans for the purpose of promoting investment within the Community.   European Parliament written question No. 815/78 by Mr. Ansquer to the EEC Commission, 30.11.78. Financial Times, 26.9.79: EIB Press Release, 29 January, 1980.

23. EIB Annual Reports, 1977, 9, 15, 16; 1978, 9-11. Bank of International Settlements, 1979 Annual Report, 44-48.

24. Daily Telegraph, 21 September, 1979. Harrop op.cit. 23.

25. EIB Information, No.22, July 1980, M. Le Portz, 3, 8.

26. Ibid., M. Le Portz, 3, Points 2 & 4: No.26, July, 1981, 4-5.

Chapter 5

EUROPEAN INVESTMENT BANK LENDING FOR ENERGY PROJECTS OTHER THAN NUCLEAR POWER

The great industrial expansion which the creators of the European Community wanted depended partly on increased supplies of electrical power. In support of this policy, therefore, the European Investment Bank has granted loans for a wide range of energy enterprises over long periods of time (see Table 5a).

a) EIB LOANS FOR COAL AND LIGNITE

The recipients of EIB loans for coal and lignite mining inside the Community have been Italy, Britain, Denmark and West Berlin, for which EEC economic support was laid down in the Treaty of Rome.[1] Up to the end of 1972, because of the cheapness of Middle East oil and the continuing fall in its price, together with the relatively low costs involved in its use compared with those for other fossil fuels, the coal industries of France, West Germany and the Benelux countries were deliberately run down. As Table 5a shows, the EIB did not grant a single loan for solid fuel extraction before 1973.

The Community was particularly sensitive to the oil price rise since imported oil covered nearly two-thirds - 63 per cent - of the EEC's total energy requirements. However, there were wide differences in the degree of dependence on oil imports amongst the different member states (see Table 5b given on page 83).

Interest in coal and lignite revived after the sudden increase in oil prices in 1974 (see Table 5a and Fig. 5a). The previous year, Britain with its big coal industry had joined the EEC and, in 1975, the EIB granted loans for British coal mining in Wales, Yorkshire and the Midlands, and to British Rail for special rolling stock for hauling coal. The Bank has also been helping to finance coal-

TABLE 5a: Amounts lent by the European Investment Bank for Power Projects other than Nuclear Energy and proportion of total financing they represent (Amount = mills.ua : EIB own resources : to nearest whole per cent)

Kind of Project	1958-72		1973-77		1978-80	
	Amount	% of Total Financing	Amount	% of Total Financing	Amount	% of Total Financing
Thermal Power Stations	75.1	3.0	75.9	1.5	361.6	4.2
Hydro-electric Power Stations & Pumped Storage Plants	87.7	3.6	157.8	3.2	470.2	5.5
Development of Oil and Natural Gas Deposits	2.5	0.1	304.0	6.2	172.2	2.0
Solid Fuel Extraction	-	-	16.7	0.3	23.9	0.3
Power Lines	5.0	0.2	73.6	1.5	338.8	3.9
Gaslines and Oil Pipelines	125.8	5.1	333.5	6.7	383.4	4.4
Geothermal Power Stations	-	-	-	-	29.1	0.03*
District Heating Plant	-	-	-	-	40.8	0.5 **
Solar	-	-	-	-	2.6	0.03***

SOURCES: EIB, 1958-1978, 24-5 : EIB Annual Report 1978, 32; 1979, 38; 1980, 38, 87.

* 1978 only
** 1978 and 1979 only
*** 1979 only

burning power stations.   In 1977 and 1978, it
granted loans to convert Asnaes power station, west
of Copenhagen, from oil to coal-burning and in March
1980 it announced another loan for a coal-fired
station, also in Denmark, in East Jutland.

TABLE 5b: Oil as per cent of Total Fuel Imported
            by EEC Countries in 1973

Over 99%	..	Denmark and Luxembourg
83 - 86%	..	Italy and Belgium
78 - 80%	..	France and Ireland
55%	..	Federal Republic of Germany
48%	..	United Kingdom
6%	..	Netherlands

SOURCE: EIB, 1958-1978, 37.

b)   EIB LOANS FOR NATURAL GAS UP TO THE END OF 1972

Up until 1963 natural gas was little used in
the EEC.   By the late 1970s it accounted for 16.4
per cent of all energy consumed, 156 million tonnes
of oil equivalent, and the proportion was expected
to rise to about 18 per cent, equal to the contribution of coal, by 1985.[2]
Pipelines to convey natural gas have been among
the most spectacular of the power projects supported
by the EIB.   These pipelines were planned in the
1960s with the aim of creating an EEC gas grid.   The
system originated in the Netherlands in 1964 with
the laying of a pipeline to convey natural gas from
the province of Groningen where low calorific or
'L' gas was discovered.   Most other local and imported gas in the EEC was of high calorific value,
so a separate distribution system had to be provided
for the Groningen 'L' gas, not only in the Netherlands, but in other countries in the EEC and in
Switzerland which, of course, is not a member of the
Community.   The immediate recipients of EIB loans
for the creation of a gas pipeline network have been
the public gas supply authorities (see Map 5a and
Table 5d).
The Bank has also assisted the transmission of
natural gas imports from outside the Community.   In
1972 it granted 30 million ua to Gaz de France for
a plant at Fos-sur-Mer, near the mouth of the Rhône
at Marseilles where liquid gas was brought from

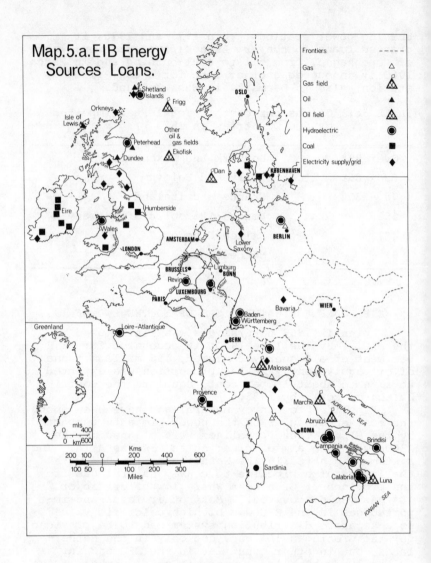

Map. 5. a. EIB Energy Sources Loans.

Frontiers — — — —
Gas △
Gas field ⬱
Oil ▲
Oil field ⬱
Hydroelectric ●
Coal ■
Electricity supply/grid ◆

Shetland Islands
Frigg
Orkneys
Isle of Lewis
OSLO
Peterhead
Dundee
Other oil & gas fields
Ekofisk
Dan
KØBENHAVEN
Eire
Humberside
Wales
BERLIN
AMSTERDAM
Lower Saxony
LONDON
BRUSSELS
Limburg
Revin
BONN
PARIS
LUXEMBOURG
Baden-Württemberg
Bavaria
WIEN
Loire-Atlantique
BERN
Malossa
Provence
Marche
ADRIACTIC SEA
Abruzzi
ROMA
Brindisi
Campania
Calabria
Luna
Sardinia
IONIAN SEA

Greenland

mls 400
km 600

Kms 200 400 600
200 100 0
100 50 0
Miles
100 200 300

84

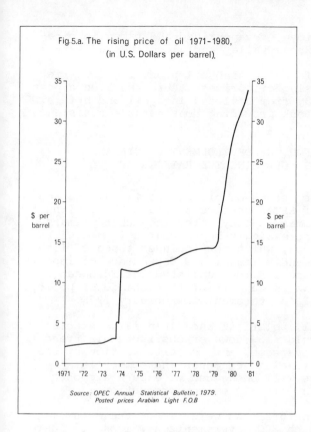

Fig.5.a. The rising price of oil 1971-1980, (in U.S. Dollars per barrel).

Source: OPEC Annual Statistical Bulletin, 1979.
Posted prices Arabian Light F.O.B

FIG.5b : Value of Oil Imports (in US $ 1000m) in 4 largest EEC countries compared with those of the USA and Japan

	1972	1973	1974	1975	1978	1979 1st Half[1]	1979 Total[2]	1980 Total[2]
West Germany)	2.32	3.40	8.87	8.02	9.94	6.72	16.84	26.93
France) EEC	2.70	3.54	9.86	9.71	12.01	7.22	18.10	29.15
Britain)	2.29	3.18	8.71	7.49	6.77	2.20	5.51	7.00
Italy)	2.45	3.40	9.65	8.20	10.77	6.06	15.19	24.44
United States	2.38	4.23	16.60	19.75	34.26	19.81	49.65	81.94
Japan	3.93	6.00	18.90	19.64	23.40	13.33	33.41	56.58

[1]Actual. [2]Estimated.

SOURCE: Swiss Bank Corporation, Prospects, No.2, 1980, 15.

85

Algeria and Libya, revapourised and taken in pipelines up the Rhône valley and along the Mediterranean coast.[3]

Thus, before the Arab oil-producing countries
commenced raising oil prices, there had been a power
revolution away from coal and into oil and natural
gas with the Bank providing considerable assistance
for gas projects.

c) EIB LOANS FOR THE DEVELOPMENT OF OIL AND
   NATURAL GAS FOLLOWING THE RAISING OF OIL
   PRICES

The Arabs' stand on oil prices in 1973 caused
governments of EEC countries to press ahead with
energy programmes. They determined that primary
energy must increasingly be generated from EEC
domestic sources, which now included those of Ireland, Denmark and Britain, and dependence on imports
must be decreased. They enlisted the European
Investment Bank in support of this change of policy,
witness the EIB's statement in February 1975:

> Technical, political and financial obstacles
> which could slow down or obstruct this trend
> must be overcome, and concerted action by the
> EEC, national governments and commercial
> interests will be needed to ensure a smooth
> growth in domestic energy production.[4]

Oil and natural gas were two of the main
sources to which EEC governments now looked. There
were indigenous Community sources to be developed,
but also new sources other than those held by Arab
countries.

There was a sharp distinction between the two
fuels. Until recently, natural gas has remained
relatively cheap because it has not been used in a
number of countries. It is still considered uneconomic to use in some places. In parts of the North
Sea and other sites where gas is a by-product of oil
extraction, it is often simply burnt off. However,
because of the oil price rise, natural gas has become more attractive and because of its cheapness,
demand for it has risen.

Since both oil and natural gas resources are
found in similar areas in EEC waters and require
similar equipment and installations for their exploitation, the EIB's loans for these purposes have
often been intended for either type of fuel. In
October 1973, just when the Arab initiative in

raising oil prices was beginning, the EIB provided
loans to Italian state agencies of 27.8 million ua
(L.22,650 mill.) for two semi-submersible drilling
platforms to be built by a Hamburg firm, Blom & Voss.
In December 1974, it granted a direct loan to the
Italian state agency, SAIPEM, of 12.4 million ua for
the construction, in a Trieste shipyard belonging to
Italcantieri, of a semi-submersible pipe-laying
barge, <u>Castoro VI</u>.   It was intended to operate in
Norwegian and Scottish waters for up to 300 days in
a year in place of the then usual 120 days.   The
Bank also granted Istituto Mobiliare Italiano a loan
of 15.7 million to finance the vessel.

Also, in December 1974, the Bank granted a loan
of 7.7 million ua for the construction in the Isle
of Lewis in the Hebrides of a steel fabrication complex to make semi-submersible platforms.   The
recipient was Lewis Offshore Limited, a subsidiary
of the private Fred Olsen and Aker groups.   Once
the presence of oil or gas was established, the complex was intended to produce prefabricated steel
decks for the concrete production, drilling and
storage platforms.   The EIB envisaged some 1,000
workers making and assembling a variety of offshore
equipment which could be launched from two graving
docks.[5]   The project went ahead as planned.

In 1974, the EIB granted loans for the development of the Frigg oil and gas field, partly in
British, partly in Norwegian territorial waters.   A
first loan of 19.5 million ua went to French companies, the state-owned Elf Oil Exploration and
Production & Aquitaine Oil, which contracted with
the British Gas Corporation to supply natural gas
for distribution throughout most of Britain.   The
Bank has granted several loans direct to the British
Gas Corporation for the distribution of Frigg gas.
By October 1976, these loans totalled £67.8 million,
over a third of the then cost of piping gas from the
Frigg field to the Scottish mainland at St. Fergus,
and then across country to meet the existing Scottish natural gas distribution system at Bathgate and
to north west and north east England.[6]

Since, by Article 18 of its Statute, the Bank
is empowered to fund projects outside the EEC, if
they are considered to be in the Community's
interests, it has lent not only for the development
of the British but also of the Norwegian sectors of
both the Frigg and Ekofisk oil and gas fields.   In
1977, the Bank granted a further 35.3 million ua to
Elf Oil Exploration & Production (UK) Ltd. and
Aquitaine Oil (UK) Ltd., together with 8.8 million
ua to Elf Aquitaine Norge AS, a multinational

venture for the development of the Norwegian sector of the Frigg field. Similarly, the Bank has lent for the development of the Norwegian Ekofisk oil and gas field, to a group which included the Italian state enterprise, AGIP and the UK Phillips Petroleum Company, in which the British-based chemical transnational, ICI, has a 51 per cent stake. The Bank stated:

> ....the interest to the EEC is clear since the entire gas production - it will meet 7% of total consumption - and the bulk of the oil production of the field are intended for the Community.[7]

The gas from Ekofisk is now landed at Emden in West Germany and the oil on Teesside, near one of the big ICI production complexes (see Chapters 8 and 13).

The Bank has also been granting loans for the development of oil alone in the British Thistle and Beryl North Sea fields and, in 1975, for the small Danish field, Danfelt. As with liquid natural gas, it has assisted the distribution of oil with a loan to the Shetland Islands Council for the construction of an oil tanker terminal in Sullom Voe.[8] The Bank stated that it was expected that by 1982 a minimum of 65 million tonnes of oil would be landed there by submarine pipelines and shipped out to refineries in the United Kingdom and on the Continent. It was hoped that this supply would reduce the dependence of EEC countries on oil imports by providing 50 per cent of the UK's estimated needs and about 10 per cent of those of the other EEC countries.[9]

The EIB supported similar ventures in the Mediterranean. By 1975 five small gas fields had been found in Emilia Romagna and the Adriatic, off the Abruzzi and the Marches. A sixth was found in 1978 in the Ionian Sea. The Bank lent for the development of all of them.[10]

Prospecting is also taking place on land. One result has been that AGIP has discovered large oil and gas deposits at much deeper levels and at much higher temperatures than any previously found, in the Malossa Field in the valley of the River Po, 25 km. from Milan. In January 1975, the EIB lent AGIP 30 million ua for the development of an anticipated 15 wells, each over 6,000 metres deep. They were expected to produce about 3,000 million cubic metres of gas and 2.5 million tonnes of oil a year.[11]

d) EIB LOANS FOR THE TRANS-EEC GAS PIPELINE SYSTEM

i) Inside the EEC

The EIB also provided a loan for a new section of pipeline running via Maastricht on Holland's southern frontier, across West Germany, through Switzerland and into Italy. Towards the end of 1975 the Bank gave another loan for a similar pipeline project to distribute the 'H' gas from near Maastricht across Belgium to France.[12]

ii) Outside the EEC

In the second half of the 1970s, the EEC countries negotiated supply contracts for natural gas with Libya, Iran and the USSR, and also agreed to purchase both natural gas and oil from Algeria. The Bank granted a large loan of 91.7 million ua for laying pipelines to convey both oil and gas from Algeria to the Italian mainland, a project still under way at present.[13]

In 1973 the EIB began to fund a pipeline on land outside the Community but seen to be in the Community's interest. This was the Trans-Austrian Gasline (TAG), a section of the pipeline running across the European Continent from east to west. TAG is jointly owned by Austrian, Italian and French interests, and brings Soviet gas into the EEC. The Bank lent 23.5 million ua for the scheme via the Italian ENI and 19.8 million ua via Gaz de France.

In 1974, the EIB granted the West German Ruhrgas AG a further 19.9 million ua for the construction of pipelines from the Czechoslovakian frontier to bring gas from the same source and then to distribute it. Three years later, it lent 43.2 million ua (Dm 110 million) to the Mitelleuropaische Gasleitungsgesellschaft - MEGAL - for the construction of pipelines from Waidhaus on the Czechoslovakian frontier (one of two transfer points for Soviet gas)[14] to Medelsheim on the French frontier, and from Oberkappel on the Austrian frontier to Schwandorf in Bavaria. In 1977, the EIB granted a further loan for the TAG pipeline.[15] According to the EIB, the amount of Soviet gas piped to the EEC was still small in 1980 and the main supply from Iran via the Soviet Union has not materialised[16] although moves are afoot to increase supplies.[17]

The EIB has also been giving large loans, mainly to Italy and Britain, for the development of liquid natural gas. Inevitably, the increase in oil prices raised prices for gas and other fuels.[18]

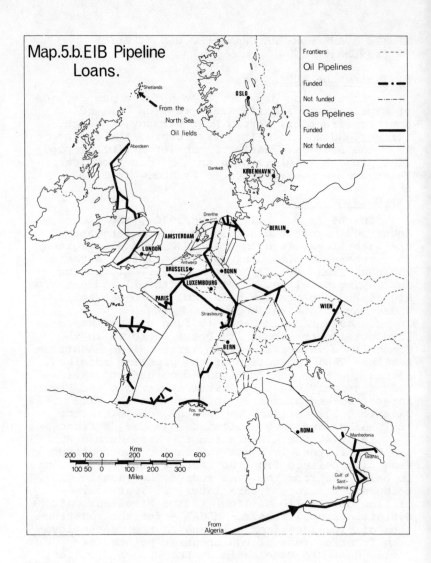

Map.5.b. EIB Pipeline Loans.

Frontiers	
Oil Pipelines	
Funded	
Not funded	
Gas Pipelines	
Funded	
Not funded	

Shetlands

From the
North Sea
Oil fields

OSLO

Aberdeen

Danfeldt

KØBENHAVN

BERLIN

Drenthe

AMSTERDAM

LONDON

Antwerp

BRUSSELS   BONN

LUXEMBOURG

PARIS

Strasbourg   WIEN

BERN

Fos sur
mer

ROMA   Manfredonia

Taranto

Gulf of
Sant -
Eufemia

Kms
200 100   0   200   400   600
100 50 0   100   200   300
Miles

From
Algeria

e) THE RISING COSTS OF ENERGY

Between 1970 and 1976, oil prices in then current terms rose by 500 per cent. Since most of the
oil used in the EEC was imported, the increase had
a considerable effect on the overall balance of
payments:

	1970			1976		
	Value mua	% of GDP	% of total imports	Value mua	% of GDP	% of total imports
NET ENERGY IMPORTS	8,200	1.3	17	43,300	3.7	31

SOURCE: EIB 1958-1978, 37.

By the end of August 1979, the EEC countries' total
trade deficit, with the rest of the world, was considerable - £4,559 million[19] largely because of the
rise in oil prices.

Although prices of oil fluctuated, the general
tendency was for them to rise. The trend was further stimulated by stockpiling of oil by industrialised EEC countries, since oil was not only essential for heat and light, but was also the foundation
of their transport and chemical industries[20] (see
Chapters 7 and 11).

As for other projects, EIB loans have gone to
firms from countries outside the EEC, notably in
1976, when recipients included United States
interests: 27.2 million ua to North Sea Inc. for
the development of the Beryl oilfield and 27.0
million ua to Santa Fe (Minerals) UK Inc. for the
development of the Thistle oilfield. EEC governments, of course, benefitted through licence fees
and taxes paid by oil development companies. In
view of the profitability of oil production, it
might have been thought possible, however, to raise
money for such ventures on the international money
markets without having recourse to the EIB's low
interest loans.[21]

f) HYDROELECTRIC POWER

From the start of the European Economic Community, the EIB has lent for hydroelectric power
schemes. The first loan was in 1959 for a pumped
storage power station at Vianden in the north of
Luxembourg. A barrage was built across the River
Our, the boundary between Luxembourg and West Germany, to create a reservoir of 10 million cubic
metres. Nearly 300 metres higher on the plateau of

Mont St. Nicholas, a second reservoir of 7 million
cubic metres was created.[22] The plant has been expanded since.

In 1963, the Bank granted three loans for
hydroelectric schemes in Italy, in Sardinia, Gallo
Campania and Brindisi.   All three were combined
with irrigation schemes (see Chapter 8 & 13,& Table
8a).   The Bank has also granted three loans for
hydroelectric equipment projects in Provence in
France and, in 1971, lent Electricité de France 16.0
million ua for a pumped storage station in the
Ardennes at Revin.   The power was used to help
operate two nuclear power stations at Chooz in
France and Tihange in Belgium (see Chapter 6).   A
7 million cubic metre reservoir was created in the
valley of the River Fau, a tributary of the Meuse
and, as in Luxembourg, a second, higher reservoir of
about the same size was built on the plateau of
Marquisades de St. Nicholas.[23]

Following the oil price rise, EIB loans for
hydroelectricity increased substantially.   In 1974,
the Bank provided a loan for a pumped storage
station in the south of the Black Forest in the
Federal Republic of Germany.   Again, this involved
a lower reservoir, this time in the Wehr valley and
an upper one near Hornberg village.   The
Schluchseewerk (Black Forest), Vianden and Revin
stations all contribute power not only to the EEC
grid but also to the whole continental electricity
transmission system.   In 1976, the Bank began to
lend for the Dinorwic pumped storage scheme in
Wales in the UK, the largest it had so far financed.
The scheme will be capable of delivering 1,500 mega-
watts of electricity.   It involves the excavation
of a mountain as well as the building of two large
dams to increase the capacities of two natural lakes,
Marchlyn Mawr and Llyn Peris.   From 1974, lending
for hydroelectricity in Italy also increased and by
the early part of 1980 amounted to 90 billion lire.

In addition, the EIB handled loans for hydro-
electricity in Italy, amounting to 40 billion lire,
from the Ortoli facility.   Inevitably, these
schemes also involved the building of large dams.
While the earlier projects provided irrigation, as
well as power, these recent North Italian projects
are purely for the generation of electricity.[24]
These North Italian loans are good examples of the
use of EEC funds for non-repayable grants to reduce
interest payments.   Both loans from the EIB are for
12 years at fixed interest rates of 11.9 per cent.
But an EMS subsidy of 3 per cent of the interest
reduces the amount Energia Nazionale Ellectrica must
pay to 8.9 per cent.

g) GEOTHERMAL POWER

In 1979, the Bank lent to ENEL, the Italian
state electricity authority, for the development of
geothermal power.   The loan covered half the cost
of five geothermal power stations, the two most important sites being in Tuscany, near Sienna.   One
great advantage of these geothermal stations is
that they use no fuel. Unless it is linked to a
heat distribution scheme, a cooling tower is needed,
but external water is not required for it.   About
20 per cent of the water taken out of the ground is
returned to it; however, there is waste since the
remainder escapes into the air in the form of steam.
Such power stations may be remote controlled and can
be moved to different sites.[25]

i) PEAT

The Bank has lent 33.8 m.ua for an age-old
power source - Irish peat.   Peat-fired power stations supply 20 per cent of Ireland's electricity
consumption, and Bord Na Mona, the Irish peat development authority, claimed that, in 1978, peat
production was the equivalent of 936,000 tonnes of
oil imports.   The Bank, in 1979, provided two loans
towards the cost of putting into production peat
bogs in five new areas.   Once worked out, Bord Na
Mona and An Fora Taluntais, the Irish Agricultural
Research Organisation, plan to bring the land under
cultivation.   It had previously been unfit for
farming.[26]   However, the project is not acceptable
to everyone, for environmentalists are unhappy
since the bogs are of outstanding significance for
wild life.

h) RENEWABLE ENERGY SOURCES

In the financing of solar, wind and other renewable sources of energy, the EEC and the Bank
have made a very small and cautious beginning.   It
was not until 1978 that the EEC Commission began its
scheme for Loans for the Development of Alternative
Energy Sources, mainly solar power (see Table 1a).
Of the renewable sources, solar is now accepted as
the most promising.[27]   The EIB gave a small loan
for its development in 1979, of 2.6 million ua
(L.3,000 mill.) to the Italian firm, La Metalli
Industriale SpA, for the reorganisation and
modernisation of two factories in Tuscany producing
solar panels and pyrotenax cables.   In addition,
the Bank has acted as agent for other EEC loans in
this field (see p.224).

h) CONCLUSIONS

The environmental impacts of the various energy projects for which the EIB has granted loans are massive. They have included oil and natural gas platforms, transmission lines, terminals, and huge hydroelectricity projects. A project on the scale of the Dinorwic pumped storage scheme entails considerable disruption to the local environment, even though steps have been taken to reduce the impact (see Chapter 13). Not only has the Bank lent for the production of electricity but it has also assisted the installation of high voltage transmission lines. EIB loans have been instrumental in the destruction of homes, farmlands and forests, the flooding of valleys, and the loss of highly valued landscapes. Dams, taking headwaters out of rivers, may adversely affect the aquatic environment by reducing the oxygen content of rivers downstream at low flows.

The number of accidents involving oil tankers is increasing, as is the cost to the public of dealing with spillages. It should be noted that the main terminal the EEC envisaged for shipments of Algerian liquid natural gas is not on French or Italian Mediterranean coasts, involving a relatively short sea crossing, but at Wilhelmshaven, in the north of the Federal Republic of Germany.[28] Risks arise also from EIB loans for submarine and on-land oil and gas pipe-lines. Procedures for maintenance and stopping of fuel in the event of damage to pipes are not known.[29]

The Bank's funding of various kinds of electricity generating stations encourages polluting emissions of various substances into the air and water. Even with geothermal plants, sulphurous emissions have been a problem.

The Bank has not, of course, been alone in this sort of financing and development. It has acted in accordance with the wishes of the member states' governments. Particularly since the 1973 oil price rise a conflict has sharpened between energy supplies deemed essential for industrial development and the maintenance of living standards, and conservation of natural resources.

The rise in oil prices called into question the future of much of the existing industry in several member states. In determining EIB loan policies, their governments apparently failed to take into account the effects of a likely future decline in some of the kinds of manufacturing industry in the EEC, especially chemicals and transport on

demands for energy. Nor, conversely, has there
apparently been much attempt to link energy planning with a possible revival of less prosperous
industries, such as that now predicted for shipbuilding, because of the greater need for coal-
carrying vessels.

It is questionable whether the EIB's lending
for energy is, as yet, promoting the best mix of
sources. The slowness to react cannot but raise
serious questions about Community planning in
general, and about energy policies laid down for the
Bank by its Board of Governors. Despite the creation of committees since the mid-1960s, there still
appears to be an alarming lack of medium, let alone
long-term energy strategy.

NOTES

1. Treaties Establishing the European Communities, EEC 1973,
   p.498, Joint Declaration on Berlin: EIB 1959 Ann.Rep., 17.

2. EIB, 1958-1978, 40.

3. There were similar terminals for liquid gas shipments at
   La Spezia in Italy, Barcelona in Spain, Le Havre in
   France and Canvey Island at the mouth of the Thames. The
   Belgian Distrigaz, a member of a consortium interested in
   Fos, decided to import gas also through Zeebrugge. EIB
   Information, No.5, May 1976, 4-5.

4. EIB Information, No.2, February 1975, 6.

5. EIB Information, No.7, October 1976, 2-3.

6. Ibid, 3.

7. EIB Information, No.5, May 1976, 2. ICI also has a
   stake in the Ninian field, The Times, 29 February, 1980.

8. EIB Information, No.4, February 1976, 3.

9. EIB 1977 Ann. Rep., 31. Information, No.5, May 1976, 1.

10. Ibid.
    EIB Press Release, March 1980, No.28 March 1980, No.19/
    80. See also Financial Times, 8 November, 1979. The
    Italian government's efforts at energy conservation by
    introducing rises in fuel prices were blocked mainly by the
    left-wing Radical Party. To deal with the crisis, ENI
    began arranging bilateral deals which by-passed the
    major oil companies. Furthermore, in order to buy oil,
    ENI was swapping technology through its energy engineer-
    ing subsidiary, Nuove Pignone. It agreed to supply a
    complete gas processing system to Iraq and compressor

equipment to China.

11. EIB, 1977 Annual Report, 31; Information, No.5, May 1976, 2.

12. Ibid.; Information, No.1, February 1975, 6; No.17, June 1979, 6-7.

13. EIB, Annual Reports, 1977, 31; 1978, 25; 1958-1978, 40.

14. The other is at Baumgarten on the Czech-Austrian border.

15. EIB, 1958-1978, 40; Information, No.5, May 1976, 4.

16. Following the revolution against the Shah in 1979, the Iranians cancelled the contract to feed natural gas through the USSR into the MEGAL pipeline.

17. Sunday Times, 5 March, 1980.

18. Financial Times, 26 October, 1979. North Sea operators were then producing about 3.2% of total world oil output.

19. Times, 22 February, 1980, IMF idea of exchanging petro-dollars for its Standard Drawing Rights as a way of lessening Western monetary instability failed: oil-exporting countries prefer lending to developing coun-tries in deficit; also 26 February, 26 April, 1980.

20. Ibid., 4 June, 1980: 'Oil - learning to live with uncertainty'; 28 June, 1980.

21. Financial Times, 7 November, 1979; EIB Information, No.23, November 1980, 7.

22. EIB Information, No.8, February 1977, 6. This was a joint project, the Sté. Elec. de l'Our (SEO) and Rheinisch-Westfälisches Elektrizitätswerk (RWE) which ultimately provided off-peak power to work the pumps. In return, it received about 75% of Vianden's output to meet West German peak demand.

23. Ibid.

24. EIB Press Release, No.25/80, 2 May, 1980.

25. EIB Information, No.17, June 1979, 6-7.

26. Ibid.

27. Times, 21 February, 1980, claim that by 1980 a quarter of French homes will be solar heated, saving 15 mill. tonnes of oil imports; Financial Times, 12 October,1979, Lucas Industries new solar-electric power division; 20 Nov. 1979; Grants and Loans from the European Community,37-9.

28. EIB 1958-1978, 40.

29. IMCO has no knowledge of monitoring arrangements for sub-marine pipelines which are not yet regulated by any inter-national agency. No international organisation covers risks - mainly explosions - arising from LNG.

APPENDIX 5A: Oil and Gas Developments in the EEC assisted by the European Investment Bank (Millions national currencies, except Italy: billions lire. Millions ua)

Country	Kind of Development etc.	Name and Place of Project	National Currency	u.a.
		Loans Total:	£S 192.7	325.6
U.K.	Oil and gasfield development	Thistle oil field in the British sector of the North Sea (1976)	£S 17.9	27.0
		Beryl oilfield, North Sea (1976)	16.8	27.2
		Frigg gasfield, North Sea (1974)	10.4	19.5
		Development of the Sullom Voe oil harbour in the Shetlands, Scotland (1975, 1979, 1980. three loans)	34.2	56.6
		Development of a construction yard on the Isle of Lewis, Scotland for assembly of steel structures for offshore oil installations (1974)	4.0	7.5
		Harbour installations in the Orkneys, Scotland (1979)	1.5	2.2
		Construction of wharf and engineering facilities in Dundee, Scotland, for the manufacture of equipment for offshore oil and gas platforms (1979)	1.0	1.5
	Gas and oil pipelines	Development of system bringing gas from the Frigg field in the North Sea to Scotland and Northern England with connections to national network (1975, 1976: six loans)	67.8	120.1

		Pipeline bring North Sea gas from East Anglian coast to SW England (1976: two loans)	£S	25.9	44.1
		Oil pipelines from Ninian oilfield in the North Sea to Sullom Voe petroleum harbour, Shetland, Scotland (1976)		10.7 20.5	16.2 33.3
Netherlands	Gaslines	Transmission system for conveying Dutch and Norwegian natural gas to Belgian and German frontiers (1974)	Fl	100.0	31.9
Denmark	Oil and gasfield development	Development of DAN oil field, off the west coast of Jutland (1975)	Kr	43.0	6.1
Belgium	Gasline	Gasline across Belgium from Dutch to French border transporting natural gas from North Sea and Dutch fields to Southern Belgium and Northern France (1975)	Bfrs	500.0	10.8
France	Oil and gasfield development	Equipment for laying underwater pipelines (1975)	Ffrs	10.0	1.8
		Loans Total:	DM	282.0	107.6
F.R.G.	Oil and gasfield development	Factory for the manufacture of drilling equipment at Uetze, Lower Saxony (1973)	DM	–	0.6
	Gaslines (1)	Gaslines across Germany from Czechoslovakian and Austrian frontiers to French frontier, conveying natural gas from the USSR for both German and French consumers (1978, 1979: two loans)		220.0	87.1

APPENDIX 5A (contd.)

Country	Kind of Development etc.	Name and Place of Project	National Currency	u.a.
		Gasline to bring USSR natural gas from German/Czechoslovakian frontier to the Bavarian distribution system and the main Germany interconnecting network	DM 60.0	19.9
Austria	Gasline (1)	Trans Austria Gasline (TAG) conveying natural gas from the Soviet Union to Italy and, via Italian network, to France (1973, 1977: three loans)	Ffrs 110.0m Lit 17.35 billion Sfrs 13.0m	Total Loan: 48.0
			Loans Total: US$ 73.1	62.5
Norway (1)	oil and gasfield development	Development of Frigg gasfield in Norwegian sector of North Sea (1977: two loans)	US$ 50.0	44.1
		Development of Ekofisk oil and gasfield in Norwegian sector of North Sea (1974)	23.1	18.4
Tunisia (1)	Gaslines	Construction of section of the Algeria-Italy gasline from the Alberian border to Cap Bon where the pipeline goes undersea to Sicily (1980)	US$ 25.0	17.3

			Lire billions	
		Loans Total:	Lire 596.7	571.9
Italy	Oil and gasfield development	Semi-submersible barges and other equipment for oil and gas production (1973, 1974, 1979: six loans)	75.6	84.4
		'Malossa' gas and oilfield, Lombardy (1975: two loans)	36.2	44.5
		'Cavone' oilfield, Emilia Romagna, 'Settala' gasfield, Lombardy, and 'Amelia', 'Davide' and 'Barbara' offshore gasfields in the Adriatic – loan from New Community Instrument resources for development works at all five fields (1980)	20.0	16.7
		'Squalo' offshore gasfield in the Adriatic (1978, 1979: two loans)	19.8	18.0
		'Anemone', 'Azalea', 'Antonella-Antonio' offshore gasfields, Adriatic (1977)	18.0	17.9
		'Settala' gasfield, Emilia Romagna and 'Amelia' offshore gasfield, Adriatic (1979, 1980: two loans)	18.0	15.6
		'Barbara' offshore gasfield, Adriatic (1977)	15.0	14.9
		'Fratello' offshore gasfield, Adriatic (1978)	14.0	13.2
		'Nilde' oilfield off Sicilian coast (1980: two loans)	13.0	11.2
		'Cavone' oilfield, Emilia Romagna (1979)	9.0	7.9

APPENDIX 5A (cont'd.)

Country	Kind of Development etc.	Name and Place of Project	National Currency		u.a.
Italy	Oil and gasfield development	'Campo di Luna' offshore gasfield, Ionian Sea (1974: two loans)	Lire	8.0	9.8
		'Hera Lacinia' offshore gasfield, Ionian Sea (1978: two loans)		8.0	7.4
		'Santa Maria' oilfield and 'San Giorgio' gasfield, Adriatic (1980)		8.0	6.7
		'Davide' offshore gasfield, Adriatic (1977)		6.5	6.4
		'Rospo Mare' offshore oilfield, Adriatic (1978, 1979: two loans)		4.0	3.5
		Equipment to treat 'sour gas' from 'Cupello' field, Abruzzi (1980)		4.0	3.4
		Development of 'Emilio' offshore gasfield, Adriatic (1978)		2.5	2.3
		Extension and modernisation of three factories at Florence and Massa, Tuscany, and Talamona, Lombardy, producing equipment for the oil and gas industry and other energy equipment (1978)			
	Gaslines/storage	Construction of the Algeria-Italy gasline in Sicily, Calabria, and across the Straits of Messina (1978, 1979, 1980: five loans including one — Lit 50 billion/41.7 mua — from New Community Instrument resources)		10.0	9.2
				240.0	210.3

Italy	Gaslines/storage			
	Interconnecting gaslines, bringing gas from the Netherlands and the USSR, with main transmission network (1976, 197: two loans)	Lire	39.0	39.6
	Expansion of two gas storage reservoirs in Lombardy and Emilia Romagna (1976, 1978: two loans)		16.0	15.7
	Laying of four gaslines in Calabria (1975)		7.6	8.6
	Various works to improve gas transmission system in different areas of the Mezzogiorno (1976)		4.5	4.7

SOURCE: EIB, Information, No.23, November 1980, 5-9.
Annual Report, 1980, 44-9.

Chapter 6

THE EUROPEAN INVESTMENT BANK'S LENDING
FOR NUCLEAR POWER PROJECTS

The European Investment Bank began to lend for
nuclear power projects in 1967, nine years after its
inception.   Until 1972 total financing for energy
production accounted for only 12 per cent of the
Bank's lending.   However, EIB loans for nuclear
power production alone over the six years, 1967-72,
amounted to not far short of all its financing of
energy projects.   This high percentage was due to
early West German commitment to this form of energy
and partly to the high costs of schemes.

a) THE EFFECTS OF THE OIL PRICE RISE

In the next four years, the proportion of the
EIB's total loans for all kinds of energy more than
quadrupled in line with the quadrupling of oil
prices in 1974.   But within this increase, the
total financing of nuclear power projects rose more
than fivefold.   This trend continued to 1980 but
with nuclear energy occupying a less important place
than in 1973-77.

TABLE 6a: EIB loans for nuclear power projects
             compared with loans for all power
             projects in the EEC (own resources)
             1967 to 1980

Years	Amounts of EIB Loans mills. ua		% of all EIB Loans	
	All Power	Nuclear	All Power	Nuclear
1967-72	294.4	129.1	12.0	5.3
1973-77	1,311.3	756.8	26.5	15.3
1978-80	2,258.9	975.3	26.0	10.1

SOURCE: EIB, 1958-1978, 24 : EIB Annual Reports, 1978, 32;
           1979, 38; 1980, 38.

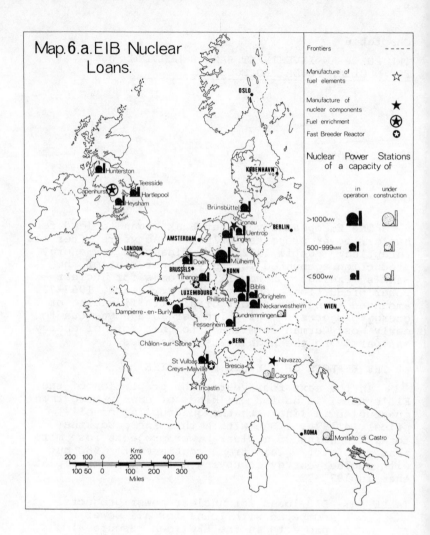

Map.6.a. EIB Nuclear Loans.

Frontiers   -----

Manufacture of
fuel elements   ☆

Manufacture of
nuclear components   ★
Fuel enrichment   ✪
Fast Breeder Reactor   ✪

Nuclear Power Stations
of a capacity of

	in operation	under construction
>1000 MW		
500-999 MW		
<500 MW		

OSLO

KØBENHAVN

Hunterston
Teesside
Capenhurst
Hartlepool
Heysham

Brünsbüttel
BERLIN
Gronau
Uentrop
Lingen

AMSTERDAM

LONDON

Doel
Mülheim
BRUSSELS
Tihange   BONN
LUXEMBOURG   Biblis
Phillipsburg   Obrigheim
PARIS   Neckarwestheim
Dampierre - en - Burly   Gundremmingen   WIEN
Fessenheim

Châlon-sur-Saône   BERN

St Vulbas   Brescia   Navazzo
Creys-Malville   Caorso
Tricastin

ROMA   Montalto di Castro

Kms
200 100 0   200   400   600
100 50 0   100   200   300
Miles

In addition to its own loans, the EIB also manages Euratom and New Community Instrument loans making the necessary assessments of projects before recommending they should be financed. Thus, the Bank carries some responsibility for the whole nuclear programme of the European Economic Community.

In 1978, the EIB set out changes then envisaged in the proportions of primary energy expected to be derived from different fuels by 1985 in the EEC:

TABLE 6b: Changes in uses of Energy in the EEC:
            % of Total Primary Energy

Year	Oil	Natural Gas	Solid Fuels	Hydro-Electricity	Nuclear Power
1963	37.5	2	35	5	-
1973	61.0	12	23	Less than 3	1.4
1985 Projection	40.50	18-23	17		13-17

SOURCE: EIB, 1958-1978, 37.

In 1978 renewable sources were not considered as of any significance. In support of this programme of expansion of nuclear generating capacity, the EIB has granted most finance to French nuclear projects, with the UK in second place and the Federal Republic of Germany third.

The French commitment to nuclear power is at present unequalled in west Europe. Under is VIth Energy Plan, France was already committed to building light water nuclear reactors capable between them of producing 8000MW. The EIB had contributed to the Plan in 1972 with a loan of 30.0 million ua for the construction of Fessenheim nuclear power station in Alsace. Higher oil prices forced up the value of French energy imports, which rose from 12 per cent of total imports to 21 per cent between 1973 and 1976. The French Government reaction to the oil price rise was to increase nuclear energy production above that envisaged in the Plan. Accordingly, the state concern, Electricité de France (EDF) was authorised by the Government to place orders for nuclear plants with production capacity as follows:

            1974-75 ... 13,000 MW
            1976-77 ... 12,000 MW
            1978-79 ... 10,000 MW

TABLE 6c: European Investment Bank Loans from own resources for Nuclear Energy Projects in the EEC, 1967 to 1980
(Millions own currencies, except Italy: billions lire - Millions u.a.)

Country	Type of Project - Location - Year	National Currency	u.a.
Belgium		Loans Total: Bfrs 10,230	251.1
	Tihange power station, Liège (1974, 1979: two loans)	2,730	65.8
	Doel power station, Antwerp (1978, 1980)	7,500	185.3
France		Loans Total: Ffrs	629.9
	Fessenheim, Alsace, power station (1972)		30.0
	'Super Phénix' power station, Creys-Malville, Rhône-Alpes (1977, 1978, 1979: three loans)	1,126.4	195.9
	EURODIF uranium enrichment plant, Tricastin, Rhône-Alpes (1977, 1978, 1979: three loans)	836.3	146.3
	Bugey power station, Rhône-Alpes (1973, 1974, 1975, 1977: seven loans)	772.4	139.5
	Dampierre-en-Burly power station, Centre (1977, 1980: two loans)	629.4	109.6
	Equipment for improved operating procedures at Chooz power station, Champagne, Ardennes (1979)	23.0	4.0
	Factory to manufacture pressure vessels and steam generators for nuclear power stations, Châlon-sur-Saône, Burgundy (1975)	25.0	4.6

F.R.G.

	Loans Total: DM	816.9	336.2
Darme Lingen power station, Power, Saxony (1967)			6.3
Obrigheim power station, Baden-Württemberg (1968)			6.2
Brunsbüttel power station, Schleswig Holstein (1972)			26.1
Philippsburg power station, Baden-Würtemberg (1972)			30.0
Gundremmingen power station, Bavaria (1976)(1), 1980)		336.0	115.6
Neckarwestheim/Gemmrigheim power station, Baden-Württemberg (1973: three loans)		153.0	45.8
Biblis power station, Hessen (1973: two loans)		153.0	45.8
Uentrop power station, North Rhine-Westphalia (1973)		90.0	28.0
Mülheim-Kärlich power station, Rhineland Palatinate (1977)		74.9	28.4
Construction of uranium enrichment centrifuge assembly plant at Gronau, North Rhine-Westphalia (1979)		10.0	4.0

(1) Two guarantees on loans from other sources

United Kingdom

	Loans Total: £S	259.5	414.9
Power station at Heysham, NW England (1977, 1979: two loans)		102.3	156.6
Hartlepool power station, NE England (1974, 1975, 1978, 1979: four loans)		96.3	156.0
Torness power station, Scotland (1980)		25.0	38.6
Hunterston power station, Scotland (1975: two loans)		23.4	43.7
URENCO uranium enrichment plant, NW England (1978, 1980: two loans)		10.0	15.8

TABLE 6c (cont'd.)

Country	Type of Project – Location – Year	National Currency	u.a.
United Kingdom	Whessoe, Ltd., Middlesborough, Teesside and Darlington, Co. Durham, manufacture and assembly of major components for nuclear plant (1980)	£S 2.5	4.2
Italy		billions Lire	
	Loans Total:	95.2	101.6
	Power station at Montalto di Castro, Latium (1978)	40.0	37.6
	Power station at Caorso, Emilia Romagna (1975)	36.2	44.5
	Uranium mining at Novazza, Lombardy (1976)	9.0	9.7
	Expansion of factories in Florence and Massa, Tuscany and Talamona, Lombardy, producing equipment for the nuclear sector (1977)	8.0	7.9
	Construction of plant for producing equipment for the nuclear sector in factories at Brescia and Roncadelle, Lombardy (1978)	2.0	1.9

SOURCE: EIB Annual Report, from 1967–1980 Annual Report, 44–5.
EIB, Information, No.23, November 1980, 5–8.

In 1978 it was envisaged that installed nuclear capacity in France should reach 40,000 MW by 1985 or over 40 per cent of generating capacity, compared with 6 per cent in 1976.

There is general agreement that the production of nuclear energy involves risks to the environment and human health. Those who favour nuclear energy believe that safety precautions have reduced hazards to an acceptable level. The risks in the working environment are considered by some to be less than in some other occupations. Those who oppose nuclear energy do so partly on the grounds that safety precautions are not as foolproof as supporters claim.[1]

Although the Community has supported the nuclear programme through Euratom, the EIB and latterly the New Community Instrument, there has been little EEC legislation to diminish the risks of pollution. The EEC Decision (26 June, 1975), stopping a programme on the management and stocking of nuclear wastes, of course, had no binding force.[2] References to nuclear hazards do not figure in either the EEC Commission's First or Second Statement on the Environment. Until 1979 there was an unusual measure of agreement between the governments of most member states, the EEC Commission and the European Investment Bank on the promotion of nuclear power. In line with this consensus, the EIB has fulfilled its mandate to encourage the development of new technologies, to a considerable extent through its investments in nuclear projects which range from uranium mining through to re-processing spent fuel.

b) EIB LOANS FOR URANIUM MINING IN THE EEC

Only a small amount of uranium is mined in the present EEC countries, in the French Alps and in Italy. Most uranium is imported (see Chapters 14 and 15).

In 1975, the EIB granted a loan of 9.7 million ua (9,000 mill.lire) to the Italian state concern, AGIP, A.S., for the development of a uranium deposit at Navazzo in Lombardy. The radio-activity of crude uranium bearing ores is low, but the risks involved are considerable. For example, a United States trade union study in 1967 stated that, uranium miners were then exposed to 57 times the officially admissible dose of radiation.[3]

c) THE EIB'S LOANS FOR URANIUM PROCESSING
   AND USE IN NUCLEAR POWER PLANTS

The European Investment Bank has granted loans

for the processing of uranium in Europe required for
the production of nuclear fuel.   Thus, about a
quarter of the EIB's loans for nuclear energy to
France, amounting to 146.4 million ua, have gone to
the construction of a uranium-enrichment plant using
the gaseous diffusion method, at Tricastin in the
Rhône-Alpes Département. The constructors are a consortium of French, Italian, Belgian, Spanish and
Iranian* promoters.   When it comes into operation,
in 1981, it is estimated that EURODIF, as this plant
is called, will have an enrichment capacity of 10.8
million tonnes USW (units of isotope separative
work).   In addition, up to 1980, the EIB had
granted loans of 158 mill. ua to British Nuclear
Fuels Ltd. for the development of the uranium-
enrichment plant at Capenhurst in North West England,
which has an initial capacity of 400 tonnes USW.
These loans financed BNFL's participation in the
West German-based international's subsidiary, URENCO
UK.[4]   The combined output of both plants by 1978
was considered 'about sufficient to keep abreast of
the annual rate of commissioning of nuclear power
stations in the Community in 1985'.[5]   The EIB's
loans have been in line with the 1973 Resolution of
the Council of Ministers of the EEC, calling for
the creation of adequate uranium enrichment capacity.
     The transport of uranium ore to processing
plants is not considered dangerous, but even so
risks to health and the environment increase once
uranium reaches the processing stage.   For immediately uranium leaves a mine, it is not only the
mineworkers who may be affected, but increasing
numbers of the public.   In the fission process now
used in nuclear reactors almost everywhere, from
the first stage of the process of obtaining the required materials, there are emissions of radio-
active substances into the air and the aquatic
environment.   There is considerable difference of
opinion as to how hazardous these emissions are,
but it is generally agreed that there is a serious,
though unknown risk, of cancer among those exposed
to increased levels of radiation.[6]   The argument
turns on whether or not the risk of an increased number

* It is unknown what has happened to the Iranian contribution
  since the institution of the new régime in Iran.

of cancer cases is worth taking in order to ensure a relatively firm supply of energy to a highly indus- trialised country.

c) EIB LOANS FOR NUCLEAR REACTORS

The EIB has contributed to the development of various kinds of nuclear reactors (see Table 6c), including the French fast-breeder, Super-Phénix, at Creys-Malville, between Lyons and Grenoble. The Centre Nucléaire Européene à Neutrons Rapides S.A. or NERSA project is being developed by EDF in part- nership with its Italian counterpart, ENEL, and a group of electricity generating concerns from West Germany, Belgium, Netherlands and the United King- dom. Up to the end of 1980, nearly a third out of the total 629.9 mill.ua which the EIB has granted for nuclear undertakings in France, has gone to Super-Phénix in three loans in 1977, 1978 and 1979 (see Table 6c). The Bank endorsed the official argument in favour of fast-breeder reactors: 'Fast breeder reactors make optimal use of uranium and will enable the Community to make most sparing use of an energy resource with which it is far from well endowed.'[7] Super-Phénix has also, of course, received Euratom finance, but Euratom loans have been based on the European Investment Bank's apprai- sal and managed by the Bank 'in accordance with the terms of Euratom/EIB co-operation' since 1977.

In January 1979, the Economic & Social Commit- tee of the European Communities unanimously adopted a proposal for an EEC Council decision aimed at making gradual progress towards eliminating dissimi- larities in codes and standards for fast breeder reactor components by making it...

possible for the regulatory authority in one member state to accept components licensed by the regulatory authority in another member state.[8]

Fast-breeder reactors pose four particular problems: firstly, the fluid used to transport heat in fast-breeders is sodium which creates a violent chemical reaction as soon as it is in contact with air or water;[9] secondly, they are expected to be exceedingly costly to build; thirdly, they produce large quantities of plutonium, which is one of the most highly radio-active substances known; and lastly, they require the construction of special processing and fuel fabrication facilities.

e) THE PROBLEM OF RADIO-ACTIVE WASTES

All nuclear power stations to date use the fission process, as a result of which they produce considerable quantities of spent fuel, some of which, including, in most cases, plutonium, is radio-active. This spent fuel is either stockpiled or reprocessed.

By funding nuclear energy plants, the Bank has contributed to the problem of the disposal of spent fuel, including a proportion of radio-active wastes. A variety of waste disposal methods are being used in the Community and it is not uncommon for radio-active wastes to be embedded in glass or concrete and dumped into the sea. Obviously, the quantity of wastes and the problems of its disposal increase with the growth in size and number of nuclear power plants.

There is officially no connection between the civil and military nuclear programmes. However, plutonium, which is a by-product of the fission process, is also an element used in nuclear explosive devices. [10] Therefore, there is a possibility that the civil programme, which the EIB has supported, may be producing fuel used in nuclear armaments.

Example of Impact of EIB Loans on the Nuclear Fuel Cycle in the U.K.:

EIB Loan 1978	EIB Loans: 1974, '75, '77, '78 & '79		
Uranium enrichment and fuel fabrication at Capenhurst →	Nuclear reactors at Hartlepool, Hunterston and Heysham →	Reprocessing at Windscale →	Wastes including Plutonium
	MAIN RISKS OF THIS PHASE		
Radio-activity	Low level emissions accidents	Low level emission leakages	

The same connection exists between the EIB's loans to the French uranium enrichment and fuel fabrication establishment at Tricastin, the building of nuclear reactors in France, West Germany, Belgium and Italy, and the reprocessing of the resulting spent fuel at the La Hague plant on the tip of the Cherbourg peninsula.

112

f) ACCIDENTS AT NUCLEAR POWER PLANTS AND INSTALLATIONS

There have been a number of accidents at nuclear power plants throughout the world, including, of course, some of those in the EEC. For example, in the autumn of 1979, French trade unions tried to block the development of the national nuclear programme because of defects discovered in a pressurised water reactor being built by the steel company, Creusot-Loire, under the Framatome-Westinghouse agreement.[11] The EIB in 1974 had granted a loan to Framatome, which is controlled by the Belgian group, Empin, through its associate, Creusot-Loire.

The EIB maintains secrecy about the safety precautions which it requires as a condition of its loans. However, in September 1979, following the accident in March that year at the Three Mile Island reactor in Pennsylvania, the Health and Safety Director of the British Central Electricity Generating Board announced a new approach to public safety at the Heysham nuclear plant for which the EIB has granted loans. This amounts to a tacit admission of a lack of adequate precautions when the first EIB loan was granted in 1977.[12]

g) EIB INVOLVEMENT IN OTHER RISKS

Just as the European Investment Bank is involved in the creation of nuclear wastes through its loans to nuclear reactors, as Map 5a shows, because of the spread of nuclear enterprises it has funded, the EIB inevitably is involved in the problems of disposal of the wastes resulting from fission processes. These wastes are much more radio-active than uranium ores, and the risks involved in their transportation are therefore much greater. The dangers are implicitly acknowledged by the very strict regulations and precautions laid down by the UN's International Atomic Energy Agency to ensure that containers will withstand every kind of accident. EEC countries being UN members are bound by these rules. Highly radio-active fissile material from nuclear plants, such as those the EIB has been and is helping to fund, cannot be left at the plant. It is transported over long distances inside the Community, being sent basically to two central sites for reprocessing - Windscale in North West England, and La Hague on the Cotentin peninsula in Normandy on the west coast of France.[13] Despite all the precautions, accidents, both on road and rail, have been known to occur. The transportation of wastes from nuclear power stations also gives rise to one of the greatest fears of nuclear specialists, the theft of radio-active material.

The EIB is involved in another risk from nuclear power generating stations besides that of radio-activity, a threat to the aquatic environment. Nuclear plants require more water than those that are fossil-fuelled because of the very high temperatures which the various types of reactors demand. The water once used may be emitted at a temperature of 30°C, the exact temperature being determined by the type of cooling system employed. [14] Most British reactors are sited on coasts and it is held that emissions into the sea do not give great cause for concern since the vast mass of cold sea water quickly cools the sudden rush of hot water and only small areas near the reactors are affected. A growing body of opinion is now questioning this view. But in other EEC countries, many reactors are sited on rivers, as Map 5a shows, and the impact of thermal pollution is much greater. The Bank has lent for every nuclear installation shown on the map and cannot be exculpated from responsibility for some of the environmental problems arising from hot water emissions which are now the cause of some concern.

There are many risks associated with the production of nuclear power and no space to list them all here. The question is whether the Bank, under its mandate to assist the building of infrastructure could not have put more emphasis on less risky sources, and particularly on renewable power sources.

h) THE ALLOCATION OF THE EIB's LOANS FOR NUCLEAR PROJECTS

The European Investment Bank's loans for the production of nuclear energy have mainly been granted to state enterprises, such as Electricité de France and the Italian ENEL, which, in turn, have used some of the EIB finance to award contracts to private enterprises. The EIB also lent to the transnationals, Siemens and AEG, to assist the West German nuclear power production programme in the late 1960s. The big EEC-based international companies have links with United States companies in the nuclear power plant and processing business. For example, Siemens, a West German chemical firm, established licensing agreements (which eventually lapsed) with the US Westinghouse company for building pressurised water reactors.[15] Siemen's partner,

114

AEG, built boiling water reactors under licence from the US General Electric Company.[16]

The concentration of nuclear power production in France must be seen against the background of uranium deposits currently available to that country in its former colonies of Zaire, Chad and, above all, in Niger. Under the Presidency of General de Gaulle, the emphasis was heavily on the building of a national industry. But immediately on his resignation, in 1968, French nuclear interests, like those in West Germany, sought links with the United States nuclear industry.[17] The French then dropped gas-cooled reactors which they had been developing, in favour of light water reactors widely used in the USA, but held by some to be less safe.[18] The EIB gave loans for both types.

The European Investment Bank claims to make its loans conditional upon observance of Community laws and regulations, as well as those of the EEC member states. Yet it continued to finance the French nuclear programme while the French were breaking the Euratom Treaty both directly and indirectly. When, in 1977, the Commission of the European Communities was given the power to raise Euratom loans, it was with the proviso that the European Investment Bank should act as agent on its behalf. The Treaty empowered the EEC Commission to organise a Community nuclear market, by giving Euratom a monopoly over fuel supplies through the Euratom supply agency. It also conferred the sole right to conclude contracts for the purchase of fuel, together with a mandate to see that all Community customers have equal access to fissile fuels and that a strict balance is maintained between supply and demand. However, these provisions were ignored until, in November 1978, the Belgian Government brought a test case in the European Court of Justice which ruled that the Euratom Treaty must be fully implemented in this respect.

This decision particularly alarmed the French who feared that insistence on observance of the EEC law would severely limit their freedom to exploit fully the commercial advantages of their rapidly developing nuclear industry, for it contained a threat that France might have to share its nuclear fuel production interests in a common pool. Indeed, the French government had for some time been blocking an affirmative response to a Commission request for a mandate to negotiate, on behalf of the Community, a nuclear safeguards agreement with Australia on the transport of uranium ore.

The European Investment Bank, through its

assessment and inquiry procedures in respect both of its loans to EEC member states and those of the EEC Commission must have been well aware that EEC countries, not only France, were calling the role of Euratom into question.

In the summer of 1979 France proposed that the Euratom Treaty should be changed. This, in turn, alarmed the West Germans, who feared that amendment of the Euratom Treaty would set a dangerous precedent in that any other member country dissatisfied with the controls exercised by the Community could seek alterations and so weaken the legal basis of the Community. The French, however, had their way and thus a precedent of alteration to an EEC Treaty by the independent action of a member state was set. [19] It was yet another proof that, as far as the EIB was concerned, the wishes of individual governments overrode Community law, for the EIB continued to lend for French nuclear energy projects while France did not abide by the Euratom Treaty.

i) RECENT CHANGES IN THE EIB's LENDING
   POLICIES ON NUCLEAR PROJECTS

However, in its loans for nuclear power projects, the EIB has been affected by public opinion through its effect on governments. The assumption that governments can usually proceed at will with nuclear programmes was first shaken by the Austrians in 1978, when they forced their government to arrange a referendum before proceeding with the operation of a nuclear power plant at Zwentendorf. The majority voted against operating the plant, and it has subsequently stood idle. They are now reconsidering the matter. The Swedes also forced their government to a referendum which blocked the creation of nuclear powered district heating schemes in 1979.[20]

Among the EEC countries, the Danes have now turned their backs on nuclear power. There has also been opposition to the nuclear programme in West Germany where public protests virtually stopped the nuclear programme in 1973. Sensitive to popular alarm, West German nuclear research centres, by 1977, were allocating 9 per cent of their activity to reactor safety and 3 per cent to environmental research.[21] However, these safeguards were not enough to avert a demonstration - an expression of popular disapproval at all social levels - in March 1979 against a nuclear 'park' at Gorleben, near the Polish border. The government was sufficiently impressed to halt its reactor programme abruptly.

In turn, the interruption caused a short break in
EIB loans for the programme.

The EIB resumed its loans to the Federal Republic in 1980.   But both there and in France, environmentalists have emerged as a political force
in recent national elections, partly because of
their determined opposition to nuclear programmes.[22]
The Bank, in its assessments of loan applications,
has now to take into account the increasing degree
of political uncertainty over nuclear power programmes.   Its continued loans to France and Britain
particularly, are proof that it feels sure that the
investments are safe because the majority of the
population accepts nuclear energy.

j) THE ARGUMENTS IN FAVOUR OF LENDING
   FOR NUCLEAR POWER

Official support for nuclear power in the EEC
is based partly on the argument that it reduces dependence on imported oil as a fuel and that assists
balances of payments.   Secondly, supporters of
nuclear power at the EEC Commission argue that by
engaging in a continuous building programme for the
completion of, say, 6 plants every 5 years, requiring a workforce of about 5,000 for each, 30,000
people would be employed in the medium-term and far
more in ancillary trades.   The numbers required to
run a plant are, of course, small.[23] However, it
could be argued that the EIB is contributing to the
creation of employment in the medium-term partly by
its support for the EEC nuclear energy programme.

There are suggestions that the hot water wastes
from nuclear power stations, instead of endangering
the aquatic environment, could be utilised in district heating schemes.   The idea is, however,
highly controversial and no EIB finance is known to
be involved in district heating by this means.

The nuclear energy industry might ultimately
dispense with the fission method currently used,
and thus avoid the resulting safety problems.
The fusion method does not require uranium but can
manufacture fuel from ordinary water, albeit at a
very high cost.   But then, a fast-breeder reactor,
such as Super-Phénix (see Table 5c and Map 5a) are
also very dear.   The EIB may have been involved in
its agency role in a £900 million EEC study of the
fusion process due to be carried out at the Italian
Euratom research centre at Ispra, which has been
blocked by France.   However, in 1980, the EEC Commission reiterated its commitment to the fusion
method.

117

k) CONCLUSIONS

The European Investment Bank's strong support, especially since 1973, for the EEC countries' nuclear power programmes is part of its effort to assist member states to become much less dependent on foreign oil imports.

A comparison of energy output per unit of account invested by the Bank in the various forms of energy production is scarcely possible. For claims that nuclear power is less costly than traditional power sources and vice versa are very difficult to assess, as a number of different elements enter into estimates: for example, whether power stations are sited near fuel sources and, if not, the costs of transporting fuels, costs of imported fuels and materials, local labour costs, etc. Moreover, these costs fluctuate and are bound to vary over the period of years that it takes to build a power station. Part of the difficulty is that power stations have to be planned well in advance of need and long-term costs are extremely difficult to forecast. For these reasons, caution is advisable and it is perhaps unwise to undertake a large long-term commitment to any one source of power.[24] However, a large long-term commitment is precisely what all but two of the EEC countries are undertaking with the help of the European Investment Bank and, it may be added, with the blessing of the OECD.

However, the EIB's Technical Staff must be aware that the efficiency of nuclear power plants is questionable in that few have so far operated at estimated maximum capacity. They generally appear to reach their peak, typically 75-80 per cent of their planned capacity, three years after they come on-stream and decline after that. Structural flaws, errors and accidents can cause long shutdowns. Hence the unit costs of electricity they produce can be very high. Thus, on financial grounds alone, the EIB's investments may be questioned. There is the further cost arising from the fact that the useful life of a nuclear power plant is a mere 20-30 years. Thereafter, it will remain an environmental and health hazard for hundreds and, in some cases, for thousands of years, and for that reason will require, during that time, to be guarded and monitored. Conventional power plants, at any rate, avoid this cost. There are also the social costs of accidents and cancer cases arising from nuclear power installations. Presumably, up till the present, these have been considered of an acceptable level.

The EIB must also know that concern is increasing, especially in France and West Germany, over the strict security systems operating in and around nuclear power plants. The fear is growing that, as a result, democratic rights in these countries may be curtailed.[25]

All EEC states contribute indirectly to the European Investment Bank's financing of nuclear power schemes through their subscriptions to the Bank's capital and to Euratom with whose funding the Bank has latterly been involved. Yet Ireland has no nuclear programme and the government of Denmark is positively opposed to nuclear power. It could be argued that the contributions to subscribed capital of both these countries are much smaller than those of the countries committed to nuclear power programmes. Nevertheless they represent a part of the resources used by the EIB as a means of financing nuclear power, along with other projects. It is unknown whether the Bank's accounting system is required to deal with opposition to a particular aspect of its lending.

The strengthening public opposition to nuclear installations is an indication of increasing alarm at the risks involved. It is another factor which the EIB has now to take into account in its loan assessments. When the safety measures laid down in the Community's 1980 Directive on Environmental Impact Assessments come into force in 1982, general safety standards will be laid down for the Bank to follow. Meanwhile, in view of the EIB's strong support for this energy sector, it would be useful to know what safety standards the Bank has required for those nuclear power projects it has already funded.

NOTES

1. C.M.Vadrot, Larousse Encyclopèdie de l'écologie, 1977 Ch.14, 282.

2. EEC JO L178, 9 July, 1975.

3. V.E.Archer et al, Lung Cancer among Uranium Miners in the United States, Pergamon, 1973, vol. xxv, 351-71. The maximum threshold doses fixed for human beings by the International Commission for Protection against Radiation are:

    0.17 rems per year for the population generally.

    5.0 rems per year for workers in nuclear power stations or laboratories.

    The rem is a coefficient for the measurement of different

levels and force of penetration of various radio-active
elements.   The usual natural dose per person per year is
0.1 rems.   A watch with a luminous dial produces 2-3
millirems of radio-activity, well below the threshold,
and ecologists point out that in the mid-1970s, the manufacture of such watches was stopped.
See also Vadrot, op cit.
See Commission of the European Communities, Grants and
Loans from the European Community, 36, for a scheme begun
in 1976 for financial aid for uranium prospection projects 'to improve the Community's uranium and hence
energy-supply situation.'

4. Uranit Uran-Isotopentrennungs GmbH of which URENCO Ltd.
    is an associate company and URENCO UK a subsidiary.

5. EIB Annual Reports, 1977, 30-1; 1978, 29 : EIB 1958-78,
    39, 42-3.   Eurodif has also received some finance from
    Crédit National of France, Istituto Mobiliare Italiano of
    Italy, and the Sté. Nationale de Crédit à l'Industrie of
    Belgium, like the EIB, all members of the 'Club' of Com-
    munity institutions specialising in long-term credit.

6. Dissenting Report of the Somatic Sub-Committee of BEIR
    111 235 ff.
    See also Times, 8 March 1980, Report of findings of
    Colorado School of Medicine on increase in cancer in
    areas downwind of the plutonium reprocessing plant, Rocky
    Flats.
    Daily Telegraph, 1 February 1980, Swedish county authori-
    ty of Halland reported as issuing iodine pills to people
    living around one of the country's 4 nuclear power plants
    as protection against thyroid cancer.
    Gunther Altner and Inge Schmitz-Feuerhake, eds. 239 PU,
    Die Gefahren der Plutoniumwirtschaft, 1979, Schmitz-
    Feuerhake & Kollert, 'Das Risiko der Beschaftigen in der
    Atom-industrie....', 142 ff.
    Jean-Claude Barreau, L'Escroquerie Nucléaire, eds. Stock,
    Paris, 1978, 29: at this time Electricité de France had
    recognised that it was impossible to trap totally the
    inert gas, krypton.

7. EIB, 1958-1978, 43.

8. Bulletin of the Econ. & Soc. Committee of the EEC, No.1,
    1979, 7-8.

9. Vadrot, op. cit. 289.

10. See Nuclear Non-Proliferation: Failures & Prospects,
    Paper, Rockefeller Foundation & Royal Institute of
    International Affairs, 1980.

11. Financial Times, 24 September, 3, 5, 6 October, 1979.
    It was not the first strike for improved safety in France.
    See Révue d'écologie politique, No.14, 29, for an account

of the strike for better and safer working conditions at
the Comhurex plant, Pierrelatte, Provence, December 1976.
Despite this there were accidental escapes of highly toxic
uranium hexafluoride in January and on 1 July, 1977 - the
'Pierrelatte cloud' - and further accidents on 26 September and 25 November that year.
See also W. Patterson, The Fissile Society, 136-38, 140-
41, 158-256; Vadrot, loc. cit.; Barreau, op. cit. 268,
287, including an account by a worker at the La Hague reprocessing plant of radiation hazards, taken from La
Guele, No.49; Le Monde, 15 March, 1980, Special Suppl.
interviews with workers at La Hague; Safety standards at
British nuclear plants seem to have been brought to a
reasonable level, but the 1977-78 Report of the Chief
Inspector of Nuclear Installations, Mr. R. Causden, dis-
closed an overdose of radio-activity of four workers at
Windscale in 1978: Health & Safety - Nuclear Establishments, 1977-78, HMSO, 29 January, 1980.
See also Financial Times, 3 October, 1979, award of
£67,000 to the widow of a Windscale worker.
For risks in the Federal Republic of Germany, see Altner
and Schmitz-Feuerhake, op.cit.

12. Financial Times, 13 September, 1979.

13. Additionally a small amount goes to Marcoule in France.
Some reprocessing was done for a time at the Carlsruhe
plant in the FRG, but now all reprocessing by British
Nuclear Fuels Ltd., French CEA and Carlsruhe is organised
as one commercial venture, United Reprocessors.   20-30
consignments are transported a year.   A typical 1000 MW
light water reactor plant discharges 30 tons of fuel a
year.   A lorry carries up to 10 casks of 3-5 tons of
material, i.e. 30-50 tons, but the protective covering
made from lead greatly adds to the weight.   20 tons of
uranium concentrate being transported by lorry from the
French mining base at Arlit, North Niger, to the port of
Cotonou in Benin, was removed and taken via Libya to
Pakistan.   As a protection, the means of transport is
varied.   For rail transportation, see Barreau, op. cit.:
Address of the Ecological Committees of the Rhône Valley
to Railway Workers and their Families.   See also Le
Point, No.130, 17th March, 1975, 86 ff.; CEA YS/SL.
23.8.75, Annexe 21, Nuclear Transportation, Authorisation
Transportation Authorisation, e.g. the Orsan branch of the
Marcoule Atomic energy plant on 1 July, 1976 notified
contamination of Wagon No.24.87.097.0020-2 as a result of
carrying irradiated fuel.   The wagon, still contaminated,
was dispatched on the morning of 6 July to Spain via
Cêrbère.   Decontamination was due to take place only in
the afternoon of that day.
For British rail transportation, see Daily Telegraph,
1 January, 1980.

14. Vadrot, op. cit., 291. E.V.Giusti & E.L.Meyer, Geological Survey Circular 745, Water Consumption by Nuclear Power Plants & some Hydrological Implications, 1976: Daniel Merriman, 'The Calefaction of a River', Scientific American, May 1970, Vol.222, No.5.

15. op. cit. Altner & Schmitz-Feuerhaker, eds., G. Michelsen, 'Der Weg in die Sackgasse', 34-6.

16. Kraftwerkunion was a joint subsidiary of Siemens and AEG, building nuclear and non-nuclear power stations. (See Table 6b.) By 1976, AEG was losing so much money it pulled out of Kraftwerkunion and paid Siemens about DM.614 mill. compensation. See Financial Times, 20 September, 1978, 5 December, 1979. (I am indebted to Steven Hahn for some of this information.)

17. Co-operation of course occurred at government level, e.g. the US Dept. of Energy and the French Commissariat à l'Energie Atomique have a co-operative agreement on a French chemical exchange uranium enrichment process.

18. W. Patterson, op. cit. 201, 215.

19. Financial Times, 3 August, 1979, Guy de Jonquières, Common Market correspondent.

20. Financial Times, 24 March, 1980; 28 March, 1980, following pressure to continue the programme, e.g. that nuclear power was vital to the pulp industry. Ibid., 13 November 1979, that a retreat from it could cost £8.2 billion. Ibid., 27 November, 1979.

21. Press & Public Relations Dept., Bonn, Ministry for Research & Technology, Energy and Energy Technologies Program, 1977-78, Ralf Friese trans., diagram, p.166.

22. See Alain Touraine, La prophétie anti-nucléaire, March 1980: Environmentalists won 6 seats in the Baden-Württemberg state elections in March 1980, Times, 17 March, 1980; Financial Times, 15 October, 1979 and 21 December, 1979. In a park, nuclear processing takes place on site; risks of transporting irradiated fuel are eliminated; wastes are buried.

23. Interviews, July 1979 with M. Jean-Claude Morel, Director, Directorate B, Directorate General 11, Commission of the European Communities; Mr. Rolf Gradin, Head of Energy Conservation, OECD. M. Dominique Finon, Inst. Juridique et Social, Univ. des Sciences, Sociales, Grenoble, July-August 1979.

24. Dominique Finon, 'Evolution comparée de la competivité de la production d'electricité d'origine nucléaire aux États-Unis et en France, Revue d'économie industrielle, No.3, Dec., 1976, 82-129; No.4, Jan. 1977, 22-56.

Chapter 7

THE EUROPEAN INVESTMENT BANK'S LENDING
FOR TRANSPORT

The European Economic Community's long-term aim
is the economic and political unity of member states.
More than trans-frontier gas and oil pipelines,
electricity supplies or nuclear energy, transport
has promoted that unity. Roads and railways have
been built to tie the EEC together in one great
economic network. In this process, as in other
kinds of infrastructure, the European Investment
Bank has been heavily involved as the Community's
provider of long-term loans. By 1960 the EEC Commission had drawn up a first outline of a common
regional economic development policy and recommended
to the member governments a list of investment projects considered of common interest for improving
transport infrastructure. Despite differences in
their transport planning agencies and methods of the
Community countries, a definite transport pattern
emerged after 20 years of the Community's existence.

a) LOANS FOR RAILWAYS

i) Railway Lines

The EIB's loans for transport began in 1961
with aid for railways. A network was gradually
built up: Italy to France and the Rhône Valley via
the Genoa-Modane-Chambéry line, modernised and
improved so that goods reached Lyons for forwarding
north and west without having to cross the
southern littoral of France and the southern section
of the Rhône valley: Italy to the Federal Republic
of Germany via the Bolzano-Brenner line: the
lines from the big ports of the north of West Germany to Scandinavia, Switzerland and Austria, and
from Bonn to Luxembourg;   and modernisation .
of the railways in Brittany and the west of
France.   Railways were driven the length of Italy
to connect the new industrial complexes and

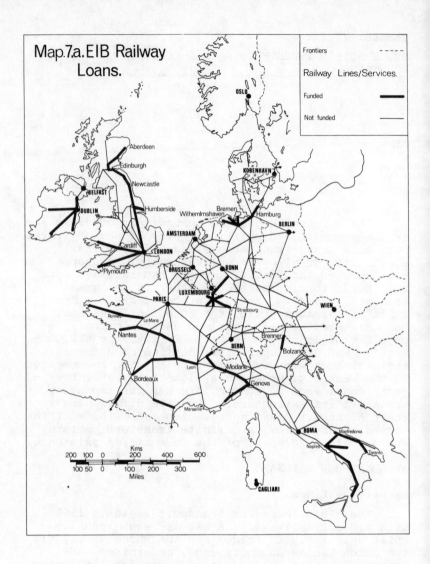

Map.7.a. EIB Railway Loans.

Frontiers — — — —

Railway Lines/Services.

Funded ▬▬▬▬

Not funded ——————

Aberdeen
Edinburgh
Newcastle
BELFAST
DUBLIN
Humberside
Cardiff
LONDON
Plymouth
OSLO
KØBENHAVN
Wilhelmlmshaven
Bremen
Hamburg
AMSTERDAM
BERLIN
BRUSSELS
BONN
LUXEMBOURG
PARIS
Strasbourg
WIEN
Rennes
Le Mans
Nantes
Brenner
BERN
Bolzano
Lyon
Modane
Bordeaux
Genova
Marseille
ROMA
Manfredonia
Naples
Taranto
CAGLIARI

Kms
200 100   0   200   400   600
100 50   0   100   200   300
Miles

commercial firms in the south with the rest of the
EEC.   Besides this north-south network, rail links
were improved in the industrial heartland of the
north, through the modernisation of the Moselle line
linking the Saar-Lorraine-Luxembourg region with the
Rhine-Ruhr area.

All these developments were begun in the 1960s
with the help of EIB loans.   Thus the produce of
the Mediterranean and of Brittany had improved
access to the markets of the great cities of the
Community and to the North Sea, Atlantic and Baltic
ports.   Similarly, the movement of imported raw
materials and of aggregates such as sand and gravel,
was facilitated, while the manufactures of the north
could be conveyed to the southern and western outlets.

In time, with EIB help, the old Mediterranean
coast railway line running east to west was also
improved and rail links modernised and developed
across France to Bordeaux/Aquitaine and from Paris
to the Spanish border.   When the three new countries, Britain, Denmark and Ireland, joined the
Community in 1973, the Bank provided loans for the
development of Irish railways.

ii) Rolling Stock

At the same time, the Bank lent for the development of new railway technologies.   In 1967, it
gave two loans for the introduction of engines
driven by gas turbines, developed first in France
on the Paris-Caen-Cherbourg line, and in 1973 introduced on lines radiating from Lyon to Bordeaux,
Nantes and Strasbourg.   France is so far the only
country in the world where gas turbine railway
engines are in regular use.[1]   By 1976, the maximum
speed reached was 200 kilometres per hour.   But
speeds of 300 kph were planned, partially using gas
turbines.[2]

In 1976 the Bank lent £11.6 million to the
British Railways Board for the development of the
first three high speed electric trains.   It is
hoped these advanced passenger trains may be in regular service on the western Glasgow-London line by
1982.   They are being introduced on other main
routes.   In March 1980, the Bank granted a further
loan of £25 million for the construction of 18 high
speed diesel-electric trains for use on the main
line linking Scotland and North East England with
South West England and South Wales.[3]

The EIB's loans for high speed rail transport
are now taking on a significance beyond the economy

125

of the Community and efforts at passenger appeal.
For Britain, France and West Germany they are proof
of engineering excellence which, it is hoped, will
sell rail products abroad despite massive competition.[4]   One of the new features of both French and
British high speed trains is that the coaches are
modelled on aircraft bodies and have a similar
seating design, together with air conditioning in
place of the old ventilation systems which were
under passenger control.   The aim is partly to enable railways to compete with air transport and to
cut noise.   While some of those obliged to use the
trains may have reservations about comfort and ame-
nity, the fact remains that from the points of view
of the environment and the conservation of energy
and other natural resources, railways are preferable
to road or air transport.

b) LOANS FOR WATER TRANSPORT

The same is true of water transport.   In the
EEC, coastal and inland shipping has traditionally
been important in the transport of freight.
In 1968, the EIB made its only loan for the
strengthening of internal water transport.   It lent
24 million ua for the construction of the Bamberg-
Nüremberg section of the Rhine-Main canal with the
aim of providing a freight route to the frontier
region, the Bavarian Zonenrandgebiet.
The EIB has made several loans for a variety of
sea transport projects (see Table 7a).   These have
included loans to Ireland and Denmark from 1973
onwards for the development of harbour installations
including some financial aid for Denmark's far-
flung province of Greenland.   The Bank has also
been granting loans to the Shetlands Island Council
for the development of Sullom Voe oil terminal.   In
addition, the Bank has made a few loans for the
actual building of ships of which two have been for
testing docks at Gelderland in Holland and at
Bremerhaven.   It also assisted a Danish factory
making propulsion systems for ships and granted
loans for ships for the Danish-Greenland service and
one for the British-Irish service.   In 1976, the
EIB provided a loan for the 'stretching' of two
hovercraft and a new terminal at Dover.   Finally,
in 1967, the Bank granted two loans for the building
of oil tankers, one to modernise and redevelop a
Bremen shipyard, and another for the Monfalcone yard
near Trieste.   The last was arranged shortly before
the President of the Italian Naval Italcantieri re-
tired from the EIB's Board of Directors on which he

126

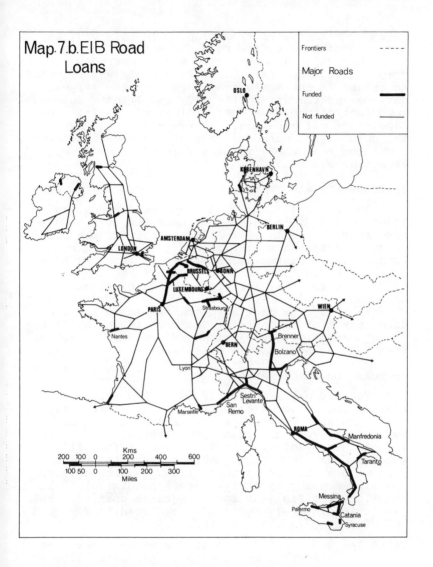

Map. 7.b. EIB Road Loans

Frontiers ----

Major Roads

Funded ▬▬▬

Not funded ▬▬

OSLO

KØBENHAVN

BERLIN

AMSTERDAM

LONDON

BRUSSELS BONN

LUXEMBOURG

PARIS

Strasbourg

WIEN

Nantes

Brenner

BERN

Bolzano

Lyon

Sestri
Levante

Marseille   San
           Remo

ROMA

Manfredonia

Taranto

Messina

Palermo

Catania

Syracuse

Kms
200 100   0   200   400   600
100 50   0   100   200   300
Miles

served for ten years from 1958. In this way, the
Bank contributed to the readjustment of the Community's shipbuilding industry to severe overseas
competition, especially from Japan. It was intended
to transform the Monfalcone yard into the largest,
and most up-to-date in the EEC, and Trieste into an
important oil port as the terminal of the Trieste-
Ingolstadt oil pipeline. Between 1966 and 1969,
the quantity of cargo handled at the port rose from
6 million tons to 24 million tons of which 20 million tons was oil.[5]

c) LOANS FOR AIR TRANSPORT

The European Investment Bank has made a few
loans in aid of increasing or improving air transport services. In 1972-1974 it lent for the purchase of large passenger aircraft in Britain and
France, the last two loans being for three B2 Airbuses. While, in 1980, it gave a large loan of 48
million ua to Italy for the purchase of eight B4
Airbuses.
In 1978, the Bank also granted loans for the
development of airports at Sumburgh in the Shetlands
in support of oil extraction and exploration activities, and at Godthaab in Greenland.

d) LOAN FOR ROAD TRANSPORT

The EIB has lent nearly twice the total
granted for these three forms of transport (rail,
water and air) to a single other sector: roads.
Besides motorway and road construction, it has, on
top of this, lent over half as much as for rail,
water and air transport combined for motor transport manufacture of various kinds, particularly to
the Fiat Company in Italy[6] (see Appendix 7a). In
addition, the EIB lent for integrated port/road/rail
facilities in Italy and guaranteed credits for road
building also in that country.

TABLE 7a: Total EIB financing for various forms of
          transport and transport projects, 1958-80
          (mills. ua)

Railways & Trains	Shipping & Inland Waterways	Air Transport	Road Con- Struction	Motor Manu- facture
335.3	294.0	144.2	999.9	395.6

TOTAL Rail, Water & Air: 773.5   TOTAL Road/Motor: 1,396.5

SOURCE: EIB, 1980 Annual Report, 96, Table 14.

Total financing for road construction and motor manufacture has been about 41.4 per cent higher than for all other transport over the past twenty-two years.

The south of Italy, in 1958, presented the Italian government and EEC planners with a virtually clean slate as far as transport was concerned. The large loans the EIB provided in this area gave a considerable boost to private sector road and rail building firms. At the other extreme, the EIB has lent very little for roads in West Germany and not a great deal in Britain, although the M1-A1 link is now listed as a priority for EEC aid.[7] EIB finance was not required because of the vigour of West German and British government support for national road building programmes.

The Bank's loans for road building have also been focussed on motorways radiating from the EEC's main industrial area, Saar-Lorraine-Ruhr-Belgium-Netherlands. It was towards this area that motorways were driven up both sides of Italy through the Alps, through France and south from Denmark. Further, it is envisaged that Britain should be part of the system designed to reach the 'golden triangle's' westernmost point, Birmingham.

e) THE SOCIAL AND ENVIRONMENTAL COSTS OF
   MOTOR TRANSPORT

Local opposition to new road schemes gained strength in the 1970s. There has been increased questioning of the economic value of new roads as well as growing concern about the social and environmental impacts of large motorway schemes. The true economic return on a new road is notoriously difficult to calculate involving as it does many variables, such as by how much travelling time is cut. Critics of the motorised society, such as Martin Burckhardt, who put a high valuation on health, safety and environmental quality, suggest that the costs of roads have been greatly underestimated. In a study published early in 1980, Burckhardt put the costs of running the road system in the Federal Republic of Germany in 1977 at 57,441 Deutschmarks, broken down as follows:

Costs of building and maintaining roads,
including charges for traffic police ..   .. DM 22,400 mill.

Full traffic insurance premiums   ..   .. DM 12,041 mill.

Costs of accidents   ..   .. DM 23,000 mill.

                  TOTAL: DM 57,441 mill.
                                      8

He compares this figure with the total public transport subsidy for the same year of DM 10,300 million
and points out that the total value of production,
also in 1977, from the Saar industrial region was
only DM 18,800 million.[9]

i) Noise Pollution

One of the first EEC Directives on limitations
on environmental pollution, agreed in 1970, was on
changes in member states' laws to allow the
establishment of permissible sound levels.   Yet in
1980, proposed limits on traffic noise to be introduced two years later[10] would still permit noise
levels considerably higher than those established as
causing annoyance.   The OECD Report, The State of
the Environment, published in 1979, showed that dis-
turbance due to noise begins at 55 dBA* and affects
about half the population in several EEC countries,
while the EEC Commission proposed limits of as much
as 91 dBA for some vehicles, as Table 7b.1 shows.

In some EEC countries, legislation limiting
noise already exists.   In the Federal Republic of
Germany there is the 1971 Noise Control Act and the
1974 Pollution Act.   In the Netherlands there is
the 1979 Noise Nuisance Act.   In the United Kingdom,
the 1973 Land Compensation Act provides some protection.   A Noise Advisory Council was set up in
1970, but disbanded in February 1981 after it issued
a report calling for expenditure of £200 million to
insulate houses against noise.[11]   In France there is
as yet no protective Act.[12]   But in February 1980,
the Cabinet agreed anti-noise measures and has in-
stituted a local complaints procedure in the towns.

Thus, if the Bank sticks to its declared policy,
as from 1982 it will have noise level standards, the
observance of which it can make a pre-condition of
its loans for vehicle manufacture.

* dBA is a decibel - a unit of measurement of sound pressure
level related to a standard reference level of 0.00002 Newtons
per sq.m.A-weighted in which greater emphasis is given to
medium and high frequencies to which the human ear is most
sensitive.
Leq means equivalent continuous sound level in A-weighted
decibels.

TABLE 7b.1:   EEC Limits on Traffic Noise proposed
               for 1980 as measured under ISO Test
               Conditions

Type of Vehicle	dBA
Heaviest lorries	88
3.5 tonne buses	89
Heavy buses	91
Motor cycles according to cylinder capacity	80-85
Cars	82

SOURCE: OECD draft paper May 1980, Noise
           Abatement Conference, 'The Cost of
           Noise Abatement', ENV/NC/79/.2,
           pp. 3-5.

TABLE 7b.2: Per cent of population exposed to aircraft and road traffic noise, selected countries or regions, mid-1970s

| NOISE LEVEL in Leq (dBA) outdoor measures | ROAD TRAFFIC NOISE % of national population exposed to given noise levels | | | | | | | | |
| | | | EEC Countries | | | | | | |
	U.S.	Japan	Belgium	Denmark	France	W.Germany	Netherlands	Spain	U.K.
> 55 Sleep can be disturbed if windows are open	40	80	68	50	47	72	-	74	50
> 60 Sleep and conversation can be disturbed if windows are open	18	58	39	-	32	46	30	50	27
> 65 Sleep and conversation can be disturbed even if windows are closed	6.4	31	12	20	14	18	7.4	23	11
> 70 Sleep and conversation disturbance; possible complaints	1.8	10	1	-	4	4	1.6	7	4
> 75 Possible long-term danger for hearing ability	-	1	-	-	0.5	-	0.1	1	1

Data for various years in the 1970s. Errors due to attempts to translate data into Leq measurements have probably produced an important margin of error, particularly at the lower levels where it may be about ±10%.

SOURCE: OECD Report, State of the Environment, Paris, 1979.

132

ii) Air Pollution

Concern about air pollution in the Community also began in 1970, with agreement on no less than three Directives. That on <u>air pollution by gases of positive ignition systems</u> was updated in 1974 and again in 1978 (see Table 7c). Therefore, the harmful effects of vehicle air pollution were recognised and their extent reasonably well established. Burckhardt gives estimates for 1972 for emissions of toxic elements from motor vehicles in the Federal Republic of Germany:

	Approx. mg per cu.m of air	Toxicity Rating [13]
Carbon monoxide	6.3	1
Hydrogen carbons	0.26	103
Nitrogen oxide	0.46	50
Sulphur dioxide	57.00	75
Lead	10.00	150

The toxicity rating is a measurement of the amount of contamination contained in a given quantity of a pollutant, since some polluting substances are more toxic than others. For example, as the figures quoted above show, 10 mg of lead present in 1 cubic metre of air are twice as toxic as 57 mg of sulphur dioxide. Lead is added to petrol to permit easy ignition and prevent 'knocking' in the engine. However, suitably adapted cars can run on lead-free petrol.

Just as in the case of noise pollution, by the late 1970s, some EEC countries had established new standards of emissions of lead into the atmosphere:

	Amounts of lead per milligram per cubic metre of air
Federal Republic of Germany	0.15
Netherlands/Denmark	0.4
United Kingdom	0.45

Furthermore, an EEC Directive requiring a maximum of 0.4 mg per cu.m for all member states was due to come into force in January 1981 and the United Kingdom Government has now decided to reduce the level to 0.15 over the next four years.

Lead is not the only pollutant emitted by motor

vehicles subject to controls agreed by the EEC countries. Representatives of Community governments have agreed Directives setting standards of emission for other noxious substances (see Table 7c). As in the case of noise pollution, the EIB therefore has national and Community standards whose implementation it may require as a condition of its loans. It would seem, however, that the Bank's support for motorways and motor transport in Italy have not been inhibited by the Italian government's reluctance to observe certain legally enforceable Community standards on air pollution. For Italy is the country to which the Bank has lent most in both these spheres, notwithstanding the fact that the Italian government has been taken to the EEC Court of Justice for its failure to observe the Council Directive on the reduction of sulphur in gas oil, which would involve vehicle emissions.[14]

f) CHANGE IN EEC TRANSPORT POLICIES

By 1977, it was accepted in the EEC that changes in transport policies were necessary. Over the next few years a number of studies were launched in member states and Commission departments to try to determine the best means and mix of transport methods in order to reduce pollution, road accidents and consumption of petrol.[15] There have been indications that the Commission and member states' governments may be moving away from motor to other forms of transport despite pressure from the car and oil lobbies.[16] In September 1979, the Commission of the European Communities issued a policy statement based on on-going studies on future developments in transport. The statement included a list of then current 'inadequacies', such as the failure to develop links between member states and other neighbouring countries, and the fact that national transport policies were 'sometimes primarily determined by considerations other than those of transport policy.' However, perhaps the greatest step forward was the admission that 'taking a global and rather simplified view, a disproportionate priority had been given to the development of roads and motorways.'[17] In its projections for the future allocation of finance for Community transport, the Commission envisaged that proportionately less would be spent on roads than in the past, and referred to the importance of inland waterways in supplying the 'missing links' in its grand Community transport strategy. Nonetheless, the plan proposed a greater amount of expenditure for the further devel-

TABLE 7c: EEC Directives intended to diminish noise and air pollution arising from motor traffic

Date and Number of Directive	Subject of Directive	Date of Implementation
20. 3.70 : 70/220/EEC	Air pollution by gases of positive ignition engines of motor vehicles	1.10.71
28. 5.74 : 74/290/EEC	Amended: Definition of specifications for acceptance tests	1.10.74
30.11.76 : 77/102/EEC	Amended: Fixing permissible levels for carbon monoxide, hydrocarbon fuels and nitrogen oxides; establishing methods of measuring these substances	1. 1.77
14. 7.78 : 78/665/EEC	Amended	1. 1.79
2. 8.72 : 72/306/EEC	Measures against emissions of pollutants from diesel engines used in motor vehicles: requirements for their approval	10. 2.74
6. 8.74 :	Amended: Definition of standards for acceptance test and fixing permissible levels for fumes; determing methods & etc. of measuring fumes	
24.11.75 : 75/716/EEC	Definition of two types of gas oil in order to provide for reduction in their sulphur content in two stages and for spot checks; to provide for exemptions where appropriate	26. 8.76
28. 6.77 : 77/537/EEC	Measures against emission of pollutants from diesel engines used in wheeled agricultural forestry tractors; requirements for type approval; fixing permissible values for fumes and methods of measuring fumes	30.12.78
29. 6.78 : 78/611/EEC	Fixing the lead content of super grade petrol at 0.4 g/l; laying down a reference measuring method; providing for Ireland to be exempted and for other exemptions	5. 1.80
6. 2.70 : 70/157/EEC	Fixing permissible limits for the sound level and the methods of measuring this level	10. 8.71
7.11.73 : 73/350/EEC	Adaptation: prescribing measures for exhaust systems	1. 3.74
8. 3.77 : 77/212/EEC	Amendment	1. 4.77

135

Date and Number of Directive	Subject of Directive	Date of Imple-mentation
4. 3.74 : 74/151/EEC	Fixing permissible limits for the sound level of wheeled agricultural and forestry tractors and methods of measuring this level	7. 4.75
29. 3.77 : 77/311/EEC	Fixing permissible limits to the driver-perceived noise level of wheeled agricultural or forestry tractors and methods for measuring this level	1.10.79
23.11.78 : 78/1015/EEC	Fixing permissible sound levels and prescribing measures for exhaust systems of motorcycles and methods of measuring sound	1.10.80

SOURCE: Commission of the European Communities, Progress made in connection with the environment action programme and assessment of the work done to implement it, COM(80) 222 final 7 May, 1980.

opment of road transport than for any other kind of transport. Thus, while future expenditure for railway and inland waterway development were set at 11,564 and 4,269 million ua respectively, the provision for roads was estimated at 13,987 million ua.[18] In its plan, the Commission listed three EEC institutions as funding transport developments: the Bank, the Ortoli Facility and the European Regional Fund. But the Commission also proposed a fourth:

> a new financial instrument for supporting transport infrastructure projects of Community interest will complement the existing instruments. [19]

The recession has led to the postponement of this addition to the Commission's financial instruments. If it is ever set up, three of the Community's lending instruments will be under the control of the Commission, and the EIB's importance as an autonomous lending instrument may be further reduced, although its borrowing expertise will probably be used more than ever, and its agency role in handling loans increased.

g) CONCLUSIONS

The European Investment Bank's loans for transport infrastructure give cause for concern in two respects. The first is that there is some uncertainty about how far the Bank has upheld Community Directives on motor transport pollution as these have come into force since 1971 by ensuring that its loans were granted only to those prepared to observe Community standards (see Table 7c). Secondly, the EIB granted loans for private motor manufacture, including components firms, partly on the grounds that the motor industry provided a large amount of employment. While this was true when the Community was set up,[20] West European car production, like everything else dependent on oil, has been affected by the increase in prices. Thus, the Bank's Board of Governors in transport, as in other sectors of the Community's economy, showed little awareness of the Club of Rome's 1972 warnings that resources, such as oil, were finite. They did not, for example, give priority to loans for more fuel-efficient forms of private transport, such as small cars, or shift the emphasis from roads to other transport developments less wasteful of a precious raw material and less questionable environmentally. However, there was encouragement from the Bank for new railway developments in Britain and France in the later 1970s.

The Bank has contributed to the reduction of employment by the concentration of car production in fewer units and by the introduction of automated processes as a way of meeting overseas competition, particularly from Japan.   But in doing so it permitted the growth of excess production capacity in the motor industry which cannot, in the face of Japanese competition, secure a sufficient proportion of the world market to make it economically viable.[21] Lastly, there are doubts about the extent of social costs of private motor transport, such as congestion in urban areas resulting from the convergence upon them of traffic from large motorways like those financed by the EIB.

Possibly, the recession may assist a reappraisal of the Bank's loan policies for transport by slowing down investment.

NOTES

1. One loan each to Energieversorgung Weser-Ems (1965) and Gaz de France (1967) as part of the gas pipeline programme for 'natural gas mains for gas turbine railway engines'.

2. EIB Information, No.6 July 1976, 4-5.   200 kph = 125 mph.

3. Ibid. Press Release, 13/80, 17 March, 1980.   (The EIB also provided a loan to British Railways in 1973 for the acquisition of some 'merry-go-round' wagons to convey coal from mines to power stations.)   EIB, 1980 Annual Report, 49.

4. EIB, Information, No.6, July 1976, 4-5.

5. EIB, 1969 Annual Report, 160-61.

6. The European Investment Bank granted a considerable number of loans for various aspects of motor vehicle manufacture, see Annual Reports and Appendix 7A.

7. EIB, 1980 Annual Report, 4.

8. Martin Burkhardt, Die Gesellschaftlichen Kosten des Autoferkehrs, Bundesverband Burger Initiativen Unweltschutz e.V., Freiburg, 1980, 21 ff.

9. Ibid 43-6; Daily Telegraph, 7 February, 1980, '5m. motorists on the black list'.

10. The Times, 29 February, 1980.

11. Noise Advisory Council, A Study of Government Noise Insulation Policies, HMSO, February 1981.

12. OECD Draft Papers for May 1980 Noise Conference, ENV/NC/ 79, No.6, 9. No.7, 5-6. Noise pollution from railways and aircraft is more localised and has elicited less widespread protest.

13. Burkhardt, op. cit., 54-5.

14. Herr Stieftauch, EEC Dept. of the Environment. Mr. Lawrence, EEC Dept. of the Environment. Directive of 24 November, 1975 on approximation of laws of member states relating to the sulphur content of certain liquid fuels. OJ L 31, 27 November, 1975.

15. Financial Times, 1 February, 1979. Dept. of Transport study comparing 1968 and 1978. The use of energy for transport had outstripped energy consumption generally.

16. Not unfortunately in the UK, see Financial Times, 31 October, 1979, 'More roads needed', for European traffic. 1 April, 1980, 'Victory for private road transport'.

17. Bulletin of the European Communities, Suppl. 8/79, 7. The EEC was looking at a rail, not a road, tunnel link across the Channel.

18. Ibid, 27.

19. Ibid, 12-13.

20. The British Road Federation in 1979 estimated it at 10 per cent of all employment, but included the workforce in certain firms not exclusively devoted to motor vehicles, for instance, Lucas Aerospace. Transport 2,000, an independent transport research and planning pressure group, put the figure at 4 per cent for those directly employed, but excluded departments in mixed enterprises, such as Lucas which manufacture parts for vehicles.

21. Daily Telegraph, 11 September, 1979; Times, 26 April, 8 May, 1980; Financial Times, 8, 24 September, 1979, Special Suppl., 'Commercial Vehicles', 11; 26 September, 31 October; 7, 15 November, 1979 (Firestone), 7 December (Daimler-Benz), 31 December, 1979; 8 March, 1980 (Dunlop), etc.

APPENDIX 7A: Main EIB Loans for Car Manufacture

Year & Place	Beneficiary	Amount mill.ua	Purpose of Loan
ITALY			
Modugno 1970	Fiat Group	16.0	Construction, motor vehicle & truck component complex
Cassino, Latium 1971, 1978		62.3	Motor vehicle assembly plant construction & reorganisation
Sulmona, Abruzzi, 1972		15.8	Electrical components factory
Bari, Apulia 1977		5.9	Steering gear factory
		7.4	Enlargement fork-lift truck factory
Ufita valley, Campania 1977		24.8	Coach work factory
Termini Imerese, Sicily, 1978		7.5	Reorganisation & expansion of car factory
Termoli, Molise, 1979		3.5	Expansion gear-box factory
Turin area, Piedmont, 1980		10.0	Measures to cut energy consumption in factories
Modena & Cento, Emilia-Romagna 1980		13.0	Rationalisation & modernisation, 3 tractor production units
Villafranca, Tirrena, Sicily 1971, 1979	Pirelli Group	13.1	Production unit lorry radial tyres, construction & reorganisation & modernisation
Tivoli, Latium 1979		7.0	Reorganisation & modernisation tyre factory
Foggia, Apulia 1976, 1977	SOFIM (Sociéta Franco-Italiana Motori, SpA)	25.2	High-speed diesel engine factory
Abruzzi 1979	SEVEL (Societa Europea Veicoli Leggeri, SpA)	87.3	Light commercial vehicle factory
Battipaglia, Campania 1971	Sociéta Meridionale Accessori Elastomerici SpA	4.0	Car accessories factory

APPENDIX 7A (cont'd.)

Year & Place	Beneficiary	Amount mill.ua	Purpose of Loan
ITALY (cont'd.)			
Cagliari, Sardinia 1971	General Cable-Riva Products, SpA	4.6	Tyre cord factory
San Salvo, 1972	Fabricca Italiano Magnetti Marelli, SpA	4.4	Car accumulator factory
Emilia, Romagna 1979	Ferrari	7.9	Diversification & enlargement two car body factories
Bari, Apulia 1979	Weber, SpA	5.3	Extension diesel engine pump factory
FEDERAL REPUBLIC OF GERMANY			
Wittlich, Rhineland, Palatinate, 1970	Dunlop A.G.	10.9	Tyre factory
St. Ingbert, Saar, 1971	Kleber-Colombes Reifen und Technische	5.5	Tyre factory
Dingolfing, Bavaria, 1973	Bayerische Motorren Werke A.G.	15.5	Motor car assembly plant
Saarbrücken	Deutsche Bendix	4.3	Brakes & cylinders factory
UNITED KINGDOM			
Belfast & Ballymena, N.Ireland 1979, 1980	Michelin (Belfast) Ltd.	19.4	Extension & modernisation of 2 tyre factories

Chapter 8

THE EUROPEAN INVESTMENT BANK'S LENDING FOR
WATER SUPPLY PROJECTS IN THE EEC

The European Investment Bank has assisted the
provision of water in the Community under the heads
of regional development, the building of infrastructure and promotion of projects of common interest to
several member states.   Besides water supplies for
hydro-electricity, mentioned in Chapter 5, the Bank
has granted loans for the provision of water for
agriculture and industry, and for sewage and
sewerage schemes (see Chapter 13).   Industry has
benefitted directly from supply schemes linked to
plants.   The chemical, petrochemical, paper and
pulp, leather and tanning, metallurgical and glass
industries all use vast amounts of water, and the
EIB has granted loans to all these kinds of undertakings.   In addition, many industries use water
indirectly through their need for large amounts of
electricity, since all types of power stations require huge amounts of water.
Domestic demand has, however, also risen as a
result of rising living standards and the greater
availability of water through improved supplies.
Consequently people use more water in their homes
and buy products which require large quantities of
water for their production.   Tourism, a new growth
industry, also adds a little to the pressure on
water supplies.

a) WATER RESOURCES AND DEMAND IN THE EEC

There is no overall water shortage relative to
society's demands in the total EEC area.   The
average rainfall is many times greater than needs.
Nonetheless, there are problems.   France has plenty
of water in its alpine areas, but little in the
north and in Provence, hence the Provençal saying:
'Here water is gold'.   The north of Italy is rich
in water, the south poor.   The Mafia's power in
the south of Italy, Sicily and Sardinia was built on

142

TABLE 8a: Loans from the EIB's own resources for water supply projects

Type of Project	Area	Years	Amount lent mill.ua
I T A L Y			
Irrigation & Water Supplies (drinking water)	Metaponto Plain	1965, 1968 1975-80	600.00
	Molise	1979	22.00
	Sardinia	1978, 1980	115.2
	Campania (Naples & Caserta)	1978	46.2
	N. Apulia & Abruzzi	1980	87.5
Irrigation & Water Supplies to industrial zones	Sicily, Campania, Apulia, Abruzzi, Latium	1966, 1978-80	240.00
T O T A L:			1,110.90
F R A N C E			
Irrigation & Water Supplies	Provence	1964, 1969-70, 1973, 1977, 1979	85.9
	South-West	1965-66	5.6
	Brittany	1973, 1975	10.2
T O T A L:			101.7
U N I T E D K I N G D O M			
Water Supplies, sewage & sewerage	N.W.England	1975-80	168.2
	N.E.England	1975-80	171.0
	Yorkshire*	1978-80	114.6
	Wales & West Midlands	1978, 1980	39.1
	South West	1975-80	31.2
	Scotland	1977-80	165.5
T O T A L:			689.6
I R E L A N D			
Water Supplies, drainage, sewage & sewerage	Whole country	1977-80	158.0
LUXEMBOURG	Esch-sur-Sûre	1968	4.0

SOURCES: EIB, Ann. Reps.; 1958-1978; Information, Aug. 1977
* It is not clear whether some of the loans to Yorkshire are
  for the transportation of water from the Kielder Forest Dam
  as shown in Map 8a.

its control of water supplies.   In the United
Kingdom, rainfall is often heaviest where population
is least concentrated.   Ireland has a lot of rain,
but a small population, so that in this respect it
is the opposite of Belgium, and is better off for
water than Italy or the Netherlands.[1]

Interest in the conservation and cleaning up
of water supplies and long-term needs for water in
the EEC became serious only as a result of the 1976
drought.[2]   Shortly afterwards, in 1977, the EEC
Commission made a preliminary study on the basis of
which it announced that it was taking steps to
ensure sufficient water supplies.   These measures
included an expansion of research on water resource
problems, the setting up of a 'Water Resources'
Working Party of experts from member states, and
examination of the possibility of a 'European Water
Plan', with direct Community participation in large-
scale water management schemes of interest to
several member states.   Among its conclusions, the
Commission mentioned...

> The need for the European consumer to be
> conditioned to an idea - new for most - that
> water is a precious, increasingly expensive
> commodity, to be used wisely and not
> squandered.[3]

To date the main beneficiary of EIB loans for
financing water projects has been Italy.   Up to
the end of 1980, EIB financing from its own resources for irrigation, drainage and water supplies
in that country amounted to some 1,111.0 million ua.
The Bank provided funding for these purposes as
part of its support for infrastructure, to industrial estates in Sicily, Campania, Apulia, Latium
and the Abruzzi.   Equally striking, because they
have been concentrated over a shorter period of
time, have been the Bank's loans for water projects
in the United Kingdom.   In the seven years, 1973-
80, loans for all types of water projects, quality
as well as supply, amounted to nearly 700 million
ua, over £400 million.[4]   While this financing has
been of considerable benefit to the areas concerned,
there is some question as to whether assessments of
need for water were in every case soundly based.
One notable example raising such a doubt is that of
the dam in the Kielder Forest in the north of
England (see Table 8a).

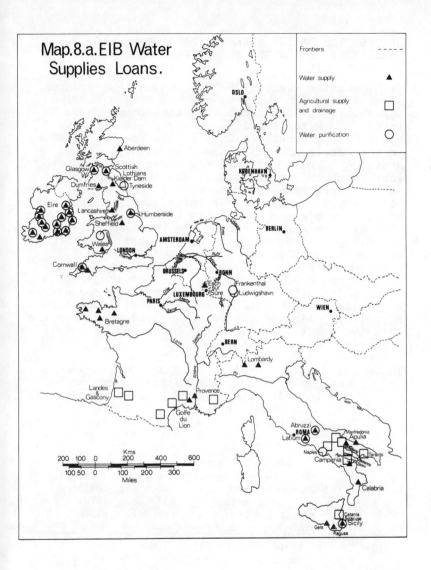

Map. 8. a. EIB Water Supplies Loans.

b) THE CASE OF THE KIELDER FOREST DAM: AN
   EXAMPLE OF A WATER SUPPLY PROJECT ASSISTED
   BY THE EIB

Over the years 1975-78, the Bank has granted
about 88 million units of account (£56.3 million
approx.) to a single project, the scheme for
increasing water supplies in north east England
based on the Otterstone dam on the North Tyne River
in the middle of the Kielder Forest. The final
decision to build the dam was taken in 1973, the
year in which Britain joined the EEC, but studies
had been proceeding for some years previously, since
water supplies, like other infrastructure projects,
have to be planned many years ahead. In 1970, the
then British national body, the Water Resources
Board,[5] published predictions on water demand to the
year 2001 which formed the basis for the 1973
decision on Kielder. The choice was by no means
an easy one. Using information from the various
local water authorities in the area, the Board drew
up fourteen different plans of ways of increasing
supplies. All had drawbacks. Table 8b shows the
relative costs of some of the other more likely
projects compared with Kielder.

TABLE 8b: Estimated Storage Capacity, Storage Cost,
          Yield per day and Capital Costs of
          building some of the proposed reservoirs
          considered as a means of making up the
          predicted shortfall in water supplies by
          2001 in North East England (mills. cu.m.)

Proposed Dam	Estimated Storage capacity -mill. cu. metres stored	Estimated costs per 1000 cu. metres stored. £s	Estimated Yield -1000 cu. metres per day	Estimated capital costs of building - later 1960s prices, £s mills.
Kielder Forest	188.0	48.00	995	9.05
Irthing	72.7	36.00	332	2.60
Middleton, for Teesside	83.4	158.00	364	13.20
Kielder Burn*	43.1	93.00	236	4.0
Lewis Burn*	43.6	208.00	236	9.1

SOURCES: *Northumbrian River Authority, Report on Survey of
         Water Resources, 1973; other, Interim Report on
         Water Resources in the North, 1967, HMSO.

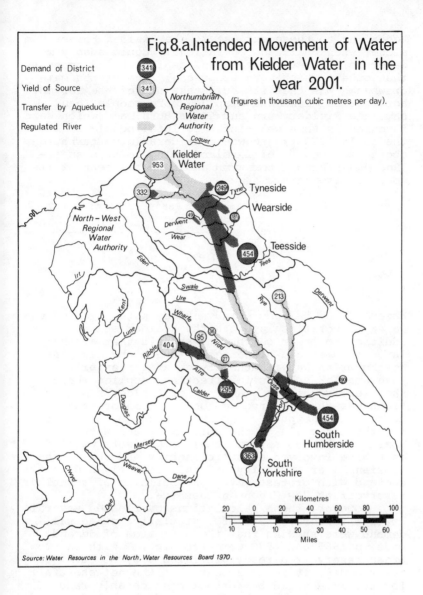

Fig.8.a.Intended Movement of Water from Kielder Water in the year 2001.

(Figures in thousand cubic metres per day).

Demand of District

Yield of Source

Transfer by Aqueduct

Regulated River

Northumbrian Regional Water Authority

Coquet

Kielder Water

North – West Regional Water Authority

Tyneside

Wearside

Teesside

Eden

Derwent

Wear

Tees

Irt

Kent

Lune

Swale

Ure

Wharfe

Ribble

Nidd

Aire

Calder

Rye

Derwent

Ouse

Douglas

Mersey

Weaver

Dane

Clwyd

Dee

South Humberside

South Yorkshire

Kilometres
20   0   20   40   60   80   100

10   0   10   20   30   40   50   60
Miles

Source: Water Resources in the North, Water Resources Board 1970.

According to these estimates, the Kielder Forest Dam
alone, when built and operational, could supply more
water relative to storage and capital building costs
than others which were proposed.   One of its main
drawbacks was that it would take out of use far more
agricultural land and displace more people than,
say, the Kielder Burn and Lewis Burn Dams which were
favoured by some well-informed local people.   By
the early 1970s there was considerable perturbation
about the amounts of farmland being lost in an island which then had to import about 50 per cent of its
food requirements.

	Amount of land lost (acres)	No. of people displaced
Otterstone, Kielder Dam	1,896	130
Kielder Burn & Lewis Burn Dams	216	6

However, the balance of advantage in the eyes of the
water authorities lay with the Kielder scheme.   In
addition to lower costs, it was held that a single
large scheme held economies of scale and gave the
Northumbrian Water Authority greater flexibility
than smaller schemes in directing supplies where
they were required.   Another of Kielder's attractions was that it involved only one major reservoir,
hence only one public inquiry and one major fight
for the officials of the Northumberland Water
Board.   Whereas several smaller projects would
each have involved a public inquiry and the Northumbrian River Authority had only recently had to
contend with protests over the building of a smaller
reservoir at Cow Green on Teesside.[7]
     However, these calculations overlooked several
crucial factors.   By 1980, statistics of actual
demand were showing that the estimates of demand
made in 1967 and 1970 were too high.   With the Cow
Green reservoir already providing 450,000 cu.m. of
water a day, it would appear that the net shortfall
for the area would be further considerably reduced.
Another mistake was the failure of the water authority to react to the change in economic circumstances
clearly apparent when they took their decision.
For, it was not until 1973 that the Kielder scheme
was accepted by the government and not until May
1974 that the order was formally given to proceed,
well after the rise in oil prices started.   The inevitable consequences for the north eastern economy

were pointed out by Tyneside Environmental Concern.[8]
     In addition, there was growing overseas compe-
tition in two key North East industrial sectors -
steel and shipbuilding. The north east of England
is an area where, contrary to the national trend,
the industrial demand for water is greater than the
domestic demand.[9] Forecasts of future North East
water needs made in the mid-1960s were based on
pressing demands by the big industries of Teesside.
Above all there were the requirements of the steel
industry and the Imperial Chemical Industry's complexes at Wilton and Billingham, then the biggest
chemical plants in western Europe.[10] In addition
to ICI's own needs, water supplies were required
for Phillips Petroleum (see Chapter 5). A 1973
estimate gave average quantities of water used as:

Oil Refining .. 18.3 cu.metres per 1 cu.m. crude oil

Steel .. .. 182.0 cu.metres per 1 tonne
                                                    [11]

By 1976, ICI was taking 191,000 cu.m. a day out of
a total of 416,000 cu.m. a day supplied to the
whole of Teesside, that is, very nearly half the
total, and it has remained by far the largest Teesside water consumer.[12] But subsequently the company stated that it was not expecting to increase
its rate of water usage in its Teesside plants at
the same rate as it expects to increase production.[13]
The Northumbrian Water Authority admitted in its
1979 Plan the over-estimate in industrial demand
for water in the area. However, it was then still
looking for growth in the steel complex at Redcar,
although not expecting this for some length of time.
     Another mistake in the water authorities' de-
mand calculations, particularly on Teesside, arose
because they overlooked the fact that most big manufacturing concerns pay directly for their water
supplies through a meter system. Therefore they
have an incentive to instal plant that makes savings. Consequently, the Water Authorities' revenues were likely to be and, indeed, have been lower
than foreseen.[14]
     The Kielder scheme had been intended to pro-
vide a spin-off through tourism. In 1978, a comprehensive Plan for the Development of Recreation
& Tourism produced jointly by the Northumbrian
Water Authority and the Forestry Commission forecast recreational developments over the next 10-15
years, with an ultimate capital expenditure of £8
million at April 1978 prices. It was based on

149

national government agencies' promotion of
Northumbria as a tourist area. By 1979, the NWA
had spent about £15,000 especially on car parking,
access ways, landscaping and planting, and improvement of premises. Meantime, cuts in local authority spending have meant that approach roads and
boating, and other recreational facilities proposed
for the impounding dam in the Kielder Forest are
being dropped.[15] Thus reductions in public spending
in turn reduced expected income from a proposed
tourist attraction.

The Northern Technical Working Party Report of
1970 estimated a total shortfall by 2001 of
887,000 cubic metres a day.[16] However, on the
basis of actual demand in 1979, the Northumbrian
River Authority estimated a shortfall of only
563,000 m^3 a day and Dr. David Hitchcock, an hydro-
logist, only 438,000 m^3 a day, although he predicted
a 50 per cent increase in metred demand by industry
over that forecast in 1979. The key difference between the Northern Technical Working Party's forecast and the other two was its prediction of a rise
in population in the area of nearly a third. Whereas the Northumbrian River Authority and Dr. Hitchcock, seeing the effects of growing unemployment,
predicted a slight decline. For, by the end of the
decade, actual daily demand was already diverging
from the 1970 estimates in that it was some 150,000
m^3 a day, i.e. some 11 per cent less than predicted.

The advantage of building a series of smaller
reservoirs is that building and expenditure can be
phased over a longer period of time. If, due to
rising costs or a smaller demand for water than that
originally forecast, some parts of the scheme are
felt to be unnecessary, they can be dropped or
delayed. The forecast of the yield from Kielder
was 995,000 cu.m. a day. Whereas two of the
smaller proposed reservoirs at Irthing and Middleton,
say, would have yielded just under 700,000 cu.m. of
water a day (see Table 8c). If the yield from
Irthing alone had been found to be sufficient, there
would have been no need to proceed with work on
Middleton or any of the other 21 smaller reservoirs
which were considered.

A further cost of the Kielder scheme which may
have looked minimal in the late 1960s when energy
prices were cheap, but which should have given
cause for concern by the time the government took
the final decision to build the dam, was the cost
of energy for pumping the water through a series of

aqueducts and tunnels to Teesside, the area of greatest demand. These would have been required for some of the proposed alternative schemes, but not for all of them. The capital cost of building aqueducts and tunnels remains the same whether or not they are being used as extensively expected. In the Kielder scheme because of the over-estimate in demand, they are being under-used. Therefore, in terms of capital costs, the Kielder scheme is less attractive than anticipated.

The capital cost of building the Kielder dam water supply scheme was originally set at £9.05 million (Table 8a). By the late 1970s it was set at £120 million. Up to 1980, the EIB contributed some £71.2 million of this sum.

The European Investment Bank was uncritically enthusiastic about the whole of the British Water Authorities' operations, and about the Kielder Forest scheme in particular.[17] It rightly saw the development of water supplies as an essential part of building infrastructure in the north east region with the aim of stimulating industrial growth and diminishing unemployment. However, whatever the views of its Technical Assessment staff, the EIB, like the British Water Authorities, seems not to have considered the likely consequences of the oil price rise and overseas industrial competition, although its first loan for Kielder was not granted until 1975.[18] It was aware that unemployment was growing in the area since, partly in order to meet overseas competition in steel production, the EIB, in 1978-79, was lending for the modernisation and restructuring of the British Steel Corporation complex at Consett which has since been closed. The EIB has stated that its loans for N.E. England water supplies are intended to ease unemployment due to the rundown in steel and coal-mining by attracting new industry to the area.[19] The validity of the Bank's argument depends not only on whether new industry will, in fact come to the North East, but also on whether, if it does come, it will provide enough new jobs to compensate for those that are being lost, since much of the new technology, not least in the steel industry, is destroying jobs. It also rests on whether any new industries setting up in the area require as much water as old declining industries, such as steel and shipbuilding. The main justification for the EIB's loans would seem to be that Kielder has to be paid for and EIB interest rates are low.[20]

The Northumbrian Water Authority is remarkably

optimistic about costs.   In 1979 it...

> decided that the major factor in the deter-
> mination of an appropriate strategy should be
> an attempt to limit increases in charges after
> completion of the Kielder and Tyneside schemes
> to no more than the ruling rate of inflation.
> This was only feasible assuming continued
> inflation around 10% p.a. ..... [21]

By the early part of 1980, inflation was over 20%. [22]
Water charges are met partly by industrialists, but
also to a large extent by domestic users.   Thus the
costs of Kielder are being paid, not only by the
Teesside companies, whom it was intended primarily
to help, but also by industrial and domestic consumers in the rest of the North East region even
where demand is not rising and, indeed, throughout
England and Wales.   For, until 1980, all domestic
consumers in England and Wales, contributed to the
costs of all water schemes in the UK because Water
Authorities paid into a central fund in order to
meet the cost of projects.
      However, the cost of Kielder was not only
financial.   It involved felling a million trees
and destroying a number of homes, with resultant
upheavals for the families concerned.   The Forest
could have been opened to the public without the
dam and pumping works.   The provision of extra
water is essential, but the construction of massive
new reservoirs involves such drastic interference
with natural resources and human lives that caution
is necessary, and a slow and piecemeal approach
preferable to a bold commitment from which there is
no going back.   Selection of a plan should not be
made on the basis of avoiding trouble due to multi-
ple planning inquiries.   The Bank itself, so
cautious, could use its influence to ensure more
careful appraisals for future water projects.

c)   THE EIB'S LOANS FOR WATER PROJECTS IN THE
     SOUTH OF FRANCE AND THE SOUTH OF ITALY

      The miscalculations over water demand in the
Kielder scheme inevitably cause some unease about
similar schemes in the south of France and south of
Italy.   Of the two areas, the south of France had
the stronger industrial base, [23] but both areas were
primarily dominated by farming.   The provision of
water, with the EIB's help, while partly intended
to improve this sector through the provision of
irrigation, was also aimed at encouraging large-
scale industries.

The Mezzogiorno was the scene of some of the
most spectacular water supply projects assisted by
EIB finance.   The Bank's first loan, granted in
1965, via the Cassa di Mezzogiorno, was for a scheme
for draining the Metaponto Plain which stretches
from the southern foothills of the Appenines to the
Ionian coast and from the Apulian to the Calabrian
Peninsula.   In the first century BC this had been
one of the most fertile areas of the Mediterranean,
but from then the land deteriorated steadily due to
soil erosion and to the build-up of coastal dunes
which imprisoned water and made it stagnant, turning
the area into a malarial swamp.   As a result, the
population moved away and up into the hills, while
on the coast there were large estates on which the
land was underused.   Rehabilitation of the plain
began in 1928 but extensive work only started in
1950, following agrarian reforms and the introduction of water schemes, introduced by means of the
Cassa di Mezzogiorno, a government financing agency.
     The EIB's loan in 1965 for the Metaponto pro-
ject, followed by another in 1966 and simultaneous
loans for an irrigation project in Sicily around
Ogliastro, assisted the irrigation of 53,000
hectares of farmland.   However, the emphasis then
shifted towards the provision of water for industries as in North East England in the 1970s.   In
1969, the Bank commenced a series of loans for a
huge project north of the Metaponto Plain.   Four
rivers cross the Metaponto to flow into the Ionian
Sea and four dams were built on three of these.
Two were built on the River Agri, at Pertusillo and
Cannamo.   The water is brought south from the 155
million cu.m. Pertusillo reservoir in Basilicata by
an aqueduct which the Bank has helped to fund, to
the far south of Apulia.   A smaller reservoir of
107 million cu.m. on the River Bradano, which the
EIB has helped to finance, was built mainly to provide water for irrigation.   But on the River Sinni,
at Monte Cotugno, the EIB, in 1975 and 1976, lent
large sums for the construction of a dam and reservoir of 450 million cu.m. capacity, twice the size
of Kielder, and for another pipeline to bring water
to the industrial complexes of Taranto and Brindisi
which it had also helped'to fund.   At the same
time it has been granting large loans to improve
water supplies to the industrial zone of Syracuse in
Sicily.   In 1979 alone, the Bank provided 239.0
million lire, one half of the total lent for water
projects in the Mezzogiorno since 1958.   While
some of this money has assisted the provision of

drinking water to various communities, there is some doubt about the future of some of the newly created industrial complexes in the area, the 'cathedrals in the desert'. (See Chapters 9-12)

d) CONCLUSIONS

While the EIB's investments in increasing and improving water supplies in Community countries, have assisted developments essential to the improvement of living standards, gains, to some extent, have been offset by other factors. In the case of peasant areas, such as the south of France and south of Italy, in the main, only farmers with capital have been able to benefit from large-scale irrigation schemes. The merging of peasant farms in large latifundia has been encouraged, while displaced peasants were not all absorbed as permanent employees on these new large estates. Where they have remained in farming, some of the work is seasonal so that the seasonal under-employment, which characterised the old peasant system, has not entirely disappeared. Above all, the Bank, along with central and local authorities, seems to have been unable to adapt policies to radical changes in the world economy, known before decisions on water supply schemes were finally taken (see Chapters 9 and 10) which have affected industry, employment and local demography. With industrial growth lower than that on which infrastructure schemes have been based, there is a risk of over-estimates in demand for water supplies. Some costly consequences of such mistakes in forecasting might have been avoided if, in cases when asked to help to fund huge dams, the European Investment Bank had advised a more cautious approach especially from the early 1970s when there was doubt as to the continuing low level of oil prices.

NOTES

1. European Parliament Report, February 1979, 17-20.

2. EIB Information, No. 10, August 1977.3.

3. Commission of the European Communities, SEC (77), 1505.

4. EIB, 1958-1978, 27 and Annual Reports.

5. A Water Act in force from April 1974 reorganised many of the private and public water undertakings and created new regional water authorities responsible to a National Water Council for England and Wales. They were responsible for all aspects of the water cycle in major natural

drainage basins. In Scotland, water and effluent were made the responsibility of existing regional councils which deal with general policy.

6. Ministry of Agriculture, Fisheries & Food, Agricultural Statistics, 1972. About 600,000 acres of grazing land disappeared during 1965-71. See evidence of Dr. Colin Marsh on behalf of Tyneside Environmental Concern to the 1973 Inquiry. See Tyne River Authority Estimates, App. 1, Evidence to Dept. of the Environment Inquiry, 1973. The reservoir proposed for Irthing would have taken even more agricultural land than Kielder, 2,700 acres. The very high capital cost of the proposed Middleton reservoir was due largely to the compensation that would have to be paid for land lost to farmers.

7. 160 km. up-river from Darlington.

8. Dr. Colin Marsh, Tyneside Environmental Concern to 1973 Inquiry, etc. Financial Times, 24 March, 1973; Report by Fuel Economy Consultants (advisers to local authorities, Rolls-Royce, Hawker-Sidleley, etc.).

9. Water Data, No. 77, Table 2, p.5.

10. The ICI Teesside plants are the largest single installations, but the biggest producer of chemicals in Europe is now West Germany, New Scientist, 10 July, 1980, 94. ICI has just opened a huge new plant at Wilhelmshaven.

11. E. Hill, M.Sc., Thesis, Dept. of Civil Engineering, University of Newcastle-upon-Tyne, February 1973, 'A pilot study on the potential for the reclamation of sewage effluent for increasing the available water resources in England & Wales.'

12. Northumbrian Water Authority, Annual Plan, 1979, para 4.4.3.

13. ICI Head Office, Press Dept., Millbank, London.

14. Domestic users pay a water rate according to the rateable value of properties. Industrial users have a 2-part tariff, a fixed amount, payable however much is used, at a low tariff, plus a higher rate for supplies used over and above this amount. The Northumbrian Water Authority inherited several special water supply agreements with industrialists. These were revised in 1978-79 when prices were raised and guarantees improved.

15. Northumbrian Water Authority, Annual Plan 1979, paras 4.4.2-4.52.

16. The North East: A Programme for Development. Cmnd.2206, November 1963, Secretary for Industry, Trade & Regional Development: Industrial Expansion, Cmnd. 3509, Secretary

155

for Economic Affairs & Ministry of Technology.

17. EIB, <u>1958-1978</u>, 27-8.

18. Ibid.

19. Ibid.

20. EIB, <u>1958-1978</u>, 27-8: <u>Information</u>, No.10, August 1977, 4.

21. Northumbrian Water Authority <u>Annual Plan</u>, 1979, p.1,
    para 5.3.1.

22. See H.M. Government, <u>Monthly Digest of Statistics</u>: Cost
    of Living Indices, Dept. of Employment, <u>Monthly Press</u>
    Notices: Dept. of Employment, <u>Gazette</u>, etc.

23. EIB, <u>1958-78</u>, 18-19: <u>Information</u>, No.10, August 1977,
    4-5.

Chapter 9

THE EUROPEAN INVESTMENT BANK'S LOANS FOR LARGE-
SCALE INDUSTRIAL ENTERPRISE WITH SPECIAL REFERENCE
TO EMPLOYMENT

Industry has received an important share of the
European Investment Bank's loans.   Up to the end of
1972, EIB financing in this sector amounted to
997.9 million uas, or about 40.6 per cent of total
lending inside the EEC, more than the Bank provided
for energy, transport or any other aspect of infrastructure.[1]   Thereafter the proportion of the
Bank's lending to the industrial sector declined as
the emphasis shifted to energy and transport so that,
during 1973-80, it amounted to 17.8 per cent of
total financing for all sectors.   Even so, the EIB
lent a total of 2,245.0 million uas, far more in
cash terms, during the eight years 1973-80, than
over the preceding fourteen years, the increase
being partly due to inflationary pressures.[2]
The range of industrial enterprises supported
by the Bank has been extremely wide, encompassing
Italian ice-cream manufacture and the production of
both soft drinks and whisky in Scotland, besides the
creation of large cement, steel and chemical works.
During the years 1958-80, the largest investments
have been made in:

Metal production and semi-processing	...	801.3 mills. ua
Metal working and mechanical engineering	...	352.9 " "
Motor vehicles and transport equipment	...	395.6 " "
Chemicals	...	530.4 " "

Thus, over a third of total loans has been for metal
production and mechanical engineering, and about one
sixth has been for chemicals.[3]
EIB loans in the industrial sector have gone to
public as well as private enterprises since certain
industries or enterprises are state-owned, for
example, the British Steel Corporation and the
Italian ANIC, a subsidiary of the Ente Nazionale
Idrocarburi.

The Bank makes a distinction between large
enterprises seeking loans generally of at least 2
million ua on the one hand and, on the other, small
and medium-sized enterprises seeking smaller loans,
dealt with in Chapter 12 below.

a) EARLY EMPHASIS ON LOANS TO LARGE-SCALE
   ENTERPRISES

In the early boom conditions in the EEC, the
EEC Commission and the European Investment Bank won
the confidence of international business because of
the possibilities at the time for expansion in the
Community, so that foreign interests were taking
the initiative in investing in the EEC, either by
participating in existing industries or by creating
new enterprises.
By 1959, it was clear to the Bank

that the initiative in creating new industries
can in practice come only from fairly large
concerns or groups of concerns

because only they had sufficient capital resources
to provide investment in plant, equipment and in
labour.

Also (the Bank went on) the wider territorial
and financial scope they have, the more they
can appreciate the economy of an investment
in an under-developed area.[4]

That is, international enterprises and multinationals understood the benefits of cheap land and
services, and of cheap labour available in areas of
peasant economy.   Large local industrial plants
would, it was thought, create a demand for local
services through a greater local prosperity.   In
this way, eventually all Community areas would
attain a uniform economic level and the EIB would
be fulfilling Article 130 (a) of the Treaty of Rome
by providing aids intended to promote economic development of regions where the standard of living
is abnormally low or where there exists serious
under-employment.   It would also be carrying out
the Protocol concerning Italy, which recommended
the use of the EIB's resources to support the programme already in progress to create 'new opportunities for employment with a view to eliminating
unemployment' in the south of the country.

b) CONTRADICTIONS BETWEEN THE BANK'S AIMS OF
    FOSTERING EMPLOYMENT AND OF ENCOURAGING
    INDUSTRIAL DEVELOPMENT

The extent of the problem of creating and encouraging industries as a means of increasing employment has varied since 1958, with technological
and structural changes in manufacturing, changes in
economic policy, fluctuations in the terms of trade
and an increasing population continually raising
the numbers of those seeking work. So long as
public sector investment kept up and generated consumer demand, manufacturing industries should have
expanded and thus should have increased overall
levels of employment: and so many of them did.
But this policy of increasing numbers of available
jobs was being eroded by various factors, among
them the financing of modernisation and conversion
of enterprises, as shown in Chapter 3.   For it en-
tailed the introduction of labour-saving technologies designed to cut labour costs and speed-up
production.
In 1958, when the EEC was set up, and for a
decade afterwards, one of the main concerns of industries in the six EEC countries was labour shortage and this policy made sense.   As the EIB remarked in 1962[5], the labour shortage itself, as well
as the success of employees in raising their earnings which resulted from it, provided employers
with incentives to invest in labour-saving devices.
Both these factors spurred them on to apply the
principle of mechanisation long established for work
done by the less skilled; they now also increasingly
applied it to work graded as skilled.   Thus employers were hastening on the point where so many
people would be made redundant that there would be
insufficient alternative work of accustomed kinds
to absorb them even if economic growth were sustained.   The EIB was committed to helping
this development.   In the early 1960s, entrepreneurs in Community countries were confident of their
ability to withstand new overseas competition provided they modernised and converted their old
undertakings.
The process of change, however, was still more
complex.   For the Bank's encouragement to prosperous enterprises to set up in less industrialised
areas of the Community gave companies a choice.
They could simply close old works, instead of
modernising or converting them, and set up quite
new enterprises in more favourable conditions elsewhere.   The growth in job opportunities in one area

159

of the EEC which the EIB was trying to promote,
might be at the expense of job losses elsewhere.
For example, in 1961-62, closures in the traditional
Belgian and Luxembourg coal and metal industries
created industrial trouble.   High labour-intensive
metal and engineering industries have been run down
in the Dutch province of Limburg.[6]   Concomitantly,
the EIB was lending for new steel enterprises at
the mouth of the Rhône in the south of France (1971
and 1977) and particularly in the south of Italy,
i.e. in areas where labour and other production
costs were cheaper.[7] (See Table 10a).   In these
new enterprises, the most up-to-date labour-saving
machinery could be installed, so that higher productivity at lower cost, fostered partly by the Bank,
created some part of the competition which was adversely affecting the Belgian and Luxembourg industries.

However, the Bank did give a little assistance
to areas of declining industries and reduced labour
requirements, occasionally using its funds to assist
new local enterprises, partly on the grounds that
they provided work for those rendered redundant.
Loans of this kind were made in Leghorn in Italy in
1962 and Nantes in Brittany the following year, as
a result of shipyard closures in both cases.   In
1966, the Bank helped to finance the construction
of a rubber factory in Lower Saxony, to provide
work for redundant miners.   So the Bank both helped
to create and preserve jobs, and to eliminate them.

c) CHANGES IN THE GLOBAL ECONOMY AFFECTING
   EEC INDUSTRIES

By the time the mid-1960s crisis broke in the
Community, industries there and in other parts of
west Europe were feeling serious competition from
Japan and other newly industrialising countries.
Those manufactures most affected were steel, shipbuilding, electronics, clothing and some branches of
chemicals and textiles.[8]   Such overseas industrial
development was partly due to an increasing tendency
of West European and United States based transnationals to move production overseas to areas which
offered them the lowest labour and other production
costs.   At the same time, entrepreneurs, who were
nationals of such countries as Japan, Taiwan, Hong
Kong and South Korea were themselves fast introducing western industrial technologies, always of the
most modern kinds so as to enable them to keep their
outgoings to a minimum.   By the early 1970s, it was
clear that there was, not only in EEC countries but

in the world as a whole, a surplus production
capacity for the then market in cars, television
and radio sets, washing machines and refrigerators.
The EEC's Medium-Term Economic Committee, set up to
find ways of dealing with the mid-1960s crisis,
recognised these changes and recommended meeting
them principally by greater structural adaptation
of firms and more rationalisation. [9]
    It was in support of this recommendation that
the EIB increased its assistance in the late 1960s,
to traditional industries in northern EEC countries
by loans for modernisation and conversion, especially in steel, while, of course, continuing to lend
in south Italy.
    The resumption of the Community countries'
economic boom in the later 1960s made re-thinking
about the kinds of work in which the EIB was investing seem unnecessary. So despite the realisation
of overseas competition, apparently little thought
was given to diversifying into new technologies and
products where competition would be less. By the
early 1970s, numbers unemployed were lower than in
the previous decade, although the total population
of working age within the Community had risen. The
only major new departure was the development of
nuclear power. Large enterprises, such as the
Franco-German Pechiney-Ugine-Kuhlman, the French
glass firm, St. Gobain-Pont-à-Mousson, and the
Italian Fiat motor company, expanded into nuclear
energy, partly to ensure their fuel supplies [10] following the oil price rise.
    The higher prices and the recession, which had
begun in the early 1970s, did not inaugurate, but
hurried on the new international division of labour
by providing yet another incentive to companies to
cut labour and other production costs. Wilhelm
Haferkampf, Vice-President of the European Communities, admitted in June 1979:

> the tendency to shift labour-intensive production out
> of Western Europe to other parts of the world....
> European industry is feeling the effects. The de-
> mand for structural policy which has dominated econo-
> mic policy discussions for some years, is a result of
> this worldwide development. [11]

By that date, the 'export of employment' had reached
a point where Ministers from the 24 OECD countries
called on multinationals to stop trying to influence the settlement of labour disputes by threaten-
ing to remove operations to other countries. This
recommendation was the only major amendment to come
out of a meeting called to discuss revisions in the

OECD's 1976 guidelines for multinationals and companies under foreign control.[12]

d) GROWING UNEMPLOYMENT IN EEC COUNTRIES
FROM 1975

In recent years, the Community, enlarged by
Denmark, Ireland, Britain and Greece, has experienced growing unemployment.   The total number of
registered unemployed in the EEC countries rose to
4.3 million in 1975.   As a result, Community institutions, including the EIB, put greater emphasis on
slowing the increase, but to little effect, partly
because it was difficult for firms to stop large
developments to which they were already committed
and for which they had arranged finance from the EIB
and other sources.   Ambulance operations were
mounted, but the underlying causes of unemployment
were not tackled.
By the spring of 1977, governments of the EEC
countries were insisting that the Bank and the Commission do more to sustain their flagging economies.
They sought action at three levels to combat growing
unemployment, as we have seen (p. 30):

1.   Aid for those worst affected by growing
unemployment, i.e. women and young
people of both sexes.

2.   Greater investment in member states'
existing industrial sectors, along
with measures to create monetary stability and expand international trade.

3.   Less encouragement for the economies of
the strong currency EEC countries, i.e.
the Federal Republic of Germany and the
Netherlands.[13]

The third point proved that the pull of the strong-
currency states had been too great to permit the
levelling up of the economies of poorer countries.
So the EIB's efforts to fulfil that part of its mandate were not, by 1977, altogether successful.
Even following the 1977 EEC Government's policy
statement, the Bank's investments in depressed areas,
such as North East England and the South of Italy,
where it has lent most heavily, have had little impact on growing unemployment.   Furthermore, the
policy of favouring large capital intensive projects,
unquestioned for many years, has meant that a dis-

162

proportionate number of jobs have been temporary, rather than long-term. Indeed, the picture is similar for all the Bank's investments inside the EEC, since infrastructure schemes, like those for large industrial projects, tend to create short-term jobs in construction work. With the completion of the project, these come to an end. Thereafter the operational and maintenance work has required far smaller numbers of workpeople.

Estimated Employment created by EIB Investments, 1977-78:

	Permanent Jobs	Temporary jobs in energy and infrastructure projects		Jobs saved
1977	16,590	100,000	2-6 years	2,750
1978	11,000	150,000	declining after first 2 years	10,000

SOURCE: EIB Annual Reports, 1977, 21: 1978, 21.

The EIB's President, Yves Le Portz, claimed that the investments in 1979 would have created some 35,000 permanent and 145,000 short-term jobs, while those in 1980 should provide 49,000 permanent and about 120,000 short-term jobs.

However, by the end of 1980, the registered unemployed in four of the member countries numbered millions, not hundreds of thousands.[14]

TABLE 9a: Numbers of registered unemployed in European Community countries at December 1980 (to nearest 100)

	Total	Men	Women
Belgium	430,500	171,900	258,600
France	1,632,000	765,700	866,300
Federal Republic of Germany	1,118,300	583,200	535,100
Italy (p)	1,820,300	951,300	869,000
Netherlands	322,400	219,700	102,700
Luxembourg	1,451	733	'718
United Kingdom	2,244,200	1,585,700	658,500
Ireland	122,200	98,200	29,000
Denmark (p)	222,800	131,300	91,500
TOTALS	7,914,200	4,502,700	3,411,400

(p) = provisional

SOURCE: Commission of the European Communities

Within six years, by 1981, the numbers of registered unemployed in the EEC countries had virtually doubled, to over 8 million.[15] The world recession, together with public expenditure cuts, continues to push the total upwards. The worst affected areas in the EEC include some of those most dependent on traditional manufactures.

e) CHANGES IN THE PATTERN OF EIB LENDING FOR INDUSTRY APPARENT BY 1980

By 1980 there were signs of change in the EIB's lending policies for industry. A decline in the proportion of total financing going to construction materials partly reflected the contraction of public works expenditure. There was also, however, a significant drop in the proportion of total loan allocations for metal production and semi-processing, and a small increase in the proportion granted for foodstuffs:

	% of total loans 1958-80	1980
Construction materials	1.1	0.6
Metal processing & semi-processing	5.6	1.1
Foodstuffs	2.0	2.2 [16]

There was a slight movement away from loans to large industrial enterprises and in favour of more support for small and medium-scale ventures (see Chapter 12). Greater emphasis was also being given to enterprises both large and small in the field of conservation, anti-pollution measures and renewable energy sources (see Chapter 13). Had this last change been inaugurated eight or nine years earlier, an increasing demand for workers in more labour-intensive types of work would have partially compensated for the losses in numbers of jobs in traditional industries.

f) CONCLUSIONS

The governments of the initial six EEC countries must bear a large part of the responsibility for failing to react to both labour-saving technologies and the growth of manufacturing in newly industrialising countries when both developments were recognised in the Community during the mid-1960s crisis. Through their Finance Ministers in their role as Governors of the European Investment

Bank, EEC governments could have then begun to di-
vert some of the finance which the Bank was channelling into the EEC from world financial markets, into
enterprises likely to have longer-term beneficial
effects on levels of employment.   Instead, although
the danger of structural unemployment was noted, the
Bank was obliged to devote a large proportion of its
resources to the modernisation and conversion of
traditional industries, particularly metal production and mechanical engineering, both of which were
increasingly under pressure from overseas competition.

In seeking either to protect traditional
national industries, such as steel and vehicle manufacture, or to convert them into large-scale enterprises in areas where they barely existed, such as
the south of Italy, member states have wasted funds
made available by the Bank.   It was not until 1979-
80 that there was a significant rise in the amount
of EIB financing for small and medium-scale enterprises and that resources for innovative technologies in environmental protection and energy conservation became available. At the same time, the EIB's
mandate to assist poor and non-industrial areas
within Community countries has been difficult to
carry out, and old industrialised areas have
deteriorated despite the Bank's assistance.

NOTES

1. EIB, 1958-1978, 24-5

2. Ibid.; EIB, Annual Reports, 1978, 32;   1979, 32;
    1980, 38, Table 3; 96, Table 14.

3. EIB, 1980 Annual Report, 96, Table 14.

4. EIB, 1959 Annual Report, 15.

5. EIB, 1962 Annual Report, 15, 20.

6. Financial Times, 7 March, 1979, Report from Charles
    Batchelor.

7. Ibid., 31 March, 1980, Survey of Italy, pp. vi, X.

8. Rudolf Buxtorf, 'L'industrie de base talonnée par la
    concurrence', Le Mois, pub. Swiss Bank Corpn. No.10,1979,
    pp. 18-21.   See also Christopher Lutz, Prospects, No.4,
    1979, p. 4.   New Scientist, 29 November, 1979, Plessey's
    UK.   EIB, 1965 Annual Report, 20, EEC Working Documents
    on shipyards and textiles.

9. EIB Annual Reports, 1965, 19-20; 1966, 19-20; 1967, 48.

10. The Annual Reports of these Companies.

11. Swiss Bank Corporation, Prospects, June 1979.

12. Financial Times, 15 June, 1979, 'Multinational code re-endorsed'; R. Caborn, Euro M.P., Report on Multi-nationals for European Parliament Economic & Monetary Committee, April 1981.

13. EIB, 1977 Annual Report, 15-16: in July 1978, this policy was re-affirmed - 'The Community's main objective was to improve employment through sustained economic growth against a background of stability....' 1978 Annual Report, 9.

14. EIB, Information, No.22, July 1980, 2; No.26, July,1981, 2; Financial Times, 12 Jan. 1981, Special Supplement, Europe, p. XI. 'Jobless toll rises relentlessly'.

15. Times, 6 May 1981, 1, 'Breakdown in Relations' between the Treasury and the Conservative Government because of officials' unease at policies leading to high unemployment: 21 May, 1981, 21, 'Business News', 'IMF Warning on Recession'; 2 June, 1981, reprint in Times of Europe, Vol. VIII, No.9, p.1, Michel Godet, 'Unemployment is not inevitable': 25 July, 1981, 4, 'Angry Tughendhat hits at "folly" of budget ministers,' etc. Mr. Tughendhat is a member of the ECC Commission with special responsibility for budget and financial control.

16. EIB, 1980 Annual Report, 38, Table 3; 96, Table 14.

Chapter 10

EUROPEAN INVESTMENT BANK FINANCING FOR
STEEL AND TELECOMMUNICATIONS

a) STEEL

One of the industries worst affected by the
introduction of labour-saving technologies and the
growth of competition outside the Community was
steel.

From 1964, when the growth of overseas competition in traditional EEC industries was recognised,
the EIB was lending for the modernisation of steel
enterprises.   In conjunction with the European Coal
and Steel Community,[1] it has followed a dual policy.
Both institutions supported the introduction of new
technologies - modernisation and conversion - and
the Bank particularly, the creation of new plants in
south Italy.   And both institutions, also partly
through modernisation and conversion programmes,
have been helping to keep old plants going through
the crisis of the 1970s so as to slow job losses.

While the EIB's total lending for steel in the
Community before 1973 amounted to 62.1 million ua.,
almost all of it in Italy, between 1973 and 1978,
EIB loans for EEC steel totalled some 399 million ua,
over two thirds of it going to the British Steel
Corporation.

b) THE EIB'S LENDING POLICIES IN THE 1970s
   EEC STEEL CRISIS

During the mid-1970s, EEC steel producers were
forced to cut back more than their competitors, as
shown below:

Change in world steel output, 1974-78

EEC	..	..	..	- 14.9%
Japan	..	..	..	- 12.8%
USA	..	..	..	- 6.4%
Developing countries of Latin America, Asia & the Middle East (i.e. excluding Africa)			+ 48.2% [2]

167

Between 1974 and 1978, EEC steel production dropped by 30 million tonnes. During this period of rationalisation and redundancy, about 100,000 steel workers in Community countries lost their jobs and another 100,000 were put on short-time working. In 1979, the industry saw some recovery, but only half the 1974-78 loss in production was made up, short-time working was still said to be affecting 40,000 workers in any one month and lay-offs were running at about 2,000 per month. A further 81,000 jobs were expected to be lost in the steel industry in 1979-81. Other industries feared the knock-on effects of the curtailments in steel production. [3]

It was only in its 1977 Annual Report that the EIB belatedly acknowledged the industrial crisis, which referred to 'Certain sectors of industry...in the Community for various reasons facing difficulties that hold serious implications for many regions.' Therefore, it remarked:

> Companies have to modernise and restructure and some of the operations by the Bank have helped, if only indirectly, to bring about the requisite investment.
> The whole of the Bank's lending in support of investment in the British, Italian and French iron and steel industries...was in practice related to modernisation and re-structuring projects, even though they were financed in consideration of their regional interest.

Through anti-dumping restrictions and arrangements with some of the EEC's strongest competitors, Japan, Taiwan and South Korea, imports of steel into the Community were forced down by 1.4 million tonnes between 1976 and 1978, while EEC exports rose by 9 million tonnes, so saving 55,000 jobs. The reduction in competitive pressures would, it was hoped, assist the re-organisation of the industry. [4]

In its 1978 Report, the Bank was referring to the fact that:

> Slackening demand for iron and steel products and intense international competition have highlighted the dire structural problems besetting European undertakings in the steel sector. [5]

The EEC Commission took the view that the re-organisation of the industry forced on by the 1973 crisis would only be effective if all the EEC countries acted together, since all were competing on the same markets. To achieve uniformity, in 1976, Viscount Davignon, who was the EEC's Commissioner for Industry, was asked to make proposals for helping the steel industry in the Community countries.

His report was published in 1978 and is summarised in Appendix 10B at the end of this chapter.

The European Investment Bank, in lending for the modernisation of steel plants, which has meant the suppression as well as the preservation of jobs, was acting entirely in accordance with that portion of its Statute enjoining support for Community policy. It was not apparently realised, when the Statute was drawn up, that Community policy might conflict with other parts of the EIB's Statute, in this instance its mandate to provide loans for viable economic enterprises. Rescue operations to shore up the British steel industry, in particular, were based on criteria other than viability.

The EIB's loans to the British Steel Corporation included 31.0 million ua (£17.5 million) in 1975 for the installation of three new coating lines at the complex in Shotton, North Wales, and, the following year, 19.0 million ua (£12.6 million) to the iron and steel complex at Port Talbot in S.Wales, and 10.9 million ua (£6.75 million) to the complex at Consett in County Durham in North-East England. (See Table 10a.)

The British Steel Corporation was the EEC's biggest iron and steel undertaking, producing 19.7 million tonnes of steel in 1976. It was created in 1973 from ten of the largest firms and inherited several old and uneconomic plants which had been starved of investment over a long period. The Corporation, in 1973, produced a 10-year plan in which it was envisaged that a number of obsolescent and badly located plants would have to be closed and that steel production would be concentrated in modernised plants, including integrated complexes, among them those at Port Talbot, Shotton and Consett on Teesside.

By the end of 1980, the whole of Consett, most of Shotton and part of Port Talbot, had been or were about to be closed. It is not clear whether the Bank's assessments of these projects failed to uncover the full extent of the British Steel Corporation's problems, or whether they were intended primarily to delay the dismemberment of uneconomic plant. The EIB's loans may have benefitted the workforces concerned in the short-term since they helped to keep jobs going a little longer than would have been the case without them. They may also have contributed to redundancy payments. But the EIB's contribution to postponement of the day when the unemployed required social welfare payments, must be set against the government's subventions to an ailing enterprise, which were similarly a charge

169

TABLE 10a: EIB Loans for the British Steel Industry

Place	Type of Project	Years	Amount mills, ua
Shotton,N.Wales	3 new coating lines at complex	1975	31.0
Consett, Co. Durham	Expansion of rolling mills	1976	10.9
	Modernisation of brickworks producing refractories for coke ovens, Templetown area	1977	6.0
Port Clarence, Cleveland, Teesside	Refinery for coking plant by-products	1977	10.5
Redcar, Yorkshire	Construction of a third ore unloader	1977	12.2
Workington, N.W. England	Construction of continuous casting mould refurbishing facilities	1976	3.2
Scotland & N. England (unspecified)	Expansion of tube mills	1976	25.6
	Rationalisation and modernisation of foundry installations	1966	*17.4
Motherwell, Scotland	Expansion of rolling mills, Dalzell works	1976	5.7
	Extension and modernisation of Ravenscraig integrated iron and steel works	1977	80.6
	Installation of continuous casting machine, Ravenscraig	1977	21.1
Port Talbot, N. Wales	Expansion of coal handling, storage and blending facilities at iron and steel complex	1976	19.0
Darlington, Co. Durham	+ Construction and equipping of factory to produce heavy structural steelwork	1980	*15.9

+ All loans were to the British Steel Corporation, the Port Clarence loan being transmitted to the BSC's Chemicals' subsidiary, except the 1980 loan in Darlington which went to the Cleveland Bridge & Engineering Co. Ltd.

* 2 loans

upon the population, repaid out of tax contributions.
By 1980, the Department of Industry, with the endorsement of Prime Minister Margaret Thatcher, was
encouraging BSC to sell off its assets, including
modernised and converted plant,[6] as failing firms
did in the 1920s and 1930s.   Meanwhile, further
questions about the utility of the Bank's loans to
BSC were raised by the uncertain future of Mother-
well in Scotland, to which the EIB has also been
giving considerable financial assistance.[7]

    By the late 1970s, competition between EEC
steel enterprises was evident.   For example, the
Italian state enterprise, Italsider (to which the
EIB gave two early loans - see Appendix 10A) was in
difficulties and the whole Italian steel industry
was beset by strikes.   The other EEC steel producers were using the opportunity to take over a
larger share of the growing Italian market for
steel, undercutting Italsider's prices.[8]   Independent EEC steel producers were demanding the swift
cessation throughout the Community of state aid
which they saw as creating unfair competition.   They
were supported by Mr. Frans Andriessen, the Community's Competition Commissioner, who wanted state
aids linked directly to a reduction in production
capacity and their complete phasing out in 1985.[9]
This policy was agreed in June 1981.   Pending the
ending of state aid, limitations on production quo-
tas were to be continued in the hopes of raising
prices, along with the policies of short-time working and early retirement for British, French and
Belgian steelworkers, supported by financial aid
from the Community.[10]   In effect, the programme
drawn up by Viscount Davignon in his 1978 Plan was
to be implemented.

    From the announcement of the 1978 Davignon Plan
the EIB's investments in EEC steel have been diminishing.   Only in the United Kingdom has there been
a loan since that year directly for the steel industry - 15.9 million units of account to the Cleveland
Bridge & Engineering Company for equipping a factory
to produce heavy structural steel work.   This project at Darlington in County Durham may be connected with a 4.2 million ua loan to Whessoe Heavy
Engineering's nuclear power plant construction
operations at Darlington and Middlesborough.[11] These
loans are to engineering firms and not to steel
works.   Hence they are different in kind from the
ambulance operations the Bank was helping to mount
in the steel industry in 1974-78.

c) CONCLUSIONS ON EIB LENDING FOR THE EEC STEEL INDUSTRY

The fate of Consett, Llanwern, Port Talbot and Shotton call into question the EIB's claim in its 20-year retrospect, 1958-1978, that its high standing rests partly on its portfolio of financing which 'covers wealth-creating, sound investments in all sectors of the economy, backed in every case by solid security....'[12] The last part of the statement is true since ultimately the Bank is backed by the entire assets of each of the member states. However, the decline in the EEC steel industry seems to indicate anomalies in the Bank's loan policies, which require clarification. Financial aid for steel enterprises earlier starved of investment by private owners may possibly be comprehended in 'progressive development of the European Community.' The curtailment or total closure of plants following such investment can, however, hardly be termed 'development', and the problem of increasing unemployment or underemployment due to rationalisation and modernisation remains unsolved. The 1981 French Socialist government of M. Mitterand is the chief proponent of the view that contraction in the steel industry must be accompanied by provision to deal with the social consequences.[13]

Up to the present, the lending policies of the European Investment Bank in respect of the steel industry in the Community, illustrate the difficulties of a unified strategy in an institution run by changing governments of a group of states with differing economies. The newer Italian industry still seems to be seen as a special case with the Italian government injecting large amounts of finance into Italsider in order to boost production, while the Belgian government is assisting the merging of two large private steel firms, Cockerill and Hainault-Sambre,[14] and the British Steel Corporation is drastically scaling down its operations. The one point of agreement among EEC governments would appear to be that the Community must retain some sort of steel industry. Especially from 1973, the lending policy on steel laid down for the EIB seems to have consisted largely of a series of responses to an apparently unexpected disruption of the industry, despite the recognition of the growth of overseas competition in the mid-1960s.

TABLE 10b: EEC regions in which the EIB has helped
to finance telecommunications develop-
ment

Regions	million ua	Loans
ITALY		
Apulia	151.2	Four loans: 1970/74/76/80
Sardinia	114.4	Four loans: 1968/73/78
Sicilia	54.2	Two loans: 1975/77
Campania	49.4	Two loans: 1972/74
Projects covering more than one region:		
Mezzogiorno	55.7	Two loans: 1979/80
(for long distance telephone links plus improved telex services throughout the South)		
Abruzzi-Molise	86.5	Guarantee on a loan provided from a German bank, 1970; two loans: 1975/78
Veneto-Trentino-Alto Adige	54.8	Two loans: 1969/75
Calabria-Basilicata	54.1	Two loans: 1976/77
Sicilia-Calabria	36.0	Two loans: 1967/71
Friuli-Venezia Giulia	20.2	1977
Campania-Basilicata	20.0	1968
Apulia, Campania	206.7	1980
FRANCE		
Nord Pas-de-Calais	100.0	1978
Lorraine	99.2	1979
Pays de la Loire	92.3	Two loans: 1971/78
Midi-Pyrenées	60.2	Two loans: 1973/77
Aquitaine	60.0	Two loans: 1972/76
Auvergne	53.8	Two loans: 1972/76
Bretagne	47.2	Three loans: 1971/75/76
Poitou-Charentes	25.0	1973
Limousin	15.0	1971
Project covering more than one region:		
Sud-Ouest (Midi-Pyrenées Aquitaine, Poitou-Charentes)	8.1	1967
UNITED KINGDOM		
Wales & The Marches	122.4	Two loans: 1975/79
Scotland	30.0	1976
North-East England	30.0	Two loans: 1976/78
Northern Ireland	27.9	1977
" "	68.8	1980

173

TABLE 10b (cont'd.)

Regions	million ua	Loans
UNITED KINGDOM (contd.) Submarine cables and equipment linking U.K. with Netherlands and Denmark	17.1	1980
IRELAND		
Projects covering the whole country:	140.6	Six loans: 1973/74/75/76/77/ 79
	32.9	1980 (from the EIB's own resources)
	17.9	1979 (from the resources of the new Community Instrument for Borrowing and Lending)
DENMARK		
Greenland	120.0	Two loans: 1974/80

SOURCE: EIB Information, No.21, May 1980.
          EIB 1980 Annual Report, 44-9.

d) THE EIB'S LOANS FOR TELECOMMUNICATIONS
   IN THE EEC

The Bank's lending for the development of telecommunications in the Community presents a contrast
for this is a new industry, unhampered by traditions.
The Bank has given far more financial support to
telecommunications than to steel, partly because it
classes telecommunications as infrastructure. It is
private as well as public enterprise, however. The
Bank's financing of telecommunications started in
1967, after the first EEC crisis. The first recipients of loans were in north Italy and not in the
south where telephone communcations were extremely
poor (see Table 10b). However, the bulk of the
EIB's total loans, amounting to 934.0 million uas,
went to the south of the country. Here and in some
of the peasant areas in France, the Bank's loans
were predominantly for infrastructure. However,
the loans to the French postal authority, the PTT,
totalling 63.7 million ua to 1980, were obviously
for the most up-to-date telecommunication systems
and assisted the PTT's own development. It is now
a $500 billion enterprise and with its Teletel and
Antiope systems has entered the international com-
puter-electronics market. Similarly, EIB loans of
296.2 million ua to the United Kingdom assisted the
updating of the Post Office's computerised Telecom
system which is now a separate nationalised concern.
EIB loans have helped to build the market for
six major telecommuncations companies: SIT-
Siemens, Telettra (a subsidiary of Fiat), Fatme (a
subsidiary of Ericsson), Olivetti, which has an
agreement with the Japanese Hitachi and two United
States companies, FACE, a subsidiary of ITT, and
the Italian branch of the General Telephone and
Electronics Company.[15]

e) THE PROBLEMS OF EIB INVESTMENTS IN
   TELECOMMUNICATIONS

There are two drawbacks to telecommunications
as a field of investment. The first is that,
although a new industry, like steel it already faces
severe competition from Japan and newly industrialising countries. This was the reason that, in
1979, Viscount Davignon's attention was switched to
this sector. At the Dublin meeting of heads of
EEC governments held that year, he submitted a plan
which has received curiously little publicity for
turning from support for uncompetitive, out-dated
industries to the more modern, computing, telecommunications and micro-electronics business in a

long-term effort to establish an EEC stake. At present the whole of Europe takes about a third of the world output of these industries, but makes only about a sixth of the products. So Davignon wants Community preference with all public ordering, especially by the post and telephone authorities, co-ordinated. A common European information network, he proposed, should be set up, jointly operating communications satellites, television and research. Davignon is vague, however, on sources of finance for this co-operative EEC effort.[16] The international nature of the industry meanwhile means that EIB finance is benefitting some of the EEC's competitors in this field.[17]

But secondly, it is in the nature of this industry to reduce employment.[18] Encouragement to small micro-electronics firms may temporarily create jobs but cannot alter the overall effect. For example in the UK and other parts of the Community, new telephone equipment is replacing the previous electro-magnetic equipment in telephone exchanges. The result will be a substantial loss of jobs, both in the factories where the equipment is manufactured and in the exchanges where it is used.[19] While the EIB's loans have helped to improve telecommunications services and sometimes to reduce costs, they are also contributing to massive new social and economic problems.

f) CONCLUSIONS

Lending for telecommunications cannot be considered apart from the whole of the policies laid down for the EIB. Improved communications for isolated communities and the elimination of repetitive and dead-end jobs will raise living standards for the Community's population only within a coherent strategy which has that end in view.

The EIB's investments, both in the case of the steel industry and the more modern telecommunications have demonstrated the need for swift reactions from its Board of Governors to the increasing speed of technological and economic change. At the same time they show, yet again, the need for caution and the difficulties posed by the large nature of some of the loan projects which require big investments and which cover a number of years. They highlight the urgency of changes to compensate for the social and economic effects of changing technologies starkly illustrated by the rising unemployment figures in the Community.

NOTES

1. E. Noël, Working Together, the Institutions of the European Economic Community, 1979, 11.

2. Main steel producing countries competing with the EEC
   countries: Asia: Japan, S.Korea.
                America: S. Africa.
                COMECON: Hungary, Bulgaria, Czechoslovakia.
                Europe: Spain

   It took 8.3 hours to produce 1 tonne of crude steel in
   the EEC in 1973, but only 5.9 hours in Japan - but even
   Japan was losing ground.   The EEC, the USA and Japan
   since 1974 have all been providing a diminishing share
   of growing world steel production.   See R. Buxtorf,
   'L'industrie de base talonée par la concurrence', Le
   Mois, pub. Swiss Bank Corporation, No.10, 1979, 18-21;
   C. Lutz, Prospects, pub. Swiss Bank Corporation, No.4,
   1979, p.4; Commission of the European Communities,
   European File, 'A Steel Policy for Europe', E 6/79,
   March 1979, 2.

	Share in world steel production, 1978 %
Comecon	30
EEC	19
USA	17
Japan	14
Developing countries (Brazil, India, Mexico, Taiwan, Argentina, etc.)	7
China	4
Other steel producers ..	9

   Source: International Iron & Steel Inst., given in Le
             Mois, pub. Swiss Bank Corpn., No.10, 1979, p.21.

   It is not clear whether the growing steel production in
   African countries is included under 'developing
   countries' or 'other'.

3. At the beginning of March 1980, the UK National Union of
   Railwaymen S. Wales Divisional Officer claimed that a
   quarter of rail jobs in his division were threatened by
   steel closures.   There will also be a drop in demand
   for some kinds of coal, so miners may be affected, etc.

4. Commission of the Eur. Communities Directorate General
   for Information, European File, 'A steel policy for
   Europe', E 6/79, March 1979; Commission for the Eur.
   Communities, Commission on Steel Prices, Working Paper
   SEC(79) 1127 Final, 16 July, 1979; Commission of the Eur.
   Communities, Background Reports: Imports were under-
   cutting prices for products from the most efficient EEC
   plants.

5. EIB, 1978 Annual Report, 31.

6. Daily Telegraph, report of speech by Mrs. Thatcher, 13
    February, 1980; Financial Times, 28 March, 1 April,
    1980; Times, 'Business News', 17-18 and 23 June.

7. Times, Business News, 30 June, 9 July, 1980; 21 May, 24
    and 26 June, 1981.

8. Financial Times, Survey of Italy, 31 March, 1980, VI, X.
    The Italian Government destroyed acres of fertile olive
    and citrus groves at Giolia Tauro on the Calabrian
    coast in order to build a giant steel works and create
    7,500 jobs. It had to abandon the project and is left
    with a desert. The people lost their original farming
    and have not been given new jobs. A small steel works
    is planned and a power station is being considered.

9. Times, 'Business News', 12 May, 1981, 16.

10. Ibid. Also 'Business News' 26 June, 1981, 21; EEC OJL
    184/1981.

11. EIB, 1980 Annual Report, 50.

12. EIB, 1958-1978, 11.

13. Times, 'Business News", 24 June, 1981, 19.

14. Daily Telegraph, 30 January, 1980; Times, 'Business
    News', 24 June, 1981, 'Last Chance to end Europe's Steel
    Industry Chaos?', 19.

15. Financial Times, Suppl. on Italy, 26 February, 1980, VI.
    The Italian government is pressing for takeovers as each
    of 5 different firms has its own switching system.
    Siemens has an agreement with the Japanese Fujitsu, see
    Times, 'Business News', 4 June, 1980.

16. Sunday Times, 23 November, 1979, 'Chips all round to end
    job starvation.'

17. Times, 'Business News', 4 June, 1980. Foreign-owned
    electronics and computer firms are starting enterprises
    in Ireland. The French Cii and Bull were originally
    both national companies. In May 1981, the Mitterand
    government was said to be considering nationalising Cii-
    Honeywell Bull, the weaker partner in the US Honeywell
    controls and computer group. The parent US company
    replied by threatening to break the existing demarcation
    agreement on products with Cii-Honeywell Bull and to
    compete in the same fields, see Times, 'Business News',
    15 May, 1981, 20. British Telecom's attempts to con-
    trol Japanese competition, see Times, 6 May, 1981, 'Tele-
    com Warning to Japan'; Morgan Stanley Electronics Ltd.,
    Letter, 31 August, 1979, lists eight EEC-based companies
    with corporate investments in US semi-conductor firms:

178

Siemens, Robert Bosch, VDO Adolf Schindling of West
Germany; Phillips of the Netherlands and Schlumberg
of the Netherlands Antilles; Ferranti, Lucas Industries and the National Enterprise Board of Britain.

18. Counter-claims that computerisation and micro-electronics
    increase employment are being made, viz. Lord Gowrie,
    British Employment Minister, speech to the Engineering
    1980 Conference, Financial Times, 7 November, 1979;
    Advisory Council for Applied Research & Development
    Report: Technological Change: Threats & Opportunities,
    HMSO, January 1980; Financial Times, 26 September, 1979,
    'How electronics is transforming the shop floor' (Sweden);
    Ibid. 6 November, 1979, Californian industry estimated
    to have created half a million jobs in last 5 years;
    Ibid. 26 October, 1979, US computing consultant, 'Effect
    of Micros on jobs'.

19. C. Hines, Automatic Unemployment, ERR Ltd., 1979;
    Clive Jenkins and Barry Sherman, The Collapse of Work,
    1979; Financial Times, 7 November, 1979, David Fishlock,
    'The robots are coming, but not in Britain'; also Ibid.
    19 October, 3 November, 7 December, 1979 and 10 September
    1979, 'Electronics in the Office'; Times, 'Business
    News', 24 May, 1980, jobs lost at Decca, etc.

APPENDIX 10A: Main EIB Loans for Steel other than UK

Place & Year	Beneficiary	Amount (m.ua.)	Purpose of Loan
ITALY			
Naples 1964	.. Italsider	24.0	Enlargement & modernisation of works
Taranto 1969	.. Italsider	25.0	Installation of cold rolling mill
Taranto 1976 & 1977	.. Siderurgica Commerciale Italiana S.p.A.	33.8	Grading & Cutting heavy steel sheet extension:plate mill reorganised & anti-pollution equipment installed
Dalmine, Lombardy 1976,1978	.. Dalmine S.p.A.	28.0	Medium-diameter seamless tube mill installed
Sesto San Giovanni & Arcore 1978	.. Acciaiere e Ferriere Lombarde FALCK, S.p.A.	4.2	Improvements to electricity installations
Catania, Sicily, 1971	.. Acciaiere Magara S.p.A.	4.0	Steel plant
FEDERAL REPUBLIC OF GERMANY			
Hamelin, Westphalia 1967	.. Hoesch Aktiengesellschaft	7.5	Construction of welded steel-tube
Völklingen 1969	.. Stahlwerke Rochling-Burbach, GmbH	7.1	Four-line drawing mill
Neunkirchen, Saar, 1973, 1976	Neunkirche Eisenwerk	17.0	Small Bar-mill; steel works restructured
FRANCE			
Toulon 1973	.. Sté. Sudacier, SA	3.6	Mini-steel works
Lorraine: Seremange 1977	.. Sté. Lorraine de Laminage Continu	19.6	Modernisation
Neuves-Maisons & Longwy:Nord Pas de Calais, Brache & Tobergues 1978	Sté, Sidernergique Châtillon-Neuves-Maisons	9.5	Rationalisation & modernisation

SOURCE: EIB, Annual Reports.

APPENDIX 10B

Summary of the Davignon Plan for Steel

a) put a ceiling on already surplus production
    capacity in the EEC.

b) establish minimum compulsory prices for par-
    ticularly sensitive products and recommended
    prices for others.

c) protect the trade by anti-dumping measures.

In the medium term, the Davignon Plan proposed to:

1. Ban national subsidies which increase production
    capacity or distort competition in the EEC.

2. Grant EEC loans for modernisation and
    rationalisation.

3. Increase EEC aid for industrial conversion and
    diversification in the main specialised steel-
    producing areas.

4. Study how to share out available work by earlier
    retirement, reorganisation of shift work,
    shortening the working week and restricting
    overtime.

5. Intensify research and innovation on products
    and production processes in order to ensure the
    better use of minerals and energy.

6. Negotiate with other major world steel producers
    in order to ensure 'an equitable division of the
    cost burden at world level', i.e. that EEC pro-
    ducers do not bear a disproportionate share of
    the cost of adjusting to a lower level of world
    steel demand.

The success of the 'Davignon Plan' is regarded in
the Commission as a test of EEC unity. If it fails
the Community would be unlikely to solve other
critical problems in the fields of textiles, shipbuilding and in energy.

Chapter 11

EUROPEAN INVESTMENT BANK LOANS FOR THE
CHEMICAL AND CHEMICAL RELATED INDUSTRIES

Between 1958 and 1972, the chemical industry
received a larger amount of assistance from the
European Investment Bank than any other single
industrial sector. The only sector that attracted
more of the Bank's investments was in infrastructure - the building of roads, bridges and tunnels. In
the next four years, 1973-77, the Bank's rate of
lending to the chemical industry increased, but to
a lesser extent than in other sectors with the result that the proportion of investment going to
chemicals fell from second to fifth place.   From
1978, the rate of investment dropped considerably
and the percentage of the EIB's total loans devoted
to chemicals declined to 0.7 per cent.

TABLE 11a: Proportion of the EIB's total loans
             devoted to chemical enterprises in the
             Community 1958-1980

1958-72		1973-77		1978-80	
Amount mill. ua	% of total loans	Amount mill. ua	% of total loans	Amount mill. ua	% of total loans
277.0	11.3	200.4	4.0	56.0	0.7

SOURCE: EIB, 1958-78, 24-5; Annual Reports, 1978, 32;
         1979, 38; 1980, 38.

a) MAIN AREAS OF EIB INVESTMENTS IN EEC CHEMICAL
   AND CHEMICAL-BASED INDUSTRIES

As Map 11a and Appendix 11a show, the bulk of
EIB finance for chemical and chemical related industries was directed to the south of Italy.   Besides
cheaper production costs, the additional geographical advantage of proximity to Middle East oil

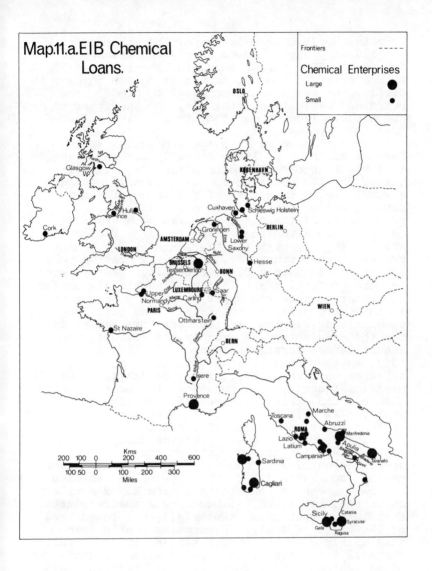

Map.11.a.EIB Chemical Loans.

Frontiers ----------

Chemical Enterprises
Large ●
Small ·

OSLO

Glasgow ●

Hull
Ince

Cork ●

KØBENHAVN

Cuxhaven
Schleswig Holstein
BERLIN

Groningen
AMSTERDAM
Lower Saxony

LONDON
BRUSSELS
Tessenderloo
BONN
Hesse

LUXEMBOURG
Saar
Upper Normandy
Carling
WIEN
PARIS
Ottmarstein

St Nazaire

BERN
Isere

Provence

Toscana
Marche
ROMA
Abruzzi
Lazio
Manfredonia
Latium
Apulia
Campania
Taranato

Kms
200 100 0 200   400   600
100 50 0 100   200   300
Miles

Sardinia

Cagliari

Sicily
Catania
Gela
Syracuse
Ragusa

supplies applied to a large part of the chemical industry as it did to energy and transport.
Two of the EIB's first loans in 1958-59, given to
subsidiaries of the United States Edison company in
Sicily, one for a cracking plant to produce the
petroleum derivative, ethylene, and the other to
use the ethylene to manufacture plastics, illustrated the point.

Some finance went to the chemical industry
further north.   In 1961, a small loan was granted
to a big Franco-German enterprise, Progil-Bayer-
Ugine, for the construction of a factory on the
River Isère, a tributary of the Rhône, for the
manufacture of synthetic foam and varnish.
As a result of the mid-1960s crisis, a greater
emphasis was given to lending to large EEC enterprises, in line with the EIB's mandate to promote
trans-national companies, loans were granted to a
second Franco-German firm, Pec-Rhin, for the manufacture of fertilisers in their industrial complex
at Ottmarstein on the Upper Rhine.   In addition,
loans were granted to the French side of a large
chemicals development in the Saar-Lorraine triangle
for the manufacture of ammonia and another loan to
a West German fertiliser concern in this area.   In
1969, another loan followed, in the same area, to
a French concern manufacturing polyethylene for the
plastics industry.   Altogether, the Saar-Lorraine
chemical industries received 16.2 million ua in two
years.   At this time, the EIB also lent 4.9 million
ua to a joint West German-Dutch-Belgian project,
the construction of a gas pipeline designed to convey ethylene to petrochemical plants in their
several countries so saving road or rail transportation (see Table 11b).   Thus the Bank assisted
the development of chemicals in the EEC's northern
industrial heartland, although to a smaller extent
than in the much less industrially developed area
of the south of Italy.   There the Bank's loans
have mainly gone to enterprises in Sicily, Sardinia,
Campania, the Abruzzi and Apulia with concentrations centred on the ports of Sant' Antioco, Gela,
Naples and Manfredonia.

In accordance with its Statute and mandates,
the Bank has supported regional and transnational
industries which, presumably turned to the EIB because they could not obtain finance from other
sources on what were considered 'reasonable terms'.

TABLE 11b: Main EIB Loans for Chemical Industry in France and West Germany

Area and Year	Beneficiary	Amount (m.ua)	Purpose of loan
FRANCE			
South of France 1958-59	Unstated	6	Construction petrochemical works
Isère 1961	Progil-Bayer-Ugine (Franco-German consortium)	2	Construction chemical works
Perl 1967	Hornstoff-und Düngemittel-werk, Saar : Lothringen GmbH*		Construction of urea factory
Haut-Rhin 1967	Produits et Engrais Chimiques du Rhin	6.1	Construction nitrogenous & compound fertiliser plant
Carling, Moselle 1967	L'Ammoniac Sarro-Lorrain S.a.r.l.*	3.1	Construction ammonia production factory
Normandy 1969	Sté Industrielle Poly-defines	4.5	Construction Polyethylene plant
Lillebonne 1969	Sté. Normande de Matières Plastiques	3.6	Extension polypropylene plant
FEDERAL REPUBLIC OF GERMANY			
Brunsbüt-teltaag Schleswig-Holstein 1965	Kali-Chemie A.G.	1.3	Modernisation & extension fertiliser plant
Neumünster 1965	Phrix-Werke, A.G. (2 Loans)	8.8 {2.5 / 6.3}	Enlargement synthetic fibre production plant
Nienburg Weser 1969 Lower Saxony	Kali-Chemie, A.G.	1.5	Construction workshop making enzymes for detergents
Fed.Republic of Germany, Netherlands & Belgium 1971	Aethylen-Rohrleitungs GmbH & Co. KG	4.9	Gas pipeline to supply ethylene to several petro-chemical plant
Munchmünster Bavaria 1972	Gelsenberg A.G.	17.1	+Olefine factory

*These two Saar projects formed an integrated whole financed by EIB and ECSC: + Paraffin product used in manufacture of ethylene and propylene

b) POLLUTION RISKS AND OTHER DRAWBACKS
OF CHEMICAL INDUSTRIES

However, from some points of view, the EIB's encouragement of chemical industries is questionable. Like other large-scale modern industrial enterprises, they tend to be capital intensive, but once the construction stage is completed, they may offer little settled long-term employment. Unlike the engineering industries of the 1960s and 1970s, they do not greatly encourage local ancillary and service enterprises. The Bank's investments in the Mezzogiorno particularly might have been more appropriately used to assist a wider range of small local initiatives, creating a larger number of permanent jobs. Planning an alternative strategy of this kind, however, is not easy and, until 1968, the view that 'big' was economically 'beautiful' was virtually unchallenged in the EEC. It was also simpler for both the Italian government and its agencies which dealt with the south, and for the EIB to concentrate on a few large projects. In addition, as already pointed out, the Bank found that only large companies had the willingness and resources to launch into large new enterprises in new areas.

A second important criticism of chemical plants, however, is that they are associated with a particularly large range of environmental problems. These include air and water pollution, in some instances the danger of explosions, toxic wastes, a variety of occupational hazards and a displeasing appearance. Strangely, the peak period of the EIB's investments in the chemical industry of the south of Italy coincided with the Community's official acceptance of the growth of environmental hazards, many of them arising from chemicals, for it was on 22 November, 1973 that the EEC Action Programme on environmental matters was inaugurated. Between 3 March, 1973 and 15 July, 1974, agreement was reached by EEC governments on eventual harmonisation of environmental protection measures.

The first and obvious risk from chemical industries and processes lies in the use of poisonous substances, some of them, such as mercury, cadmium and arsenic, well-known, others like polychlorinated biphenyls and terphenyls used in softening plastics, less so.[1] (See Appendix 11A.) Secondly, the production of perfectly harmless materials may involve great risks arising from quite simple faults in processing. For example, toothpaste and toilet soap were among the harmless products made at the works of Icmesa Givaudan, a subsidiary of the Swiss firm,

Hoffman-La Roche, at the village of Meda, just north of Milan, when an explosion occurred on Sunday, 10 July, 1976 and released a cloud of highly toxic dioxin vapour.   Within a few days, it contaminated the surrounding country, engulfing the nearby village of Seveso and spreading into the suburbs of the town of Cesano Maderno.   The damage to the health and environment of local communities were worse than they need have been because of the slowness of the Italian authorities in acknowledging the seriousness of the accident.   Consequently, evacuation of the area and safety measures were delayed.[2]

The Meda-Seveso accident, the explosions at Nypro Ltd. in Flixborough in 1974 and at Beek in the Netherlands in 1975, focussed public attention on the risks of chemical enterprises in general,   including those which the EIB had helped to finance.   For example, in August 1976, one month after the Seveso accident, the regional administration of Sicily proposed the evacuation of all the 12,000 inhabitants of the town of Priolo, near Syracuse, because they thought that the level of atmospheric pollution was a serious danger to human life, The Times of 7 August, 1976 reported:

> In an area of less than 20 square miles there are two refineries, a cement works and three chemical factories, with another chemical plant planned.

This concentration contained the two Edison plants, which had received 1958-59 EIB investment; one of them, Edison's Celene polyethylene production subsidiary, received another loan in 1965.   Part of the Sicilian administration's protest was directed against the strong United States interests.   But the immediate cause was a proposal for yet another plant to manufacture aniline, a venture in which the British Imperial Chemicals Industry and Montedison had a half-share each.   The Bank lent about 10.8 million ua (It.L.10,000 mill.) for the project, which went ahead despite the local people's protests (Table 11c).

Earlier, in March of 1976, the Bank had granted a larger loan of 20.1 million ua (L. 16,000 mill.) for the extension of the petrochemicals complex run by ANIC S.p.A., a subsidiary of the State concern, Ente Nazionale Idrocarburi (ENI) in the port of Manfredonia, in Apulia.   The complex, begun in 1971, was considered one of the most technically up-to-date in the world.   The EIB's investment was

TABLE 11c: Main EIB Loans to Chemical Industry: Italy

Place & Year	Beneficiary	Amount mill.ua	Purpose of Loan
Priolo, Sicily 1958-59	Edison-Union Carbide Group subsidiaries: Soc. Industriale Catanese SpA (SINCAT)	7.0	Construction ethylene plant
	SpA Celene Co.	4.0	Plastics factory (ethylene derivatives)
Crotone, Calabria 1962,	Montecatini Soc. Generale per l'Industria Mineral e Chemica	1.5	Enlarged chemicals factory enlarged : ferti-
1965		2.5	liser plant
Bussi, Abruzzi, 1966	Montecatini-Edison Group Montecatini-Edison SpA	2.0	Chemicals factory extended
1975	Montedison SpA	2.2	Sodium metasili- cate & hydro- carbon deriva- tives plant ex- tended
Apulia, Brindisi 1975		15.2	MDI plant (used in making rigid polyurethanes
1977		6.6	extension & modernisation polypropylene, polyethylene & ethyl oxide units
Sicily, Priolo 1976		1.6	Ancillary ser- vices for ani- line unit
	Joint enterprise with ICI	9.2	Aniline produc- tion
Manfredonia, Apulia, 1976	ANIC SpA	20.1	Construction of urea plant
Gela, Sicily 1974		19.6	Extension of petrochemicals complex
1975		10.7	" " & modernisation
Basilicata, 1974		6.1	Extension Acry- lic fibres plant
Naples, 1968,1971	Soc. Nazionale Industria Applicazioni Viscosa (Snia Viscosa)	11.6	Construction polyester plant
Salerno 1971		2.8	" "

188

TABLE 11c (cont'd.)

Place & Year	Beneficiary	Amount mill.ua	Purpose of Loan
Palario 1972	.. Soc. Nazionale Industria	4.9	Extension synthetic fibres plant
Sardinia 1962,1971	.. Sarda Magnesite & Palmas Car e SpA (SARDAMAG)	10.6	Construction & extension of magnesium oxide plant
Caltagirone Sicily, 1977	Itres SpA	3.5	Polyethylene tubing plant
Sardinia			
St.Antioco 1962	Rumianca & six other companies	24.0	Petrochemical unit
Porto Torres 1962	.. Sarda Industria Resine (SIR) & four other coy's	19.2	Petrochemical unit
Sarroch 1974	.. Italproteine	16.7	Animal feed plant
Calabria			
Crotone 1970	.. Soc. Mineraria e Metallurgica di Pertusola	14.0	Electrolytic zinc & germanium oxide plant
Abruzzi			
Bussi, 1967	·· Soc. Italiana Additivi per Carburanti SpA	2.2	Petrol additives plant
Ferentino 1970	·· Henkel Sud, SpA	4.0	Detergent factory
l'Aquila 1978	·· Hoechst Italia Sud SpA	4.7	Petrochemicals factory
Salerno 1968	·· Industrie Tessili Napolitani SpA	3.2	Factory processing polyester yarn
Caivano, Campania 1971	.. Industria Vernici ed Affini, SpA (IVI Sud)	4.0	Paint & Varnish factory
Apulia, Monte Sant' Angelo 1971	.. Chimica Dauna SpA	25.0	Caprolactàm factory
Marche,1970	Pansac-Sud SpA	4.0	Pharmaceuticals plant
Brindisi, 1977	..	3.9	Plastic packaging plant
Resigano, 1979	.. Solvay et Cie, SpA	8.8	Ethylene & acetylene production plant

specifically for a new urea plant and for the
rationalisation of the fertiliser plant which produced ammonia.   It was from the ammonia production
plant that, six months later, on Sunday, 26 September, a large quantity of arsenic compound escaped.
At that time arsenic was commonly used in the process of washing ammonia and ANIC stated that a huge
white cloud composed of 80 tons of water, 10 tons of
arsenious oxide and other materials escaped into the
atmosphere.   According to ANIC, three workers
suffered minor injuries from the explosion and two
suffered briefly from attacks of vomiting.   The
factory workers' council, however, claimed that
about 30 tons of arsenious oxide was involved and
that the number of workers who complained of sick-
ness and diarrhoea, i.e. of arsenical poisoning, was
20 and not 2.   Either way, the inhabitants of
Manfredonia were extremely lucky for the poison
cloud was blown by the wind to an uninhabited area.
However, the area round the factory, an industrial
estate, was cordoned off.   Following the measures
forced on the authorities by the Seveso accident,
the selling and eating of locally grown produce was
banned.   Police launches patrolled the coast to
see that no one fished nearby, and a committee of
experts was set up to study the extent of the contamination.[3]

The whole of the harvest had to be destroyed,
domestic and small animals died wretchedly and cows
ceased giving milk.   There were no immediate symp-
toms of acute poisoning among the population, but
there were certainly long-term risks of damage to
the skin or disruption of the nervous system, and a
carcinogenic risk for those immediately under the
cloud who inhaled the vapour, as well as secondary
risks from eating fish, vegetable or animal substances which were under the cloud.   The findings
of the Committee of Inquiry were still apparently
unobtainable in 1980.

It is notable, however, that until the Manfredonia accident, there had been little concern about
arsenic used in ammonia plant washeries.   The EIB
had given financial assistance in 1967 for ammonia
production through its loans to the French Lorraine
project and to the West German urea (i.e. fertiliser)
factory.   In 1976 the EIB also granted a big loan
of 29.9 million ua for an ammonia and urea plant
near Cork in South West Ireland (see Table 11d).
By 1976, when the Manfredonia accident occurred, the
dangers of the arsenic washery process were known.
The nascent EEC environmental protection service had
put arsenic on its black list.   A switch was

TABLE 11d: EIB Loans to other countries for
             Chemicals

Place & Year	Beneficiary	Amount mill.ua	Purpose of Loan
NETHERLANDS			
Delfzifl .. Gronigen 1968, 1971	N.V. Koninklijke Nederlandsche Jout- Industrie	18.0	Chlorine, chlo- rinated hydro- carbons & melamines
BELGIUM			
Tessenderloo 1969, 1970	Sté. Luxembourgeoise	12.0	Vinyl chloride factory
UNITED KINGDOM			
Hull, York- shire, 1976	BP Chemicals Ltd.	29.7	Acetic acid plant
Ince, N.W.	UKF Fertilisers Ltd.	7.5	Nitric acid ammonium nitrate units extended
Glasgow, Scotland, 1980	Norit-Clydesdale Co. Ltd.	3.4	Activated carbon factory for chemicals, etc.
IRELAND			
Nr. Cork, S.W.	Unstated	29.9+	Ammonia & urea plant
DENMARK			
N.Alsley 1979	Hartrig Jensen & B A/S	3.6	Expansion & rationalisation pesticide, &etc. plant
Nr. Vium 1980	Biogena A/S (Joint enterprise with Kali- Chemie of W.Germany)	1.1	Lactoserum plant

+ for which European Monetary System interest subsidy paid.

already in progress from arsenic to other washery
methods in ammonia plants in the Federal Republic of
Germany, due to a significant rise in the price of
arsenic.   West German firms were, however, hesitant
about making the change until the Manfredonia accident.[4]   Yet at the ANIC state enterprise plant, the
EIB, a Community instrument, had apparently not insisted on the use of less dangerous methods.[5]

c) PRESSURE FROM THE EUROPEAN PARLIAMENT
AGAINST TOXIC CHEMICALS

As a result of the growth in awareness of the
risks from poisons used or created by chemical enterprises, a Committee on the Environment, Public
Health & Consumer Protection, was established
within the European Parliament.   It has protested
against the slowness of procedures adopted by Councils of Ministers and the Commission for the implementation of Directives.   In particular it cam-
paigned for protection of workers on processes involving vinylchloride monomer, also known as
chloroethylene gas,[6] used in the manufacture of the
plastic, PVC, following United States reports in
1974 that it not only led to skin troubles, but also
to a terrible cancer of the liver.[7]   These reports
prompted urgent action to reduce levels of exposure
in some, but not all EEC countries.   The European Parliament Committee, however, considered that
limits, in some instances, were still too high.
The EIB had granted a number of loans, starting
with the 1958-59 loans to the Edison company, for
the production of materials involving VCM.   But its
financing of such plants increased from 1974 (see Tables 11b,c,d) after the United States reports had been
published and the full extent of the risks were
known.[8]
In 1976, the EEC issued a first proposal on
protection for workers using vinylchloride monomer
and in 1977 proposed maximum limits for concentrations of chloroethylene gas in the working area.
For new works the suggested limit was 5 ppm.* but
for old works 10 ppm.[9]   However, the European Parliament's Committee on the Environment, Public
Health and Consumer Protection, did not accept that
these limits were low enough.   They pointed out
that the Montedison company had established an
average concentration of only 1 ppm. in its works,
and some factories claimed to have eliminated the

* parts per milligram

TABLE 11e: EEC Directives on the reduction of pollution and health hazards from chemicals and other dangerous substances

Date and Number of Directive	Subject of Directive	Date of Implementation
27. 6.67 : 67/548/EEC	Approximation of laws, regulations & administrative provisions on classification, packaging and labelling of dangerous substances incl. notification of new chemical substances to be placed on the market, management and monitoring of notifications; definition of rules of confidentiality.	1. 1.70
18. 9.79 :	This Directive was subsequently amended six times. In the latest amendment the Commission was instructed to draw up an inventory of substances already on the market. This amendment combined Directive 67/548/EEC and its five subsequent amendments in one Directive.	19. 9.81
	Fixing maximum permissible levels of undesirable substances and products in animal feeding stuffs.	
26.11.76 : +	Restriction of marketing of certain dangerous substances and preparations in order to protect workers and general public and outlawing of vinyl chloride monomer as a propellant for aerosols.	
29. 6.78 : 78/610/EEC +	Approximation of laws, regulations and administrative provisions of member states on protection of the health of workers exposed to VCM. Fixing a long-term limit value with the intention of introducing it for all toxic substances.	29.12.79
27.11.80 : 80/ /EEC	Reducing to as low a level as is reasonably practical or avoiding exposure of workers to Annex 1 toxic substances.* Permitted derogations of 4-5 years.	Nov.'83 (Greece '84)

193

TABLE 11e (cont'd.)

DISPOSAL OF HARMFUL WASTES/CONSERVATION

6. 4.76 : 76/403/EEC	Prohibiting the discharge, discarding and unsupervised dumping of polychlorinated biphenyls and terphenyls; making compulsory their harmless disposal; promoting their reclamation; providing a system of authorisations for firms responsible for their collection, recycling and disposal; drawing up registers of wastes	9. 4.78
16. 6.75 : 75/439/EEC	Determining arrangements for the collection and harmless disposal of waste oils providing a system of authorisations for firms responsible for collection and disposal and a register of waste oils; recommending waste oils be re-used.	18. 6.77
15. 7.75 : 75/442/EEC	Encouraging the prevention and recycling of waste; determining arrangements for its harmless disposal; providing for its management and control, authorisations for firms responsible for its collection, recycling and disposal.	18. 7.77
20. 3.78 : 78/319/EEC	Laying down arrangements for the harmless disposal of toxic and dangerous wastes; promoting their recycling; providing administrative measures for their management and control and a system of authorisations for firms responsible for their collection, recycling and disposal; drawing up registers of wastes.	22. 3.80

*+ ANNEX 1 SUBSTANCES : 80/ Acrylonitril; Asbestos; Arsenic & Compounds; Benzene; Cadmium & Compounds; Mercury & Compounds; Nickel & Compounds; Lead & Compounds; chlorinated hydrocarbons: chloroform, paradichlorobenzene and carbon tetrachloride.

+ COM(76)556 final: Dossier:Soc/23 Vinyl Chlor. Mono., p.9; CES 900/77 he: OJ L 327/8, 3.12.80; COM(79/83 final. These 3 Directives emanated from the Directorate of Economic & Social Affairs (DG V) not the Environment & Consumer Protection Service.

SOURCE: Commission of the European Communities, Progress made in connection with the Environment Action Programme and assessment of work done to implement it, COM(80)222 final 2 May, 1980.

194

gas altogether. Mr. Vredeling, Vice-Commissioner for the EEC Commission for Employment and Social Affairs, replied, in answer to their criticisms:

> The risks run by employees who are constantly exposed to vinyl chloride monomer have clearly been demonstrated. There are economic interests at stake. If the area of application of the directive were to be extended to end-products, then the whole processing industry would be covered by it and the far reaching consequences of such a measure would first have to be considered more closely....I think that we would be overshooting our target if we were to introduce the most stringent regulations right at the start....

The Commission, he said, would accept a limit of 3 ppm.[10] for new works and 15 ppm. for old works, in spite of Montedison's much lower limits.

Finally, a Directive, passed on 29 June, 1978, proposed an action programme on the safety and health of workers exposed to VCM (Table 11e).   It was to come into force in December 1979 and was aimed at introducing uniform standards in EEC countries.   Only from then did the Bank have a legal Community standard to guide it and the workers in PVC plants, along with 350,000 processing PVC into finished and semi-finished products, have any definite Community legal standard on which they could insist.

The Commission of the European Community, in 1980, obtained agreement on a Directive intended to lessen chemical pollution.   The June 1980 Environmental Impact Analysis agreement may help to lessen VCM concentrations, although the chemical industry, particularly in Britain, has been resisting some of the more radical measures.

The EIB's agreements with borrowers are covered by the rules of confidentiality, but perhaps it is not too much to hope that its loans to Montedison in 1975, 1976 and 1977 might have led it to require that Company's standards from other enterprises.   The Bank will be aware that firms are susceptible to pressure.   For example, by 1980, cadmium was being phased out, according to the EEC Commission's Environmental Service, as witness the disappearance of yellow and orange plastics from shops and their replacement by brown, in which iron has been used instead of cadmium.[11]

PVC production still flourishes in the Community; it is one of the substances being manufactured at ICI's huge new complex opened in 1981 at Wilhelmshaven in the Federal Republic of Germany.

While safety standards have improved considerably, in some plants exposure to VCM gas has seriously damaged workers' health.   In March 1980, for example, Vinatex, a UK company in which the National Coal Board and the British Steel Corporation have indirect interests, agreed to pay £500,000 in compensation to fifteen former workers affected by VCM fumes in the PVC production process.[12] The EIB lent to British Steel (Table 10a).

Since 1973, an increasing amount of the EIB's loans for chemical enterprises has gone to small and medium-sized firms.

Amount of total loans granted as global loans to small and medium-sized chemical enterprises (mills. ua):

1958-72	...	...	1.4
1973-77	...	...	13.8
1978	...	...	2.0
1979	...	...	13.8
1980	...	...	28.0

SOURCES: EIB, 1958-1978, 24-25;
           EIB, Annual Reports, 1978, 32; 1979, 38; 1980, 38.

In these, health, safety and environmental standards may be more difficult to enforce, if only because of the large number of smaller enterprises which inspectorates have to cover.[13] The EIB's capability of seeing that companies benefitting from its loans observe both national and Community legislation is, therefore, diminished because, as shown in Chapter 12 below, the Bank does not now disburse the bulk of loans to small firms itself.

In the meantime, the Bank has greatly reduced its financing of chemical projects in the EEC.   By the late 1970s, in the chemical and chemical-related industries in the Community, there was some questioning, not only on the grounds of environment and health, but of the ratio between capital investment and permanent jobs created.   The rise in oil prices was raising prices of chemical products derived from oil, including plastics and some textiles, and that at a time when even the south of Italy, with all its advantages of State aid and cheap production costs, was suffering from growing overseas competition.[14] By 1981, Montedison was selling the State side of its operations and ANIC was having to be rescued.[15] Even if oil prices are stabilised or drop slightly, it is unlikely that this natural resource will become as cheap as it was in the 1960s, so oil-based plastics are unlikely to undercut traditional materials to the same extent.

d)   CONCLUSIONS

The chemical and chemical related industries seemed worth developing when the European Economic Community came into being in 1958.   The subsequent establishment of petrochemicals as a major industry based on large complexes in Sicily, Sardinia and a number of places on the south Italian mainland owes a good deal to EIB assistance.   By the mid-1960s, however, the risks associated with the industrial use of a number of substances had been proved (see Appendix 3A).[16]   The EIB's investments in the development of EEC chemical industries were concentrated between 1964 and 1977 when the hazards and the necessity of controlling damage and pollution from chemicals and chemical processes were known outside and within the EEC.   The rule of confidentiality makes it impossible to assess how far the EIB was responding to this growing body of knowledge by exacting safeguards for health and environment as a condition of loan contracts.   But at least in one major case, that of arsenic at the ANIC Manfredonia ammonia plant, the EIB did not insist on the least harmful known process.

Despite Middle East restiveness over oil prices and concessions by 1970[17] and growing overseas competition in oil-based plastics and other products, the Bank continued to lend for EEC petrochemical enterprises.   There was no immediate re-assessment of an industry which had come to hinge on oil.   While it is true that Community oil sources were being developed, including fields in Italian coastal waters, the time taken to alter the European Investment Bank's loans policy for oil-based sections of the chemical industry seems inordinately long.

The decline in EIB lending in the chemical sector from 1978 may have been due not only to the higher oil prices, but also to a drop in demand for loans due to alarm at the Manfredonia and other accidents and to the growing pressure from the European Parliament to introduce better safety standards for vinyl chloride monomer.   Their implementation adds to already mounting costs of production and of products.

But now, as the emphasis in the Bank's lending in chemicals is shifting from large to small and medium-scale enterprises, the question is how far the Bank will insist to loan distributing agencies that known risks be eliminated and EEC legislation observed.

NOTES

1. Commission of the European Communities, State of the Environment, First Report, 1977, 38-41; Second Report, 1979, 28-9.

2. The Times, July 20, 21, 23, 26-31, 1976; August 3-5, 7, 9-12, 18, 1976.

3. E.R.Koch & F. Vahrenholt, Seveso ist Uberall; die Toedlichen Risiken der Chemie, 1979, pp. 65-9. A reconstruction of events lays the blame on faulty welding which caused a blockage in a ventilator in a washery tower. As a result, this part of the plant finally exploded because of the excess pressure that built up, bits of the tower being hurled a considerable distance.

4. Koch & Vahrenholt, loc.cit.; Times, September 1976. Dr. Gerald Williams of the US firm, Allied Chemicals, itemised the essential safeguards for ammonia plants which included stopping the plants for 50 days of the year to avoid safety related failures. Giant private West German firms, such as the Bayer section of the Franco-German Progil-Bayer Ugine, to which the EIB granted a loan in 1961, were known to have ignored state regulatory agencies and only informed them of the introduction of new processes after something had gone wrong. See Koch & Vahrenholt, op. cit., 106.

5. Signor Natali, EEC Vice-Commissioner for Environmental Protection in Europe Environment, No.98, July 1979, 14.

6. A gas known for almost 150 years. Its polymer, PVC, has been manufactured commercially for over 40 years and together with polyethylene forms a major part of the chemical industry.

7. Angiosarcoma. The EEC Economic Social Committee Dossier Soc./23, 29 September 1977, remarked on the present state of knowledge and commented that no level of exposure to a chemical carcinogen should be considered toxicologically insignificant for humans. It wanted exposure to be reduced as near to nil as was technically feasible, with the period of adjustment for modifying chemical plants ending on 1 January, 1980 (para. 2 17).

8. For example, in the UK, urgent action was taken following US findings in 1974 and levels of exposure to VCM drastically reduced in the plants of: BP Chemicals, Barry & Baglan Bay, ICI, Runcorn & Hillhouse, British Industry Plastics at Aycliffe, Vinatex at Staveley. However, Mr. P. Baxter, UK Employment Medical Advisory Service, considered risks lower than was thought. EEC Ref. OJ C21224, August 1978, quoting Financial Times, 8 October, 1977.

9. EEC Official Journal of the Community, (OJC), Nos. 18,
   22 April, 1977, 243-44; 13, 17 June, 1977, 28-31; 10,
   14 October, 1977. See also No. C165/1, Council Resolution of 29 June, 1978; Bulletin EC, No.1, 1978, 31-
   32; EEC Econ. & Soc. Committee, Dossier Soc./23, 17
   October, 1977, Report of the Section for Social
   Questions on Proposal for a Council Directive, Doc. Com.
   (76) 556 Final.

10. EEC, OJC 13-17 June, 1977, 29-30.

11. Mr. Lawrence, EEC Environmental & Consumer Protection
    Service, Division of General Environmental Consumer
    Protection, Legal Department.

12. Financial Times, 28 March, 1980.

13. Commission of the European Communities, State of the
    Environment, Second Report, 1979, 57-8. The Commission
    laid down that it was up to the factory safety authori-
    ties to check information which manufacturers were
    obliged to give, and 'to carry out their own evaluation
    of the risks for man and the environment.' They were
    also to ensure by means of inspections that their own
    stipulations on safety procedures were carried out. And
    it was their responsibility 'to inform the public of the
    risks involved and the measures taken to reduce them to
    the minimum.'
    M. Frankel, The Social Audit Pollution Handbook, London
    1978.

14. Competition from Hong Kong, Taiwan and S. Korea was long
    established. By 1975, the effects of the Arab oil
    producers' price rises were cutting the profits of
    producers of dyes and dyestuffs. By 1978, a further
    factor reducing these markets in the EEC was a fashion
    for pale colours, which require less dye. Financial
    Times, 15 March, 1979, 10 October, 1979. See ICI
    Annual Handbooks for its non-European enterprises.
    Financial Times, 10 January, 1980, 'Half of Europe's
    Textile Jobs at Risk'; 27 March, 1980. For the French
    firm, Rhône-Poulenc, see 11 October, 1979; for UK
    chemicals, see 2 April, 1980.
    Ibid, 2 October, 1979. Viscount Davignon's speech to
    the New York Chemical Society. In order to prevent
    petrol prices hitting consumers, the Carter administra-
    tion put a limit on price increases. Thus, oil-based
    fibre producers there had cheaper feed stocks than their
    West European counterparts. It should be noted, however,
    that big EEC companies making chemical fibres also have
    plants in their main competitor, the USA. For example,
    ICI has two huge plants for turning naphtha into
    ethylene, one at Wilton on Teesside and one at Corpus
    Christi in Texas. On the other hand, the US chemicals

firm, Monsanto, has also built a plant at Teesside. Both ran into construction difficulties where the ICI Texan plant did not. See also _Financial Times_, 10 September, 1979. UK's Selincourt was negotiating sales of machinery to China with a view to low-priced exports of nets from China to the USA and S.America which will compete with EEC products. Courtaulds, the textiles firm, which has links with ICI through its fibres interests, in the autumn of 1979 was engaged in a big reorganisation of its weaving factories. _Ibid_, 26 September, 1979, 17 November, 1979. But see 31 January, 1980, rise in dividend of Allied Textiles. _Times_, 30 April, 1981, 'Business News', tougher renegotiation of Multi-Fibre Agreement; _Sunday Times_, 3 May, 1981, 'Business Supplement, outlook for ICI still uncertain; _Times_, 6 May, 1981, 'Business News' discussions on closure of Nypro UK, jointly owned by National Coal Board and Dutch state mines group, both in Co. Antrim, N.Ireland and at Flixborough.

15. _Financial Times_, 11 February, 1981, 'ANIC and Montedison face reverses'. See also 2 November, 1979, ICI's six-point plan to boost plastics profits by £20 mill. by cutting its workforce by 10%, and _Ibid_, 18 & 20 December, 1979, 10 January, 1980, to protect dividends and profits, ICI raising polyethylene prices in the UK by about 6% from December 1979; _Ibid_, 2 November, 1979; _Ibid_, 15 March, 1979, Dutch-based chemicals group, Akzo Chimie UK, planning to close PVC additives plant on Merseyside. See also _Ibid_, 7 November, 1979. _Times_, 'Business News' 15 May, 1981, 21, BASF of West Germany, one of the world's largest chemical companies, looking at ways of cutting staff.

16. _Times_, 6 August, 1976, 4, Dr. Adolf Jann, President of Hoffman-La Roche, commenting on the Seveso accident, remarked that such accidents may always happen 'unless one wants to close down all the chemical factories in the world...And chemistry has saved millions of lives.' He ignored varying degress of risk in different processes. Also there are an increasing number of queries, for example, over the safety of chemicals and chemical medicines previously considered safe, including the famous Hoffman-La Roche tranquilisers, Valium and Librium. The British National Union of Agricultural and Allied Workers has been campaigning against the use of 2,4,5-T in weed-killers. Early in 1981 the European Federation of Agricultural Workers' Unions decided to join the campaign.

17. L Anell and B Nygren, _The Developing Countries and the World Economic Order_, 1980, 99-100

APPENDIX 11A: Dangerous substances as listed for
                Directive 76/464 of 4 May, 1976, on
                the Aquatic Environment
                Date of implentation: 4 May, 1978.

LIST I: 'Selected mainly on the basis of their toxicity,
         persistence and bioaccumulation'

    organohalogen, including pesticides, particularly DDT and
                   its metabolites, aldrin, dieldrin and endrin,
                   heptachlor, heptachlorepoxide, chlordane,
                   hexachlorocyclohexane and lindane
    organophosphorus
    organotin and organostannic compounds
    mercury
    cadmium
    persistent mineral oils and hydrocarbons of petroleum
                   origin
    persistent oils and synthetic substances (particularly de-
                   tergents) which may float, remain in suspen-
                   sion or sink, and which may interfere with
                   the use of waters
    substances known to be carcinogenic in the aquatic environ-
                   ment or being imbibed via the aquatic
                   environment

LIST II:

1) zinc   selenium   tin   vanadium
    copper   arsenic   barium   cobalt
    nickel   antimony   beryllium   thalium
    chromium   molybdenum   uranium   tellurium
    lead   titanium   silver

2) Biocides and their derivatives other than those in
    List I.
3) Substances which have a deleterious effect on the taste
    and/or smell of products for human consumption derived
    from the aquatic environment and their compounds.
4) Toxic or persistent organic compounds of silicon which
    may give rise to harmful compounds in water.
5) Inorganic compounds of phosphorus and elemental phos-
    phorus.
6) Non-persistent mineral oil and hydrocarbons of petroleum
    origin.
7) Cyanides, fluorides.
8) Substances which have an adverse effect on the oxygen
    balance, particularly ammonia, nitrites.

SOURCE: Commission of the European Communities, State of
          the Environment, First Report, 1977, 384-41, 246;
          Second Report, 1979, 28-9.

Chapter 12

THE EUROPEAN INVESTMENT BANK'S LENDING FOR
SMALL AND MEDIUM-SIZED ENTERPRISES

It was only in 1963, after 5 years of operations, that the European Investment Bank began to
grant small loans, that is, according to its own
definition, loans of 2 million ua or less.

The bulk of the Bank's small loans in the EEC
have gone to small and medium-scale enterprises, but
it was only in 1968, after it had been functioning
for nearly a decade, that the EIB acknowledged their
importance:

> ....the development of the small and medium-sized
> enterprises is an important factor of regional policies
> in the Community....it is an indispensable complement
> of the vast achievements in the field of infrastructure
> and large-scale industry. Furthermore these enter-
> prises offer....the most favourable conditions for a
> rapid development. The experience of recent years
> shows that the creation of a large number of small en-
> terprises can change fundamentally the economic struc-
> ture of a region and that furthermore, they can rapidly
> acquire scope.
> Thus the promotion of these projects widens the Bank's
> field of intervention and makes possible rapid and
> effective action which facilitates industrialisation. [1]

1968 was the year in which the development of large-
scale industrialism was challenged in social upheavals in Italy and France. Particularly in the
early stages of the EIB's financing, small loans had
often been given, not to small and medium-scale enterprises, but to large companies, some based outside
the EEC. It was partly an aspect of the Bank's
efforts to attract foreign capital to the south of
Italy, although small loans to large companies were
granted elsewhere, for example:

Year	Size of Loan (mill. ua)	Recipient	Project	Country in which loan project was situated
1963	2.0	Ideal Standard	Production of porcelain sanitary ware	Italy
1964	0.4	Martin Gelber Co.	Enlargement of shirt-making factory	Italy
	0.8	Viscosa Co.	Enlargement of a Naples textile factory	Italy
1966	2.0	Olympia-Werke AG	Construction of factory for making calculating machines	FRG
	1.5	Paragummiwerke Arthur Brugger GmbH	Construction of factory for making rubber articles	FRG
	0.7	McQuay Europa	Construction of factory making air conditioning Equipment	Italy

a) IMPORTANCE OF SMALL AND MEDIUM-SCALE
   ENTERPRISES IN THE EEC

In the Community as a whole, small and medium-scale businesses dominate manufacturing industry. Their importance was highlighted by an EEC study covering the late 1960s and early 1970s, which was published in 1980. It dealt with the nine countries that made up the Community from 1973 and some of its results are shown in Tables 12a and 12b. These indicate that, as might have been expected, numerically small and medium-sized manufacturing enterprises far out-numbered large. Of greater importance, however, the Survey showed that in six of the member states, smaller manufacturing businesses accounted for 50 per cent or more of all persons employed. Only in Luxembourg and the United Kingdom did significantly fewer persons work in them, in the case of the UK less than a third of the total workforce in the manufacturing sector. In the building and engineering trades, as Table 12b shows, small and medium-sized enterprises employed an even larger proportion of the workforce in the

TABLE 12a: Small and Medium-sized Enterprises in
Manufacturing Industry in the EEC 'Nine'

i) As a percentage of total enterprises in this sector.
ii) Persons employed in small and medium-sized enterprises as
a per cent of the total.

Country	Year	% of all Enterprises	% of all Persons Employed
Fed. Rep. of Germany	1970	99.4	50.0
Belgium	1970	99.5	57.1
Denmark* **	1973	98.6	72.7
France	1976	98.6	47.7
Ireland***	1968	98.3	74.3
Italy	1971	99.9	67.1
Luxembourg	1973	99.0	38.6
Netherlands*	1973	99.3	62.3
United Kingdom	1972	97.5	31.7

* including energy and water   ** from 6 to 500 persons
*** 3 to 500 persons employed   employed

TABLE 12b: Small and Medium-sized Enterprises in
the Building and Engineering Trades in
the EEC 'Nine'

i) As a percentage of total enterprises in these sectors.
ii) Persons employed in small and medium-sized enterprises as
a per cent of the total

Country	Year	% of all Enterprises	% of all Persons Employed
Fed. Rep. of Germany	1970	98.3	64.0
Belgium	1970	99.2	69.4
Denmark)			
France)	No statistics available		
Ireland)			
Italy	1971	99.4	74.9
Luxembourg	1973	97.6	67.5
Netherlands	1973	98.3	64.0
United Kingdom	1974	98.0	45.6

SOURCE: Small and medium-sized enterprises, Artisanat
Division, Directorate-General for Industrial & Technological Affairs, Commission of the European Communities, Rep. Small and Medium Sized Enterprises &
the Artisanat in the European Community, 'Principal
Conclusions', January 1980, 744/111/80- FR/EN,8.
See part 413/11 76-E Orig: F for definitions of
small and medium-sized enterprises in the nine EEC
countries.

six countries for which statistics were available, Even in the United Kingdom they amounted to 45.6 per cent of the total. In the sphere of infrastructure in five of the EEC countries, small and medium-scale enterprises formed the great majority of energy and water undertakings and in Luxembourg made up the whole of them.

The Survey also revealed that during the 1960s and up to the early 1970s, there had been a decline in the proportion of people employed in small and medium-sized manufacturing enterprises in seven EEC countries, including the U.K. However, the decline was small, except in the case of Belgium where it amounted to 7.5 per cent.[2] On the other hand, in building and civil engineering in Italy, Luxembourg and Denmark, and in energy and water undertakings in the Federal Republic of Germany, over the decade there had been small increases in the percentages of employed persons who worked in small and medium-scale enterprises. In the case of Italy, the Survey's findings lend weight to the common observation that it is the mass of small family enterprises that keep the country going through political uncertainties and economic crises.

b) THE DEVELOPMENT OF EIB INSTITUTIONAL
ARRANGEMENTS FOR FINANCING OF SMALL AND
MEDIUM-SCALE ENTERPRISES

It is chiefly to the south of Italy that EIB lending for small and medium-sized enterprises has been directed, as might be expected. The Bank's arrangements for financing in the south of Italy determined its methods in similar cases elsewhere. Either the EIB granted the loan direct to an applicant in the same way as large loans or it passed the money to the Italian Government's special bank for the economic development of the south, the Cassa di Mezzogiorno. The Cassa did not necessarily disburse the loans itself, but passed them to a second tier of local or specialised official agencies, such as the Istituto Mobiliare Italiano or the Istituto per lo Sviluppo Economico dell'Italia Meridionale (see Appendix 12A). The Bank also, however, sometimes lent direct to one of these agencies instead of through the Cassa. Thus, during the first ten years of its operations in respect of small loans, the EIB established a system of indirect lending in this largest of the poor regions in the Community. Whereas in the prosperous and experienced industrialised countries of the north, small firms, as well as large, at first usually received EIB loans direct.

While the EIB's loans to small and medium-scale enterprises took a far smaller share of its total financing than did infrastructure or large-scale industry, by 1968, the number of applications for loans of low amounts from large or small businesses had risen to the point where the Bank's assessment staff were under some strain.

To deal with the problem, the EIB in effect institutionalised the system used in the south of Italy and applied it to almost all loans for small and medium-sized enterprises, calling it the Global Loans Scheme,which operates as follows: instead of granting a loan directly itself through this scheme, the EIB opens a credit to a finance institution or a bank which uses the credit to grant loans for projects submitted to it 'by its own clients'. The beneficiaries then are limited to those who are already known to the intermediary institution and whose projects have official approval. The intermediary institution takes the responsibility for the detailed negotiations and evaluations of projects, although the Bank must give its approval in every case. Through this formula, the Bank has contributed increasing amounts

> to the financing of investments which, although presenting economic benefits and meeting the Bank's normal criteria for lending, are nonetheless of too modest a size to merit an individual loan.[3]

In practice, the distinction is not as hard and fast as the EIB's statement suggests, since it continues to grant some small loans directly to applicants as well as to the distributing agencies (see Appendix 12A). While France and Italy have a wide range of intermediary institutions distributing Global Loan finance, this is not the case in the other EEC countries. In Denmark and the United Kingdom, other arrangements have been made by which the Bank pays over credits for distribution to small and medium-scale businesses directly to the governments. Applications for finance are made through government departments, not through intermediary institutions specialising in financing. These agreements are not strictly part of the Global Loans Scheme although the Bank classes them as such. In Britain's case, this arrangement reflects the government's highly centralised economic control. Distribution of EIB credits is through the Department of Industry, through its regional offices, the Scottish Economic Planning Department, the Welsh

Office Industry Department and the Northern Ireland
Department of Commerce.

The central control exercised by the British
government raises the question of whether small
entrepreneurs may find it more difficult to obtain
loans than in Belgium, say, where regional authorities are very strong. There is also a possibility
that the government's direct role may influence the
kinds of enterprises that are assisted. For
example, there may be little enthusiasm for co-
operatives.[4]

However, the EIB quite specifically excluded
large enterprises from benefitting from its Global
Loans scheme:

> Global loans have been reserved for assisting ventures
> where the promoter's net fixed assets do not exceed
> 30 million ua and where the new investment costs will
> not exceed 12 million ua.
> Within these parameters, the Bank gives permanent
> priority to firms employing less than 500 people and
> legally and financially independent, with no more than
> one-third of their capital held by a larger company.[5]

The EIB has thus assisted small and medium-sized
enterprises in three ways: by direct loans,
especially in the early years; through the Global
Loans credits scheme from 1968 onwards; and thirdly
through special credit arrangements with a government.

The 'Global Loan' and other credits advanced by
the EIB to agencies for distribution may be for
large amounts, anything from 2 to 30 million ua,
although the loans granted from these funds are
small, ranging from 0.1 to 2 million ua and averaging 0.5 million ua.

As Table 12c shows, the proportions of total
Bank lending inside the EEC under its Global Loans
Scheme have been small; but the number of loans made
under the Global Loans scheme is nearly as high
as the number of over 2 million ua. The EIB's
assistance to small and medium-sized enterprises
through its Global Loans scheme has increased along
with the development of economic recession. For
instance, in 1975, there was a drop in investment
generally. EIB lending for industrial projects
amounted to only 15 per cent of the average 35 per
cent for the whole period 1958-75. In the case of
the Bank's Global Loans, however, partly because of
unused credits from earlier years already in the
pipeline, intermediary institutions were able to
distribute 63.1 million ua, far above the average of

35 million ua for 1970-75.   These allocations
accounted for a third of EIB support for industry
that year.

TABLE 12c: Global Loan Allocations by the European
Investment Bank inside the Community

	1968-72	1973-77	1978-80
Number of loans under Global Loans Scheme	114	572	573
Amount of Global loans allocation (mill. ua)	51.2	268.9	377.9
% of total loans	2.1	5.4	5.4

SOURCES: 1968-72 and 1973-77, EIB, 1958-78, 24-5;   EIB Annual
Reports, 1978, 32;   1979, 38;   1980.

c) GEOGRAPHICAL AND SECTORAL DISTRIBUTION OF
EIB GLOBAL LOANS

Between 1969 and 1980, as Appendix 12A shows.
nearly half the amount of Global Loans, over 516
million ua, has gone to Italy;   almost all
of it has been directed to the Mezzogiorno.
In second place in cash terms has been France, but
in point of numbers of enterprises benefitting, Ireland comes second, well over half the Global allocations there having been made in 1980.
Inside the Community, the bulk of the EIB's
Global loan finance has been for industry with a
view to integrating smaller enterprises into
regional development plans and large-scale industrial projects.   It is no accident, for example, that
many small loans have gone to small chemical and
synthetic textile manufacturers, to motor car component firms and to makers of glass and ceramics in
the Mezzogiorno.   These loans parallelled efforts
to promote the development of large chemical and
plastics complexes, metal works and construction
schemes in the region.   There has been a similar
pattern in other parts of the Community, although
the Bank's participation has been on a smaller scale.

d) REAPPRAISAL OF THE ROLE OF SMALL FIRMS

During the first decade of the EEC's existence,
the benefits of economies of scale were generally
considered paramount so that large enterprises were
favoured, despite the bed-rock of small and medium-
scale businesses in member states.   Moreover, the

creation of large industrial complexes by firms from
more than one of the EEC countries fostered the
integration of the Community and weakened traditional national loyalties as small and medium-scale
enterprises could not.

However, the questioning of the benefits of
large enterprises and the economies of scale, which
began in 1968, increased. The development of
economic crisis and the growth of unemployment
provoked re-assessment of earlier Community policies.
The EIB, and the Social and Regional Fund Department
and Financial Directorate of the Commission came to
share a belief that small and medium-scale enterprises offered certain advantages in the matter of
employment:

1. They created more employment than large enterprises per unit of capital invested;

2. This was partly due to a greater willingness on
   the part of successful small business owners to
   plough back profits in order to create jobs as
   well as to improve plant and operations;

3. Small businesses tend to provide employment
   locally so that people do not have to move;
   thus extra funds are not required to furnish
   housing for them at a new project site.[6]

The EIB does not require that a definite minimum
number of jobs will be created in return for each of
its investments.

There is, however, some questioning of the role
of smaller businesses in creating employment, particularly in Britain where they are of less importance than in other EEC countries.[7] The UK government in administering the EIB's allocations for
small and medium-scale enterprise, does impose a condition that each investment will create a certain
number of jobs. But even in Britain, the climate
of opinion is becoming more favourable to small and
medium-scale enterprises. Large companies now
apparently see in them benefits for themselves.[8]

A second sphere in which they are regarded as
superior to large establishments is that of labour
relations. Thus, large industrial concerns are
scaling down the size of plants. For example,
with the Bank's help, Fiat and the French Peugeot-
Citroen are together now building a plant in the
Molise region in the east of Italy which will offer
employment to 3,000 people, less than half the number employed at the Fiat plant at Cassibo, south of
Rome. While modern automated technology, which

permits higher productivity per employee, is a major
reason for this change, it is also acknowledged
that one of the causes of poor industrial relations
in plants with very large workforces is simply the
difficulty of communication.[9]

By 1977, there was official admission of the
failure in the Mezzogiorno of large industrial
enterprises to generate small ancillary concerns.
Dr. Giorgio Ruffolo, President of the private financing organisation, Finanziaria Meridionale, informed the EIB that an unforeseen tertiary sector
had developed, 'a web of commercial middlemen' in
place of the expected large numbers of small concerns.   The Italian government has therefore begun
a new effort to strengthen small independent businesses with, of course, the EIB's support through
the Global Loans scheme.   It is scaling down central control and creating new authorities called
Regioni, which are intended to operate with the
participation and agreement of local interests.
They are also moving from aids and subsidies to
greater encouragement of local economic initiatives
through diversification into a wider range of enterprises.[10]

The Bank and Commission Departments have also
expressed the belief that smaller more dispersed
plants avoid the environmental problems created by
large concentrations of industry and provide <u>better</u>
working conditions.   While the first of their views
tends to be true, as already noted, the state of
the working environment and the extent to which new
standards being laid down by Community Directives
are met, depends to a considerable extent on the
strength of relevant government inspectorates.
However, since in smaller enterprises communication
between workers and management is easier, an
informed workforce can help itself in this respect.
The growing threat of unemployment and competition
for jobs, may, however, weaken the ability of workpeople to insist that legal standards be met.   This
weakness, in turn, emphasises the importance of the
Bank's insistence that legal standards be met in
small, as in large establishments, even although it
does not directly disburse its loans to them.

e) CONCLUSIONS

Small and medium-scale enterprises still do not
represent a major field of EIB financing, despite
increased allocations to them over the last ten years.
There is, too, some scepticism over support for
them through governments and the Commission of the

European Communities.   Thus, the Commission
expressed the view at the end of 1978 that it did
not think the Ortoli Facility should be used to
strengthen this sector, although it was conceded
that small and medium-sized firms merited special
attention.[11]
    The growth of recession in Community countries
must affect small and medium-scale enterprises as
it does large.   The Bank's President, M. Yves Le
Portz, in his address to the annual meeting of the
Board of Governors in June 1981 emphasised the
Bank's concern with infrastructure and particularly
with the development of new kinds of energy and the
more rational use of existing energy sources.[12]   In
view of the importance of small and medium-scale
enterprises in this sphere, a further re-appraisal
of their role in infrastructure would appear
necessary.   One result of the Italian government's
interest in energy saving has been an increase in
EIB Global Loan finance finding its way to small and
medium-scale businesses in the energy-saving field.
    Small and medium-scale enterprises have an
advantage which is rarely mentioned.   As they require a smaller individual investment, they make it
easier for a country or a federation of states to
undertake economic change cautiously and gradually.
If a mistake is made, no great interests are involved and remedies are less costly.
    Providing that the sphere of business is well-
chosen, they can contribute to easing unemployment
and to the development of poorer regions.   In the
conservationist and environmental fields, they
have been playing an important innovative role.[13]
Through its loans to small and medium scale enterprises, the Bank has an opportunity to make a considerable contribution to resolving some Community
problems, as well as to improving the quality of
life.

NOTES

1. EIB, 1968 Annual Report, 80.

2. Commission of the European Communities, Report on Small
    and Medium-Sized Enterprises and the Artisanat in the
    European Community, 1980, 'Principal Conclusions', 9;
    Financial Times, 29 October, 1979, 'Small companies
    summit', FRG and Switzerland.   See also S. Borner, Le
    Mois, published Swiss Bank Soc., No.4, 1980, 3-4,
    'Mutation structurelle et mouvement de concentration dans

l'industrie Suisse'.

3. EIB, Information, No.6, July 1976, 6.

4. This kind of lending in the UK is specifically for 'assisted regions'. Proposed downgrading of regions from this status after August 1980 and complete 'de-assisting' in 1982 would, presumably, make it harder for small and medium-sized enterprises to obtain EIB loans. cf. EIB Press Release, 9/80, 4 March, 1980; Financial Times, 16 March, 21 June, 3 September, 1979; 28 March, 10 April, 1980, for earlier support from the Conservative Government for small firms.

5. EIB, Information, No.21, May 1980, 4.

6. Ibid., No.6, June 1976, 6; No.17, June 1979, 2.

7. G. Gudgin and S. Fothergill, Regional Employment Studies on a Comparable Basis, 1952-75, Cen. for Environmental Studies, Occ. Papers, No.5, 1978; D. Storey, Job Creation and Small Firms Policy in Britain, Cen. for Environmental Studies Policy Ser., 11, 1980; C. Logan and D. Gregory, Co-operation and Job Creation, TUC, 1981.

8. Times, 17 April, 1980, Special Suppl., 'Small Businesses', 1, 'A Way Out of Economic Decline'; I & V, 'Big firms offer a helping hand'.

9. Financial Times, 31 March, 1980, Special Suppl. on Italy, VI.

10. EIB, Information, No.11, November 1977, 7.

11. European Parliament, Written Question, No. 815/78, Mr. Ansquer to the Commission, 30 November, 1978. See also Financial Times, 2 October, 1979, 'European News', AOIP.

12. EIB, Information, No.26, July 1981, 4.

13. Financial Times, 'Technical News' 1979-81, initiatives mainly of small firms; OECD, Employment and the Environment, 1978. C. Thomas, The Paper Chain, ERR Ltd., 1977; Material Gains, ERR Ltd., 1979.

APPENDIX 12A: Intermediary organisations in
Community countries to which the EIB
made Global Loan credits available,
1968-80

Intermediary institution	Global Loans		Allocations	
	No.	Amount (m.ua)	No.	Amount (m.ua)
ITALY				
Credit lines open in 1980 ..	15	272.0	315	114.6
Instituto per lo Sviluppo				
Economico dell'Italia Meridionale				
(ISVEIMER)	3	133.4	126	54.2
Mediocredito Centrale	3	42.6	58	17.4
Istituto Mobiliare Italiano (IMI)	1	17.5	34	16.6
Istituto Regionale per il				
Finanziamento alle industrie in				
Sicilia (IRFIS)	2	25.4	16	8.5
Banca Centrale di Credito Popolare	3	17.7	9	6.6
Banca Nazionale del Lavoro				
"Sezione Speciale" per il				
Credito Industriale (BNL) ..	1	13.0	-	-
Cassa per il Mezzogiorno ..	1	14.1	72	11.3
Banco di Napoli	1	8.3	-	-
Global loans wound up at 31.12.79	20	244.5	392	214.4
TOTAL ITALY	35	516.5	707	329.0
FRANCE				
Credit lines open in 1980 ..	4	51.4	50	42.7
Caisse d'Aide à l'Equipement des				
Collectivités Locales (CAECL) ..	4	51.4	50	42.7
Global loans wound up at 31.12.79	10	100.0	170	70.4
TOTAL FRANCE	14	151.4	220	113.1
UNITED KINGDOM				
Credit lines open in 1980 ..	3	84.4	85	44.5
Government (contracts of mandate				
and guarantee)	2	75.9	85	44.5
Industrial and Commercial Finance				
Corporation Ltd.	1	8.5	-	-
Global loans wound up at 31.12.79	3	56.5	57	37.2
TOTAL UNITED KINGDOM	6	140.9	142	81.7

APPENDIX 12A (cont'd.)

Intermediary institution	Global Loans		Allocations	
	No.	Amount (m.ua)	No.	Amount (m.ua)
IRELAND				
Credit lines open in 1980 ..	9	101.3	372	46.4
Industrial Credit Co. Ltd. (ICC)	6	79.1	351	41.6
Agricultural Credit Corporation Ltd. (ACC)	2	7.4	21	4.8
IDA Agency loan (contract of mandate)	1	14.8	–	–
Global loans wound up at 3.12.79	5	24.2	143	16.7
TOTAL IRELAND	14	125.5	515	63.1
DENMARK				
Credit lines open in 1980 ..	4	30.5	18	5.3
Danish Government	3	10.0	18	5.3
Kongeriget Danmarks Hypotekbank og Finansforvaltning	1	20.5	–	–
Global loans wound up at 31.12.79	10	28.2	74	28.2
TOTAL DENMARK	14	58.7	92	33.5
BELGIUM				
Credit lines open in 1980 ..	1	6.2	6	6.2
Société Nationale de Crédit à l'Industrie (SNCI)	1	6.2	6	6.2
Global loans wound up at 3.12.79	2	24.1	35	24.4
TOTAL BELGIUM	3	30.3	41	30.6
GERMANY				
Global loans wound up at 31.12.79	4	46.3	88	36.0
Sub-total - Credit lines open in 1980	36	545.8	846	259.7
of which energy saving	4	41.6	1	1.2
Sub-total - Global loans wound up at 31.12.79 ..	54	523.8	959	427.3
GRAND TOTAL	90	1069.6[1]	1805	687.0

1 - of which: balance awaiting allocation: 270.0 million;
   cancellations: 95.8 million; exchange adjustments: 16.8 m.

NOTE: Differences between annual amounts of loans and total allocations authorised have arisen due to currency fluctuations between signature of contract and date allocations authorised. Not all credits are lent out in the year of authorisation. SOURCE: EIB 1980 Ann. Rep., 98, Table 15.

Chapter 13

THE EUROPEAN INVESTMENT BANK'S LOANS FOR
ENVIRONMENTAL PROTECTION AND ENERGY
CONSERVATION IN THE EEC

The European Investment Bank has been financing
environmental protection projects since 1975 and
energy conservation since 1979. The very low proportions of total financing devoted to these sectors
over the twenty-two years, 1958-80, are partly the
result of the slowness of the Community and, in
varying degrees, of its member states to act on
either count.

The EIB, in its own estimates of its investments in environmental protection, has defined this
type of project narrowly. In fact, its lending for
environmental purposes is in excess of the amounts
shown in its annual reports, as a number of water
supply projects have an environmental dimension in
the form of sewage and sewerage schemes.[1] Since
the Bank has not, in a number of cases, published
the precise amounts devoted to these purposes within its overall loans, it is difficult to form an
approximate idea of the amounts of financing in
this area.

At the same time, it must be remembered that
there has been a crucial dichotomy in the Bank's
lending in that it allocated far larger totals for
projects which caused concern about both environmental quality and energy conservation. For
example, it assisted some questionable chemical
enterprises and the development of nuclear energy.
With EEC member countries individually and collec-
tively raising their environmental standards from
the mid-1970s and seeking ways of reducing their oil
imports, the question is whether the Bank could not
have laid greater emphasis on these two aspects of
its financing and less on others that were harmful
to the environment or wasteful of energy.

During the 1970s, West Germany, the Netherlands
and Denmark established high standards in the reduction of some forms of industrial pollution.

France now requires an environmental impact statement for every new industrial enterprise, although
this does not solve problems created by industries
established before this legislation. Italy has
tended to have lower standards, as has Britain, in
some sectors, despite progress by both countries.[2]
However, one OECD expert claimed that Britain en-
forces more efficiently such regulations as she has
and that, in practice, her standards are often better than the higher paper standards of some other
EEC countries.[3]

a) IMPROVEMENT OF WATER QUALITY

The main sphere in which the Bank has assisted
environmental improvements has been that on which
it is least informative - water quality. As part
of its infrastructure loans for water supplies, the
EIB has been granting large loans for sewage and
sewerage disposal, and for cleaning up polluted
stretches of water, since the mid-1970s. The EIB's
concern to ensure reasonably clean water is not due
solely to an interest in human health. It extends
to the economy at large:

> Industrial and agricultural development is hampered
> as much by pollution of water resources as by short-
> age of supplies; future economic growth depends on
> new sewerage and water treatment installations as
> well as reinforcing supply capacity.[4]

In 1978 alone, it lent a total of 147.7 million ua
in the nine EEC member states for water supply,
sewage disposal and irrigation combined. The main
recipient countries have been Italy, the United
Kingdom and Ireland where, in 1980, the Bank invested 53.3 million ua in the provision of sewage and
sewerage disposal schemes throughout the country.

i) Italy

The Bank's lending for water projects in the
Mezzogiorno included one of its biggest single contributions to fighting pollution. In 1975 and 1976
it made loans totalling 45.3 million ua to assist
the cleaning up of the Bay of Naples, round which
the density of population in the mid-1970s was about
ten times the national average, and which more than
doubled in the summer tourist season. Most domestic and industrial effluent entered the sea direct
or via water courses, virtually untreated. The
Bay is enclosed so that it was not diluted. Both

216

industry and agriculture suffered from the pollution of scarce water resources.

The improvement scheme covers 2,800 square kilometres, an area which includes communes in the provinces, not only of Naples, but also of Salerno, Caserta, and Avellino, together with the islands of Capri, Ischia and Procida, and 15 industrial zones. The work entails cleaning the water courses, reducing 'to tolerable limits' the amount and concentration of effluent discharged into the Bay and recycling part of the water so as to relieve pressure on fresh water sources. The project is expected to extend well into the 1980s and is providing employment for a large number of people. At the same time, the aim is 'a more rational use of water resources to encourage future industrial growth and to develop the agricultural and tourism potential'. The EIB was satisfied that 'while environmental and economic interests too often find themselves in conflict with each other, here they unite.' This conflict was highlighted by the EIB's loans for drainage, sewage treatment and effluent recycling as part of the infrastructure for the industrial zones at Avellino in Campania, Gela, Ragusa and Catania in Sicily and Taranto in Apulia (see Table 8a), which the Bank also helped to fund.[5] Steel, chemicals and paper industries use huge quantities of water and, as the Bank itself pointed out:

The greater the volume of water supplied, the greater the effluent returned. [6]

Its loans for the provision of water supplies also included piping drinking water to various localities in the Mezzogiorno. Presumably, as a condition of these loans, the Bank has required that the standards for drinking water laid down by Directives since 1973 have been met (see Table 13a).

ii. The United Kingdom

The EIB has provided loans for sewage and sewerage operations in the United Kingdom, mainly in heavily industrial areas. These interventions are welcome, but the EIB would not appear to have been altogether successful in requiring observance of Community Directives on water quality. Since 1973, EEC Directives have been setting uniform standards for member states on control of pollution in the aquatic environment. Yet, in 1975, a dispute began between the British government and its EEC partners, which has not yet been resolved. Britain

TABLE 13a: EEC Directives on the maintenance of standards of the Aquatic Environment

Date and Number of Directive	Subject of Directive	Date of Imple-mentation
22.11.73 : 73/404/EEC	Approximation of member states' laws on: i) detergents; ii) control	
22.11.73 : 73/405/EEC	of the biodegradability of surface agents	
16. 6.75 : 75/440/EEC	Definition of the quality requirements for surface fresh water used for or intended for the abstraction of drinking water; provision of plans to clean up water	18. 6.77
8.12.75 : 76/160/EEC	Definition of quality requirements for bathing water; defining sampling frequency, measuring methods & conditions in which quality is to be achieved.	10.12.77
4. 5.76 : 76/464/EEC	Providing a system of authorisations on the discharge of dangerous substances in water. Providing limit values or quality objectives for List 1* substances: Providing quality objectives for List 11 substances. Adopting anti-pollution programmes for both types of substances and communicating them to the Commission. Drawing up a list of where List 1 substances were being discharged.	4. 5.78
20. 2.78 : 78/176/EEC	Prevention and recycling of titanium dioxide waste, mainly discharged into estuaries, causing 'red mud'; providing a system of authorisa-tions for disposal operations; laying down provisions governing immersion, discharge, storage and dumping, monitoring old-established industries; providing decontamination programmes with possible ex-ceptions for new industries, authorisations possibly including pre-liminary impact assessments; determining the information to be notified to the Commission.	22. 2.79
18. 7.78 : 78/659/EEC	Laying down quality requirements for waters intended to support fish life, sampling, measuring, etc.	20. 7.80
9.10.79 : 79/869/EEC	Laying down methods and frequencies of sampling surface water intended for drinking & etc. as laid down in Directive 75/440/EEC above.	9.10.81

TABLE 13 a (cont'd.)

30.10.79 : 79/923/EEC	Laying down quality requirements for shellfish (condylicole) waters, sampling & etc.	30.10.81
17.12.79 : 80/68/EEC	Preventing the discharge of List 1 substances and restricting the discharge of List 11 substances; setting up a system of authorisations etc. for derogations; preparing an inventory of discharge authorisations granted.	19.12.81

SOURCE: Commission of the European Communities, Progress made in connection with the Environment Action Programme and assessment of work done to implement it, COM(80)222 final, 7 May, 1980.

objected to the application of the Community's high
standards for estuaries into which large amounts
of industrial effluent are poured (see Table 13a).
The government argued that less stringent controls
were needed than for inland water supplies.   Only
from 1977 did it introduce a policy of setting
'environmental quality objectives' for each stretch
of a river, but these were non-mandatory.[7]   Again,
Britain has not yet fully complied with the EEC
Directive No.76/464 on toxic and dangerous wastes
because the regulations under the 1974 Control of
Pollution Act are not yet in force.   Indeed,
recently the Northumbrian Water Authority, to whom
the Bank has been advancing large sums for sewage
and sewerage works on the north and south banks of
the River Tyne, would appear to have been lowering
its standards in respect of toxic wastes deposited
in landfills near major water sources.[8]
    The Community's 1976 Directive on quality
standards of bathing water on beaches used by a
large number of people drew from the National Water
Council the comment:

>   ....the least satisfactory EEC Directive on water
>   quality to emerge up to now....It is not well judged
>   scientifically and will be costly to administer;   it
>   would also lead to a distortion of investment in
>   environmental improvement.[9]

In 1980 the EEC Commission issued a Reasoned
Opinion stating that the UK was not fully complying
with the Directive since the necessary legislation
for Scotland and Northern Ireland had not been
brought into line with that for England and Wales.
By the summer of 1981 only 25 beaches were reported
to have been brought up to the EEC standards.[10]
    Again, in February 1979, the Commission issued
an Opinion that it was not satisfied with British
implementation of the Directive on waste from the
Titanium Dioxide industry.   These wastes are mainly
discharged into estuaries.   Two British firms
thereupon brought an action against the Commission
before the European Court of Justice, requesting
the annulment of the Opinion and a declaration that
the Directive was illegal.[11] Their action is still
under investigation.
    The nub of the argument between the British
authorities and the Community is cost.   The difficulty of meeting costs of implementing Community
standards on water quality pinpoints another anomaly
in the Community's policies.   Since 1978 the Government has been under pressure to reduce public spending.

The cutting of government subsidies to Water Authorities has inevitably been accompanied by rising costs for consumers. In 1978, the EIB was full of admiration for the way in which the British National Water Council and local Water Authorities were raising charges to consumers and reducing subsidies.[12] In most other EEC member states, water tariffs cover the real cost of water provision. However, by 1979 UK consumers were becoming restive about increasing charges. In a democratic society the 'polluter pays' principle implies the right to information and a choice on processes and products. Industrial and domestic wastes alike can, to an increasing extent, be recycled. The EIB's considerable loans to Britain give it the chance of assisting the observance of Community aquatic standards and of promoting the re-use of industrial and domestic wastes.

iii) EIB Loans for Effluent Disposal
     in other EEC Areas

Dutch environmentalists, horticulturalists, market gardeners and fishermen have become increasingly concerned about the salination of the River Rhine. One main cause is the dumping of salt wastes from the Alsace potash mines into the Moselle, a tributary of the Rhine. The mines are one of the bases of the Saar-Lorraine chemical industries for which the EIB gave several loans in 1967-69 (page 184). Although the EEC member states agreed to adhere to the 1963 Bonn Treaty for the Protection of the Rhine in 1974, and France signed the Treaty two years later, a conflict of interests is preventing a solution of the problem. The question is whether, in view of the concern about the Rhine by the late 1960s, the EIB could not, even at that time, through its Saar-Lorraine loans, have discouraged the dumping of wastes in the Moselle.[13] The EIB later supported the cleaning up of the Rhine. In 1974 it funded a large water purification plant downstream of one of the Bayer chemical group (BASF) factories. It deals with effluent from the factory and from two towns, Ludwigshafen and Frankenthal.

The Bank's 1980 loan to the Danish-West German lacto-serum project in Denmark (page 191) was partly to overcome the problem of disposal of effluent, always a difficulty at dairies. It was a sign of acceptance of a new concept - that of constructing industrial installations with pollution control systems built into them at the start.

b) LOAN TO REDUCE ATMOSPHERIC POLLUTION
   FROM INDUSTRIES

It was not until 1979 that the Commission of
the European Communities made proposals for a standard of actions to reduce atmospheric pollution
caused by industries.   Yet the government of the
Federal Republic of Germany had begun to take legal
action in this matter fifteen years earlier in
order to control dust emissions.   The steel industry to which the Bank made some loans was one of
those affected (page 180).   As early as 1973, the
Bank lent specifically for the reduction of dust
pollution from a steelworks in the Hüttental-
Geisweid area in North Rhine-Westphalia.[14]
The EIB has made several loans to Italsider, a
subsidiary of the Italian state steel enterprise,
which accounts for nearly half of Italian steel production.[15] Of these, two were specifically for the
reduction of environmental pollution; one to the
Bagundi plant in Campania in 1976 and the other for
the installation of anti-pollution equipment as
part of the reorganisation of a plate mill at the
Italsider Taranto iron and steel complex.   The Bank
also lent for the installation of pollution control
equipment as part of the rationalisation of a private Italian electrolytic zinc foundry in 1976.   In
1980, the EIB announced a loan of 6 billion lire for
the restructuring of a carbon products factory at
Narni Scalo, in Terni Province in Umbria.   The
plant is owned by Elettrocarbonium SpA, a subsidiary
of the two West German firms, Hoechst AG and Siemens
AG.   A considerable part of the project involves
the reduction of pollution.[16]
The EIB may have helped to reduce pollution in
other industrial enterprises, for instance in French
metal works, to which it has granted several loans
since 1973, and through its loans to the British
Steel Corporation for modernisation and expansion of
plants.   But as no specific reference to anti-
pollution measures is given in connection with these
loans, they must remain a matter of conjecture.

c) LOANS TO DIMINISH POLLUTION FROM ENERGY SOURCES

The environmental effects of electricity generation from fossil fuels are well known and include
the emission of sulphur, CO_2 and other substances
which have been the subject of EEC Directives (see
Table 7c).   Although the EIB has made a considerable number of loans for power stations (Chapters 5
and 6), it has only recently supported projects
specifically designed to reduce pollution.   Its
1979-80 loans to Asnaes and Kyndby power stations in

Denmark included provision for the installation of
equipment to eliminate air-borne pollution due to
the burning of coal.[17]
   The Bank has also made loans for the construction of facilities for reducing oil pollution in
French harbours.   Until recently oil tankers washed
out their cargo tanks and discharged water contain-
ing oil residues into the sea.   In addition, oil
tanks have been and continue to be quite widely used
for water ballast, which is often discharged into
harbours.   To deal with this pollution, oil-water
separation and water purification plants are now
being installed in several ports and ship repair
yards.   The Bank has helped to finance two separation plants, the first at the Fos-sur-Mer petroleum
port at the mouth of the Rhône.   Its effectiveness
led to a second similar installation, assisted by a
second EIB loan, at Brest in Brittany.   Following
the recent spate of oil tanker spills, the Brest
plant also has facilities for cleaning contaminated
sand and gravel brought to it from beaches by
lorry,[18] but as yet this aspect of EIB financing is
very small.

	Amounts of EIB Anti-Pollution Loans (energy) (mill.ua)	Total EIB Loans for development of oil and gas pipelines
Asnaes & Kyndby power stations 1977-78	55.4	
Fos-sur-Mer oil tanker ballast & water purifi- cation facilities 1977	2.7	
Brest oil tanker ballast & water purification facilities 1980	5.0	
TOTAL	63.1	1,094.3

   The Bank has helped to finance a considerable
number of hydro-electric projects, but has evinced
concern about their environmental impact only in the
case of one of them, the Dinorwic pumped storage
scheme in North Wales.   Perhaps due to the protests
of local environmentalists, the Bank publicly
announced measures taken to protect the environment,
declaring that 'a very careful and sympathetic regard' had been 'paid to the countryside'.   Landscape architects were employed to ensure that the
dams would be:

TABLE 13b: EIB Loans for Energy Saving and
Conservation in EEC member states

Type of Project	mill. ua
D E N M A R K	
Energy saving:	
Expansion of factory at Oster Doense, North Jutland, producing mineral wool for insulation (1978)	1.3
Heat & power generating plant with feeders to district heating system at Holsteinborg, Greenland (1979) ..	6.3
Power generating plant at Godthaab, Greenland (1973) ..	3.3
District heating:	
Coal-fired district heating & power plant to replace oil fired installations at Randers, E.Jutland (1980) ..	11.7
Construction of a district heating system at Kalundborg, West Zealand, using heat recovered from the Asnaes power station (1980)	7.7
Coal-fired district heating & power plant to replace oil-fired installations at Herning and Ikast, West Jutland (1980)	5.8
I R E L A N D	
Energy saving:	
Global loan for financing investment in small & medium-scale industrial ventures helping them to reduce or make more efficient use of their energy consumption (1980)	4.5
I T A L Y	
Energy saving:	
Global loans for financing investment in industry in the Central-Northern region helping to reduce energy consumption (1980: two loans)	16.7
Equipment to reduce energy consumption at a flat glass works in San Salvo, Abruzzi (1980)	12.8
Reorganisation & modernisation of flat glass factory in Casetta (Campania) (1980)	5.8
Equipment to help reduce energy consumption at various FIAT group factories (1980)	10.0
Improvement of electricity installations in steelworks at Sesto S. Giovanni and Arcore, Lombardy (1978) ..	4.2
Equipment to help reduce energy consumption at cement works at Morano Po, Piedmont, Settimello, Tuscany, and Lugagnano & Santarcangelo, Emilia Romagna (1980) ..	3.3
Installation of back pressure turbine for heat and electricity production in a factory at Magenta, Lombardy (1979)	(1) 1.7
District heating:	
Combined heat and power plant at Brescia, Lombardy (1979, 1980: 2 loans)	15.7
Solar energy:	
Reorganisation of factories producing solar panels and other energy equipment, nr. Pistoia, Tuscany (1979) ..	2.6

224

TABLE 13b (cont'd.)

Type of project	mill. ua
U N I T E D K I N G D O M	
Energy saving:	
Rebuilding of an aluminium smelter at Lochaber, Scotland, with reduction of electricity consumption (1979, 1980: 2 loans)	27.9
Construction of a mineral wool factory at Bridgend, South Wales (1980)	5.4

(1) 3% interest subsidy granted.

> compatible with their surroundings. The transmission
> lines to the nearest junction with the grid will be
> buried underground for much of their length. There
> will be a certain amount of tree-planting and rubble
> remaining from an old slate quarry will be removed.
> Power and beauty should not be in conflict.[19]

Although the small number of 'environmental' loans
the EIB has recently been making in the energy sector represent a step forward, they are still not
very significant when compared to the large sums
granted for the exploitation of oil and natural gas,
and for the development of nuclear power.

d) LOANS FOR ENERGY CONSERVATION

Since 1979 the European Investment Bank has
granted several loans for the purpose of energy conservation. Indeed, its loans to the Fos-sur-Mer
and Brest oil residue operations come partly within
this sphere since the salvaged oil can be used.
Also, one of the by-products of the Danish-West
German lactoserum operation, for which the Bank lent
in 1980, will replace oil as a feedstock.

More directly, and obviously for energy conservation, in 1980 the EIB agreed to help fund a combined heat and power plant based on the coal-fired
power station at Randers in Denmark. The plant is
expected to save something in the order of half a
million tonnes of oil equivalent over twenty years.

In Britain, in 1979 and 1980, the EIB lent 27.9
million ua to the British Aluminium Company for the
rebuilding of its Lochaber smelter, part of the project being the reduction of specific electricity
consumption. By early 1981, the UK government was
considering energy conservation initiatives and discussions were in progress between the Treasury and
the EIB on the development of a loans scheme.[20]

Early in 1981, the Italian government announced
an energy plan for the period up to 1990; objectives
included the vigorous promotion of energy saving and
the maximum utilisation of national energy resources.
The plan envisaged the increasing use of renewable
energy sources such as solar and wind energy, biomass and other alternative fuels, but the main investment is to be in hydro-electricity and geothermal power. These policies were, in fact, already apparent by 1980 and were being reflected in
EIB financing, as Table 13b shows.[21]

District heating schemes have been an important
means of energy conservation in several countries.
The EIB has contributed financing to the realisation
of one such scheme through loans in December 1979

and again in March 1980 to the municipal authority
of Brescia in the north of Italy.   This project is
designed to heat twelve million cubic metres of
housing and to   lead to fuel economies of 50,000
tonnes of oil a year.   Similarly, the Bank has
funded a district heating scheme for the West Jutland town of Herning, linked to a new coal-fired
heat and power plant. [22]
    In 1979, the Bank claimed that 15.7 per cent of
its total lending in the Community for that year was
to assist energy saving through modernisation and
conversion schemes.   Furthermore, between 1979 and
1980 it estimated that it had lent a total of 199.4
million ua for energy saving, of which 125.3 million
ua was allocated in 1980, representing 10.3 per cent
of total lending in that year.[23]   Thus, by the early
1980s, the financing of energy conservation had become an important area of EIB investment.

e) CONCLUSIONS

    Only recently in the Community have environ-
mental protection and energy conservation been recognised as of economic importance.   The European
Commission, in its second <u>State of the Environment</u>
report in 1979, declared:

> the question that should be posed is whether the expand-
> ing 'environmental industry' cannot make a contribution
> to the restructuring of our economies away from those
> traditional industries which have become unprofitable as
> a result of competition from low-wage countries, towards
> the modern, often high technology sectors which we need
> to master the problems of the future.   Just as a clean
> environment is a pre-condition of secure and balanced
> growth in the future, so the environmental industry can
> increasingly become an important source of satisfying
> job opportunities.[24]

The Community's Directorate for Employment and
Social Affairs had arrived at a similar conclusion
in a separate study.   The extent to which the European Investment Bank can assist these developments
is circumscribed partly by the view held by the
Commission and some member states' governments that
one of the main routes out of the present economic
crisis is to cut public expenditure.   Hence the
anomaly that, while many environmental protection
and energy conservation schemes aid private industries and reduce unemployment, their inauguration
largely depends on the initiatives of public authorities which are at present being discouraged

from financing, notably in the United Kingdom.

However, it is upon public expenditure that many energy programmes based on older technologies rest. Public funds are available for developing established sources of power which may be wasteful and carry serious threats of pollution. By contrast, district heating schemes are well established in only one EEC country, Denmark. However, their advantages are increasingly acknowledged although argument continues over the relative benefits they provide in terms of costs and jobs compared with accepted energy technologies. British local environmental groups have worked out such schemes as alternatives to official proposals for more environmentally dubious methods of providing heat and power, some of which merit serious consideration, but the government is unlikely to promote more than one in the next ten to fifteen years.

The provision of power stations and schemes for pollution control requires long-term investment. Local authorities and private organisations are often prepared to undertake imaginative projects, but their access to EIB funds is limited by tight governmental control over the acceptance of loans. The Bank itself, however, can encourage them through its selection of projects to be funded. The conservation of energy and pollution control fall well within its mandates in that they promote transboundary co-operation between EEC states - pollution is no respecter of frontiers. In addition, such projects encourage the development of growth sectors and increase job opportunities. It is to be hoped that the greater weight given to the reduction of environmental pollution and to energy saving by the Bank since 1979 is an indication of a long-term change in its lending policies and of the adoption of new economic imperatives more benign to the quality of life than some of the old.

NOTES

1. e.g. OJ C283/12, 3 November, 1980 Written question No. 667/80 from European MP Robert Jackson to the Commission of the European Communities on the NCI and environmental protection and Mr. Ortoli's answer of 25 September, 1980 which instanced the Lothian Sewage and Sewerage Scheme.

2. M. Frankl, Anti-Pollution Handbook, pub. Social Audit, London, 1978.

3. M. Dorin, Head of Water Directorate, OECD Dept. of the Environment, interview, July 1979.

4. EIB, Information, No.10, August 1977, 4.

5. Ibid. Also No.5, May 1976, 5-6; 1958-1978, 18-19.

6. Ibid.

7. COM (80) 222; cf. Commission of the European Communities,
    First Action Programme, Annex 1; conflict and confusion
    over definition of terms 'environmental quality standard'
    there classed as 'mandatory' & 'environmental quality ob-
    jective' which is a broader definition. There is also a
    further term: 'uniform emission standards', a step to
    achieving uniform quality throughout the EEC.   Inst. for
    European Environmental Policy, Memorandum to Sub-
    Committee G of the House of Lords' Sub Committee on the
    European Communities of their general enquiry...to
    evaluate EEC environmental policy to date and its future
    direction: 1980, p.2, paras. 2.1-2.5.
    I am grateful to the Institute for making available the
    summary of their application to the Nuffield Foundation
    for a grant for a Research Proposal on The Effect of EEC
    Environmental Policy on the Legislation and Practice of
    the United Kingdom.

8. In 1979, the Northumbrian Water Authority dropped its re-
    quirements that such landfills must be lined with imper-
    meable membranes and the leached material taken for treat-
    ment and disposal elsewhere. The only proviso now is
    that it must be 'unlikely' that leaching would harm water
    quality, while highly toxic but not readily bio-degradable
    wastes have to be buried far from water resources and
    given a thick cover of impermeable ground. The Northum-
    brian Water Authority was concerned that the disposal of
    sewage sludge would become 'more intractable' because of
    growing public concern over polluting discharges into the
    sea, air and on land, i.e. the reason for lowering stan-
    dards appears to have been simply rising costs.   North-
    umbrian Water Authority, 1979 Report, para. 3.3.8.

9. National Water Council, Water Industry Review, 1978,
    para. 43.

10. F. Pearce, 'The unspeakable beaches of Britain', New
    Scientist, Vol. 91, No.1262, 16 July, 1981.

11. Commission of the European Communities, Report, 14 July,
    1975. See State of the Environment, First Report, 1977,
    45-7, extent of titanium dioxide pollution.   Inst. of
    European Environmental Policy, Research Proposal, The
    Effect of EEC Environmental Policy on the Legislation and
    Practice of the United Kingdom, pp. 6-7, paras. 5-6.
    For effects of hot water, industrial and domestic efflu-
    ents on sea water, see studies by Messrs. William Watson,
    Civil Engineers, London: NATO, North Sea Science, E.
    Goldberg, ed. 1974.

12. EIB, 1958-1978, 27. Information, No.10, August 1977, 7.
    In Britain, before the 1974 Water Act, the government

provided 58% of total expenditure on water. After the Act, by 1978, according to the EIB, the new authorities were managing to recover all their costs, including loan charges and the building up of substantial reserve funds 'by a mixture of courageous tariff increases and a greater efficiency in cost control'. Daily Telegraph, 10 October, 1977, 'New bills for water cause angry protests.'

13. Times, 19 November, 1981. Natur en Milieu, Short History of Appeal by Environmental Organisations against dumping dredged spoils in the North Sea. European Environmental Bureau, Notes, 13 September, 10 October, 1979. Emissie registratie province of S.Holland, October 1978. Waterkwalitats plan Benenden Rivier engesned, Rykswaterstaat. July 1979. The Conventions on the west European aquatic environment lay down that if there is any possibility that pollution may be due to another source, e.g. a landfill site, the current laws cannot be used to limit discharges into water courses. The Dutch environmentalists must therefore establish the source of pollution; EIB, Information, No.22, November 1980, 9.

14. Commission of the European Communities, Second Report on the State of the Environment, 1979, 92-6; Fig. 13, 110. Between 1965-75, dust emissions due to the burning of hard coal and brown coal in industrial firing systems was cut by nearly 75%. There were also substantial cuts in dust emissions from crude steel production. In plants using the old Bessemer method, emissions dropped almost 12-fold.

15. Financial Times Survey, 31 March, 1980, vi, x. The Bank's loans for the Italian cement industry, including one in 1963 involving asbestos, ceased in 1971 when concern about the environment in EEC countries was only beginning. For cement dust pollution, see M.Frankl, op. cit.

16. EIB, Press Release, 31/80, 2 June, 1980.

17. EIB, Annual Reports, 1979, 1980.

18. EIB, Information, No.8, February 1977, 6; No.18, July 1979, 7-8.

19. EIB, Information, No.8, February 1977, 6.

20. Times, 27 January, 1981.

21. European Economy, No.8, March 1981, 74-5.

22. EIB, Press Release, No.10/80, 6 March, 1980: No.20/80, 31 March, 1980.

23. EIB, Information, No.23, November 1980, 6-8.

24. Commission of the European Communities, State of the Environment, Second Report, 1979, 12-14.cf Tyneside Environmental Concern, Nuclear Power at Druridge Bay, 1979

Chapter 14

THE EUROPEAN INVESTMENT BANK'S FINANCING IN
SOUTH EUROPEAN AND MEDITERRANEAN COUNTRIES
AND IN THE MIDDLE EAST

No more can be attempted here than to give a
brief indication of the Bank's extensive operations
in South European and Mediterranean countries outside the European Economic Community.

a) ESTABLISHMENT OF THE EIB'S ROLE IN
   NON-EEC COUNTRIES

The six countries that organised the European
Economic Community intended that it should maintain
and strengthen economic relationships with countries
outside the Community, not only their colonies and
former colonies, but independent states.[1] This aim
was made clear in the Treaty of Rome,[2] although
only a general provision was included regarding the
European Investment Bank's role in this connection
(Article 18). In pursuit of this policy, shortly
after it came into being, the Community began negotiations over an Association Agreement with Greece.
It was during the course of these that, in 1960,
a new role started to open up for the Bank in providing finance in support of EEC activities outside
the Community. In 1962, on the basis of Article 18
of the EIB's Statute, the Bank's Board of Governors
took the decision to widen its field of action by
giving it a mandate to intervene in Greece.

Meanwhile, the EEC had also opened negotiations
both with Turkey and with various African countries
and Madagascar, with which the Community countries
had colonial associations. On 12 September, 1963,
the EEC countries signed a loan agreement with the
African countries (see Chapter 15), which further
widened the EIB's sphere of financing by conferring
on it a role in arranging loans and aid for them

By 1963, the Bank had acquired experience in
financing major infrastructure and industrial projects which it seemed natural to use in support of
planned association with countries outside the Com-

munity boundaries.[3]

The aim of these agreements between the EEC and the associated countries insofar as the EIB was concerned, was to allow it to intervene in the Community's interests not only each time the nature of projects 'justified the granting of financial aid', but also when 'disequilibrium in the balance of payments' in an associated country justified it.[4]

Even at this early stage, the EEC also envisaged that other countries in southern Europe, including Turkey and Portugal, would eventually be integrated into the Community as members. So the governments of EEC countries deemed it necessary to develop in them economies modelled on those of the most prosperous of the first six Community countries. The principle of levelling up the economies of the least industrialised and most disadvantaged regions inside the Community, particularly the south of Italy, was extended to countries outside. Aid was to be channelled to these potential members of the Community, in part via the Bank, in order to enable them to cross:

> in one or more stages the threshold which still separates them from the level of the major industrial countries of Europe...It was indispensible to bridge the gap if they were to contemplate an adequate integration of their economies....' with those of other states.

that is, with the EEC states. The 'stages' were designed to fit the individual economies of each country and existing development plans which they were already implementing.

It will also be remembered that three years after the EEC was set up, the Organisation for European Economic Co-operation was widened into the Organisation for Economic Co-operation & Development of which Greece, Turkey and the United States of America were members. Within a few months of the OECD's inauguration, working parties were set up to consider the long-term development problems of Greece and Turkey. The European Investment Bank participated in these OECD groups and in consortia that were subsequently established to finance long-term infrastructure developments, co-operating closely with the World Bank and big commercial banks, over projects intended to alter the economies of Greece, Turkey and, in due course, of other non-industrialised countries. Large firms with interests in poorer countries were also involved in

232

the consultations.   A collective effort was planned
with the Bank finding the right kind of funding for
each project, checking on its economic viability and
administering its financing on behalf of the EEC.
In addition, however, the EIB also took a share in
co-ordinating loans from different non-EEC sources.
The overall impact of loans managed by the EIB in
associated countries is therefore not to be assessed
merely by the size of its loans nor by the proportion of total financing that they represent.   The
Bank's role as agent and manager for other Community
financing bodies has also been important.

Poor countries outside the EEC found even the
EIB's rates of interest high.   For the Bank's
ability to charge less than prevailing interest
rates on world capital markets was, to some extent,
limited by the fact that it was to them that it
looked when borrowing most of its funds.   Therefore
in order to reduce the burden of interest for poor
countries, EEC member states' governments introduced
a three per cent interest subsidy for certain loans.
This scheme was later extended to the least prosperous EEC countries (see p.76).

Member states also helped to keep down
interest rates on loans to poor countries by lending their own national funds on special conditions
through the European Investment Bank.   In addition,
the governments of member states sometimes undertook
to guarantee EIB loans and 'even procured for the
EIB the necessary resources at their own risk', as
indeed they did for risky operations inside the Community.   This form of financing was less usual in
the case of Greece, however, than in the other
countries with which the Community early formed
associations.   For the purpose of administering
these loans, a special department was opened in the
Bank.

b) THE SPECIAL SECTION

While Greece was predominantly a peasant agricultural country, it had a partly developed industrial and banking system which Turkey and the other
associated countries lacked.   The Bank, therefore,
had no great hopes of their making punctual repayments of loans.   Hence, it would not consider
investing its own funds in projects there as it
bluntly explained:

it became evident that the resources of an institution
which has to turn to the markets for funds as does the
Bank, were hardly appropriate to come to the aid of

233

Map.14.a. Financing by and through the EIB in Mediterranean Countries.

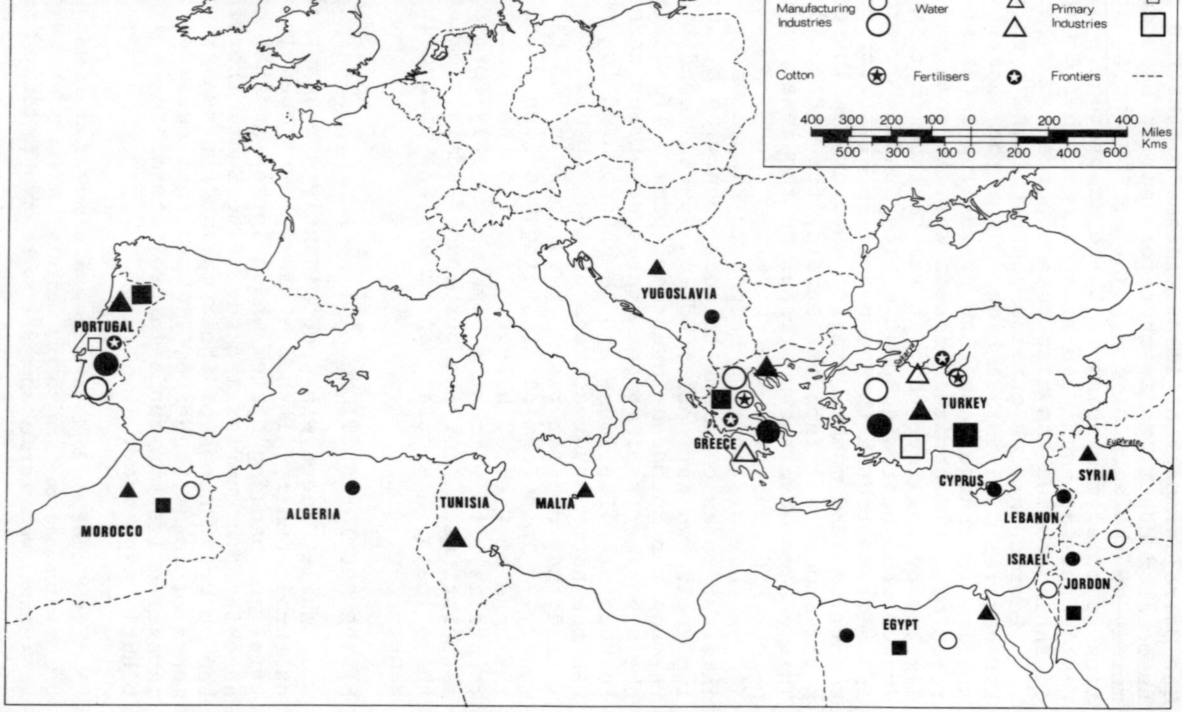
Power
Communications
Service Industries
Manufacturing Industries
Water
Primary Industries
Cotton
Fertilisers
Frontiers
400 300 200 100 0 200 400
Miles
Kms
500 300 100 0 200 400 600
PORTUGAL
MOROCCO
ALGERIA
TUNISIA
MALTA
YUGOSLAVIA
GREECE
TURKEY
CYPRUS
SYRIA
LEBANON
ISRAEL
JORDON
EGYPT
Euphrates

countries in which the balance of payments was precarious and liable to remain so for a rather lengthy
period.[5]

The difficulty was resolved by the setting up of the
Special Section, to which the Bank's Board of
Governors agreed on 27 May, 1963, three months before the Turkish agreement was signed by the Community.

The Special Section is part of the Bank, but
separate from its normal lending section.   Its
essential feature is that not only the funds lent
by the Bank, but also the repayment of these loans
is guaranteed to the Bank by one or more of the EEC
member countries.   The Bank will only arrange
loans in response to their mandates and the EEC
country or countries concerned carry the whole financial responsibility.   If any of the recipients
of loans default or are late with repayments, then
the EEC member states have to repay the Bank on
their behalf.

c) EIB FINANCING IN GREECE

The Bank felt that the Greek economy was sufficiently strong financially to enable it to lend
its own funds without undue risk.   The methods of
EIB financing were laid down in the Financial Protocol appended to the Association Agreement signed
on 9 July, 1961.   The Bank was to finance
'yielding investments' which arose through the
Greek 5-year development plan, started in 1960.
This programme was stopped and restarted in 1962,
when the new Association Agreement with the EEC
came into force.   The Agreement laid down that
loans should be granted to the value of $125 million
over the 5 years 1962-67.   A first tranche of $50
million was authorised for the first two years.[6]
These amounts were expressed in US dollars because
the EIB unit of account was still, at this time, the
equivalent of US.$1, through the medium of its gold
value.

While manufacturing industry was encouraged by
the Greek government, and by the Community from
the start of the Association, priority was first
given to irrigation works in order to raise agricultural production.   Just as eighteenth and nine-
teenth century industrial revolutions in the west
and north of Europe depended partly on increases in
food production to permit people to leave work on
the land for work in the manufacturing sector, so
in the twentieth century, a similar process was

235

TABLE 14a: EIB loans for infrastructure projects
in Greece: Transport

Year	Area	Type of Project	mill. ua
TRANSPORT			
1963	Athens-Corinth	Completion of new road (69km)*	2.0
	Corinth-Patras	Construction of new road (1,354km)*	6.2
	Antirrion-Agrinion	Modernisation of this stretch of the Antirrion-Ioannina highway, the main connection with Italy via Igonmenitsa-Brindisi, incl. 78.8km of dual carriageway	2.6
	Lamia-Larissa via the port of Volos	Construction of new road - part of the Athens-Salonika highway (146.3km) **	6.2
1979	E.Macedonia & Thrace	Construction of roads to open up forests	10.0 (Dr.497.3m)

NOTES:

*   For communication with the Peloponnese and Europe.
** The rest had already been modernised, First Five-Year Plan
    ended 1967.

All these loans benefited from the 3% interest premium.

SOURCE: EIB, <u>Annual Reports</u>.

TABLE 14b: EIB Loans for infrastructure projects
in Greece: Water projects & Energy

Year	Area	Type of project	Amount Lent (mill.ua)
WATER/IRRIGATION			
1964	Salonika Plain	Irrigation	10.3
1966	Plain of Karditsa, Thessaly	Irrigation	5.0
1967	Pinios Plain Peloponnese	Irrigation, mainly by sprinkling of 20,000 ha to develop forced fruit, citrus fruits, cotton, vegetables and the rationalisation of stock-rearing	15.0
1975	Serres Plain E.Macedonia	Irrigation, flood control	26.0 Dr.1039.8m
1979	N.W.Crete	Irrigation of 7,500 ha on coast	25.0* Dr.1243.2m
	Thrace	Irrigation of 37,760 ha, water from dam on the Ardas River & 2 aquifers in Evros	20.0* Dr.1004.9m
1980	"	" "	27.5* Dr.1668.1m
	Chalcis, Euboea	Sewerage Treatment & Water purification plant+	5.5 Dr. 336.6m
Special Loan:			
1979		Global Loan for small schemes	10.0 Dr. 525.5m
ENERGY			
1963	from the Kremasta power stn. on the R. Acheloos	Construction of 493 km. high tension cable to convey electricity	6.0
1975	Volos, Thessaly	Electrical & telecommunications cables factory	4.3 Dr. 173.1m
1979	Sfikia & Assomta, S. Macedonia	Construction of 2 hydroelectric power stations on the Aliakmon River	18.0* Dr. 895.1m
1980	"	" "	17.0* Dr.1031.2m

* Loan attracting a 3% subsidy.
+ Environmental Protection Loan

SOURCE: EIB, Annual Reports.

taking place in countries in the south.   Moreover,
the importance of farm produce as exports was a
major reason for EIB loans to increase production of
cash crops through more efficient cultivation.   Consequently, during 1965-67, the EIB provided loans of
$30 million for irrigation projects covering nearly
100,000 hectares of the Salonika, Karditsa and
Pinios plains.

The end of the first three-year plan coincided
with the Greek colonels' coup in 1967, which 'froze
relations between the Community and Greece'.   However, because the large infrastructure projects
which the Bank had helped to fund took a number of
years to complete, there was inevitably a carry-
over of financing.   For example, in 1967, the EIB
organised a loan of 20 million ua as part of the
total of 125 million ua guaranteed under the first
five-year plan.

Following the attack against the government of
Cyprus in 1974, the junta in Athens was overthrown
in the spring of 1975 and democracy restored.   This
in turn led to normal relations with the Community
and loans through the EIB resumed.   A new financial protocol for a second five-year term, 1977-81,
was then negotiated and signed.

Once lending was resumed in 1977, another
irrigation scheme, which the EIB supported, was in-
stituted in the Serres plain, adding a further
20,000 hectares.   By 1978 nearly a quarter of the
country's irrigable land had been provided with
irrigation.   Irrigation, of course, involved large-
scale alterations to water resources.   In the
case of the Serres plain scheme, not only was flood
control provided on the Strymon river, but the
capacity of the Lake Kerkini reservoir was trebled.

The government adopted measures to redistri-
bute the land, conserve the soil and provide credit
to farmers.   The kinds of crops grown remained the
same, but the volume produced and the output of
stock farming increased, thereby reducing dependence on imports and lessening the trade deficit.
As a result of modern techniques and high yields,
an agro-industrial sector is being built up.   The
Bank hoped that the modernisation and expansion of
agriculture would reduce the emigration rate,
which, over the decade 1969-78, had led to a 10%
drop in the overall population and a decline of 35%
in the farming workforce.

However, in order to achieve the goals of the
Agreement with Greece, it was primarily to industrial expansion that the EEC and EIB looked for
increasing productivity.   In 1964, the contribu-

238

tion of industry to Gross National Product was greater than that of agriculture for the first time. The Bank was surprised because, as in Italy, the vast majority of enterprises - 95% - involved only ten workers or less. There were numerous small workshops and even more artisans working in their own homes. The Greek public authorities, however, at first pursued the development of large-scale basic industries, most of which were already in existence before EEC loans started. During 1963-67 the EIB helped to finance seven of them, the most important being Aluminium of Greece. This production complex on the north bank of the Corinthian gulf utilised the large Greek reserves of bauxite. The other industries helped by the Bank included a compound fertiliser factory and three cement works. At the same time, the Bank continued to assist infrastructure development with loans for motorways and hydro-electric schemes. It was only in 1975, following the fall of the junta, that the emphasis in the EIB's lending for Greek industry was directed more towards the modernisation of small and medium-sized businesses and industries and to the production of intermediate goods.[7]

EEC interest in Greece was not, however, merely altruistic. It was and still is economic, political and strategic. Greece has minerals other than bauxite - iron pyrites, nickel, magnesite and sulphur, and British Petroleum has struck oil at Kleisoura in west central Greece. Before the Agreement with the EEC and the EIB loans, the government was already promoting a petrochemicals complex, using imported oil. Motorways were driven through the country, the EIB helping to fund the Athens-Patras-Agrinion highway along the Gulf of Corinth, the area in which industrial development was mainly located, and the Lamia-Larissa section of the Athens-Salonika route. The result, as in all rapidly industrialised peasant countries, was the increasing concentration of population around the capital, Athens, and considerable pollution problems.

In September 1979, the city's mayor, Mr. Dimitris Beis, attacked, among other things, the atmospheric pollution, absence of modern sewage systems, and lack of parks and facilities for children and the elderly. Mr. Glannis Marinos, editor of the economic weekly, Oikonomos Tahidromos, remarked that, 'Its inhabitants can no longer breathe, circulate on foot or by wheel or find rest from the onslaught of noise'. The Financial Times

reported that pollution from vehicles and industry
'is appalling....Marine life has been driven out to
sea....' and, because of marine pollution, bathing
had been banned.   Inevitably, famous ancient mon-
uments are being damaged.   Government proposals
for decentralisation were criticised by Mr. Beis,
partly for failure to include prior consultation
and co-operation with municipal authorities.[8] Despite the expectation that Greece would soon be
joining the EEC, there were seemingly virtually no
legal restrictions on pollution.   It is surprising
that the Bank did not apparently stipulate as a condition of its loans for motorways and industrial
plants, compliance with EEC anti-pollution policies
concerning motor vehicles and the sea, in support of
the effort to bring Greece into line with the other
EEC countries.
    From 1980, and especially during 1981 after
Greece had joined the EEC, the Bank's lending was
reflecting increasing concern about small and
medium-scale enterprises and about environmental
problems in the Athens-Piraeus area.   Up to October
1981, the EIB had granted six credits for providing
loans to small and medium-scale enterprises, four
of them 'to diversify the fabric of industry', two
for agricultural enterprises and one for those in
the energy-savings field.[9]   In 1980 and 1981, the
EIB provided aid for regional sewerage schemes
aimed at reducing pollution in lakes and rivers, and
thus - in line with the EEC's adherence to the Barcelona Convention - in the Mediterranean Sea.[10]   In
October 1981, the Bank announced three loans for the
Heracles General Cement Company, partly for the purpose of dispersing the firm's concentration of
operations from the 'blighted environment' of the
Piraeus, as the EIB put it, to less industrially
developed regions.[11]   This dispersal will not in
itself, of course, eliminate or diminish the pollution unless the new installations are designed to
do so.   It would be interesting to know if the EIB
has insisted on this point.   It may be added that,
in 1980, the Bank also gave a loan of 4.5 million ua
to the Titan Cement Company which it had already
assisted in 1964 and 1975, for expanding and modernising a cement works near Patras, but it does not
state with what environmental safeguards.[12]

d) EIB FINANCING IN TURKEY

    The interest of OECD countries, including the
EEC member states, in Turkey was not only political,
for Turkey has greater mineral reserves than Greece,

the main ones being coal, lignite, iron and petroleum.   By a law of 1954, private companies can ex-
plore and produce oil, although oil production at
Garzan and Raman is in the hands of the national
Turkish Petroleum Company.[13]   There are also vast
forests.

EIB activities in Turkey were covered in a financial protocol attached to the Association Agreement of 12 December, 1963.   Under this, the EIB
could grant loans of up to 175 million ua under a
first five-year plan by mandate from the member
countries and supplemented by the Bank itself with
endorsement from its Board of Directors.   Loans
have to be for a maximum period of 30 years, with a
seven year grace period before repayments begin.
Interest rates were very much below market rates.   A
second Financial Protocol of 1973 extended the provisions and laid down interest rates of:

> for infrastructure and other
> projects requiring finance
> from a variety of sources 3%
>
> for projects showing an indirect or
> long-term return 2.5%
>
> for normal production projects   ..   4.5%

For these last, the EIB adopted a two-tier procedure
as in Italy:

1.   The Bank granted loans to the Turkish
     government;

2.   The government re-lent the money either
     directly or via credit institutions, in both
     cases to private enterprises.

Infrastructure loans are channelled to various government agencies which decide the contractors who are
to undertake the work.   However, the Bank and other
foreign lending agencies have taken a keen interest
in the projects which they have helped to finance.
The Bank's Statute laid down that, 'The Bank may
make its loans conditional on international invita-
tions to tender being arranged', a provision which
the Bank has used in Turkey.   Bidding for contracts, therefore, is open to all natural or legal
persons.   As in the early years of the Community,
Turkey and other non-EEC countries borrowing on
these conditions were expected to benefit not only
from the projects themselves once completed, but
also from access to foreign technological expertise

TABLE 14c: EIB Loans for infrastructure projects
in Turkey: Energy

			Amount Lent (mill.ua)
ENERGY			
1964	Nr. Lake Kovada, N. Anatolia	Construction of an electric power station	5.0
1965	Keban Dam on R. Euphrates	Construction of dam, hydro-electric power station & transmission lines to Ankara & Istanbul	30.0*
1969	"	" "	10.0
1979	"	" "	36.0 TL.2,330.8m
Spec. Ops.	"	" "	60.0 TL.6,759.8m
1967	Sakarya River Gökcekaya, N.W.Anatolia	Construction of a dam & hydro-electric power station to meet peak demand	7.3
1968	Gökcekaya Seyitömer Izmir	Construction of a 380 kv high-tension line	7.6**
1974 spec. ops.	Elbistan, E. Anatolia	Mining of a lignite deposit and construction of a thermal power station	77.0 TL.1,338.2m
1980	"	" "	75.0* TL.5,118.9m
		Global Loan for small & medium-scale industrial projects	5.0 TL. 86.0m

Notes:
* Foreign Exchange expenditure financed by World Bank, EIB, Governments of the USA, West Germany, France, Italy. A consortium was set up to organise this financing and the finalisation of the project was coordinated by the EIB, World Bank, US Aid Administration.

** to use energy produced at Keban and Gökcekaya hydro-electric power stations

SOURCE: EIB, Annual Reports.

TABLE 14d: EIB Loans for infrastructure projects in Turkey

Date	Area	Type of Project	Amount Lent (mill.ua)
WATER/IRRIGATION & AGRICULTURAL DEVELOPMENT			
1965	Gediz Valley Western Anatolia	Irrigation & Development	15.0 (+ World Bank, USA, W.Germany, France & Italy. Total Cost: 340 mua Total foreign investment: 135 mua Co-ordination: EIB, World Bank, US Aid Admini-stration)
1974	"	"	10.0 TL. 174m
1975 Spec. Ops.	Mersin Pro-vence, S. Anatolia	Irrigation of the Berdan Valley	11.0 TL. 189.2m
1973	Nr. Antalya	Modernisation of forestry development & construction of a factory producing paper-pulp, papers & board, a saw-mill	20.0 TL. 337.8m
1976	Mediterranean Region	Forestry development	6.0 TL. 108.3m
	*Silfke, Nr. Mersin	Construction of plant making liner board, kraft paper & sawn wood	5.0 TL. 90.0m (additional loan)
		Global loan to finance pre-investment studies in the public sector	1.0 TL. 18.3m
1979	Antalya,Mersin, Adana & Kah-ramanmaras conservancies S.Turkey	Promotion of Forestry development covering 1.4m ha	10.0 TL. 677.4m
1980	*Dalaman, W. Anatolia	Papermill unit to produce coated paper & board: plant to treat effluent from mill+	4.0 TL. 450.7m

All Special Operations except*
+ Environmental Protection
SOURCE: EIB, Annual Reports.

and finance on advantageous terms.

The EEC Agreement with Turkey, which came into force in December 1964, laid down a plan for eventual Turkish membership of the Community as follows:

1964-69:   Turkey's economy was to be strengthened
                by Community aid - a preparatory stage.

The   Phased introduction of the EEC-
following   Turkish customs union and alignment of
12-22 yrs.   their respective economic policies - a
                transitional stage.

Final   Greater co-ordination of EEC-Turkish
stage: economic policies.

In 1965 only 8.5 per cent of the population were in industrial employment.   Small enterprises employed half of these workers and accounted for nearly 75 per cent of industrial production, mainly handicrafts. Turkey's modern industrial development has been beset by balance of payments problems arising from a dependence on imports of machinery, capital goods and more complex industrial products.   In addition, she has imported oil as part of her effort to industrialise since her own reserves were not being properly tapped.   Finally, her customs tariffs have been very low indeed, lower than those generally accepted by the General Agreement on Trade and Tariffs.

As in the case of Greece, the EIB expressed the view that Turkey's economic difficulties would be solved by promoting industrial development, rather than farming.   Industrialisation would create employment for 'unused reserves of manpower';   would 'ensure improved utilisation of the country's natural resources';   would make a large contribution to solving the balance of payments deficit and would be the means of establishing a customs union with the EEC. [14]

Despite outside financial aid, including EEC loans via the EIB, the economic imbalance among Turkish farmers was acute in the early 1970s: 70 per cent of farm land was in farms of over 5 hectares in size, but 75 per cent of the country's farms were less than 5 hectares, so 25 per cent of the total number of farms had 70 per cent of the available land.   As in Greece, efforts were made to encourage stock farming in place of the traditional cotton, sugar beet, fruit, hazelnuts and vegetables. The wisdom of this switch is questionable, since livestock represent a very expensive way of producing protein.

244

The first five-year plan ended in 1969, with Turkey still deep in financial crisis, although during 1963-68, GNP grew at an annual rate of 7 per cent.[15] In 1973, the Community's Second Financial Protocol with Turkey was ratified and the EIB's financing was resumed.

By the late 1970s, Turkey had received three times as much finance through the European Investment Bank as Greece. Six times more was invested in basic industries than in agriculture. The EIB also contributed finance for several huge infrastructure schemes which inevitably radically altered the environment. For example, a huge hydro-electric scheme was begun in 1966 on the River Euphrates. It involved building the Keban dam which covers 68,000 hectares with water and has a total capacity of 30,000 million cubic metres. The dam has been providing power to Ankara and Istanbul from 1974. Another hydro-electric-cum-irrigation scheme in the lower Gediz Valley north of Izmir involved building dams to create two artificial lakes, one on the Gediz, with a capacity of 1,300 million cubic metres, and one on the Alasehir of 93 million cubic metres capacity. The Bank has also been helping to finance the conversion of Lake Marmara into a 360 million cubic metre reservoir, a project which has involved building another three catchment dams and one diversion dam. This was to feed water to a 14,000 kw. hydro-electric power station, and irrigate 107,000 hectares of land, for which the EIB provided two loans of 15 million ua in 1965 and 10 million ua in 1973 towards the total cost of 172.9 million ua. Beside these enterprises, the Kielder and Italian dams appear quite modest. As they were to provide electricity, it was said they would not affect river flows.[16]

The EIB was involved in other large infrastructure projects. In the sphere of transport, it helped the building of motorways and bridges, one across the Bosporus, 1,560 metres long with a six-lane deck, and a second, across the Golden Horn, 1,000 metres long. It also funded 19 km. of motorway skirting the Istanbul conurbation to the north, but also feeding into it. The two bridges replaced two old floating bridges across the Golden Horn and numerous ferries plying across the Bosporus which cut across the flow of shipping through the straits. They were opened in 1973 and permitted a huge increase in the traffic crossing the Bosporus. By the summer of 1977, the total traffic flow in both directions was 76,000 vehicles a day, a level not expected until 1980. By 1980-81, saturation

flow of 100,000-120,000 vehicles a day was expected.
    The bridges provide a good example of the kind
of syndicate financing in Turkey in which the EIB
had a part.   In this case, the Bank was the co-
ordinator, managing loans and overseeing the main
tendering operations.   Of course, the work was
entirely carried out by foreign firms:

Consulting design engineers	..	English, Japanese
Motorway plans	..	French
Builders of the Bosporus Bridge	..	Anglo-West German consortium
Builders of the Golden Horn Bridge	..	West German-Japanese consortium
Steel tower	..	Italian
Suspension cables	..	West Germany, Luxembourg

The whole building operation was co-ordinated by the
Turkish Ministry of Public Works through its
Directorate-General for Highways.[17]
    The EIB has also assisted the building of a
petrochemicals plant by putting up loans to cover
all the foreign capital needs, and has part-financed
a synthetic fibres plant.[18]   The Bank has been a
member of a banking consortium helping to finance
the opening up of lignite deposits and the construction of a power station in Elbistan, in the
south east, using this fuel.[19]   Along with the World
Bank, the EIB has made loans totalling 35 million ua
towards forestry development in Turkey.   The Bank
remarked that Turkey's huge forests were 'still
poorly and inefficiently exploited, so that their
contribution to value added in the primary sector
is just over 2%'.[20]   The EIB's aid is intended to
support the doubling of annual production of timber
from the mature forest area of 1.4 million ha to
2.8 million cubic metres per year.   The felled
trees will supply timber chiefly to a saw and paper
mill on the Mediterranean coast of southern Turkey,
which is also being constructed with EIB help.   It
will process 170,000 cubic metres of timber a year
and produce annually 155,000 tonnes of linerboard
and 90,000 tonnes of kraft paper 'or any combination
of the two'.   The loans were conditional on the
automatic replanting of cleared areas and the planting of new forests in scrubland,[21] but the environmental impact will clearly be enormous.
    There is no doubt that Turkey needed help.   The
question is whether the projects which the European
Investment Bank has helped to finance have constituted the right kinds of help and the right amounts
of it.   In 1965, before the EIB loans had really

become effective, Turkey was able to cover all or part of her needs for a limited number of basic goods, including some manufactures. Living standards were simple, and energy, especially domestic heating, was, to a large extent, provided by noncommercial fuels such as dried dung and wood. A decade later, the country's Gross Domestic Product had grown appreciably, but the average expectation of life in Turkey was only 55 years, although ironically, some of the longest lived people in the world are to be found in her remote rural areas.

The sad fact was that, by the end of 1980, despite financial help from the EIB and other banks, Turkey's economic situation was worsening.[22] Aid from EEC sources, besides the Bank, and from other OECD countries has contributed to the disruption of the distribution of necessities. It has increased Turkish dependence on ever more expensive imported oil, gas and other products. Thus it has increased Turkey's crippling foreign debts. Financing bodies, just as in the case of the south of Italy, gave insufficient weight to assisting the base of the Turkish economy, that is the mass of small independent enterprises, although the Bank did not ignore them. From 1968, loans for small enterprises in Turkey were brought within its Global Loans scheme.[23]

In 1979-80, Turkey was reported to be making a major bid to join the EEC, a move less than welcome to the Community authorities in view of her precarious economic situation. The Turkish government was exhibiting anxiety about the amount of EEC aid that would be available to her once Greece joined the Community in 1981. Meanwhile, in 1980, the existing Agreement between the EEC and Turkey was re-negotiated and came into operation in 1981. The ceiling on the EIB's investments over 1981-86 was set at 225 million ua.[24]

e) THE EIB'S FINANCING FOR PORTUGAL

When the Portuguese people themselves joined their colonies in revolt against the dictatorship of Dr. Salazar in 1974, the EEC rushed in with aid to secure the moderates against the extreme left-wing. Aside from political considerations, Portugal has uranium reserves, as well as brown coal, lead, copper, iron and other minerals of use to Community countries and is Iberian, if not Mediterranean.

At the end of 1975, when the moderates had effectively won, the EIB was authorised to make 150 million ua available to the new government as exceptional emergency aid, on the same terms as aid to

Greece.   This amount was committed in full in 1976 and 1977, 53 per cent to energy and transport projects, 29 per cent to industrial plant and 18 per cent to agriculture.   It helped to finance two irrigation projects in the north and in the southern Alentejo, to increase and diversify the production of about 45,000 communities.   This aid was welcomed since a lack of investment over many years had been accompanied by dependence on imported foodstuffs. The Bank also provided two of its Global Loans for small and medium-scale enterprises.

In September 1976, the Bank signed a financial protocol to provide from its own resources a further 200 million ua in loans during 1978-82.[25]   Portugal's early accession to the Community is expected,[26] but with the example of southern Italy before them, there is some unease among the Portuguese people about the abrupt imposition of large-scale farming and industrialism upon a still basically peasant economy.

f) EIB FINANCING IN YUGOSLAVIA

The Belgrade Declaration of 1976 provided for the financing of projects of common interest to Yugoslavia and to the EEC.   They were to be accompanied by increased mutual trade and exchange of technology and it should be noted that Yugoslavia, too, has important mineral resources which she wishes to develop.   At the request of the Council of Ministers of the European Community, the EIB's Board of Governors authorised loans of up to 50 million ua.   The first was granted in November 1977 to assist the extension of the Yugoslav electricity network and its connection with the Greek and Italian grids.   Through the Italian network, it will be connected to the other EEC grids.

g) NORTH AFRICA AND THE MIDDLE EAST

By 1978, another ten countries in the Mediterranean area were the recipients of EIB loans.   In 1973, the Community signed an accord with Malta and began negotiations with the Maghreb - Algeria, Morocco and Tunisia.   Agreements with these countries were eventually signed in 1976.   That spring, the EEC countries started negotiations with Mashrek countries - Egypt, Syria and Jordan.   In February 1977 an agreement was signed with Israel, and in May with the Lebanon.   The Community countries, through the EEC Commission, were to grant aid for technical co-operation, rural development and social infrastructure, while there were also bilateral aid

agreements with individual EEC member countries.
The Bank was to assist with long-term, low-interest
bearing loans for infrastructure development and
industry, mainly small and medium-scale.   The EIB
saw these loans as 'a modest contribution to the
total development needs of the Mediterranean basin.'
EEC aid in general was intended 'to express soli-
darity with its southern neighbours and to help
create a vast zone of fruitful co-operation.'   There
were considerable potential benefits from the Community's point of view.   Algeria, Morocco, Lebanon,
Tunisia, Egypt and even Israel all have oil, the
Iraqi oil pipeline crosses Syria, while oil prospecting is going on in Jordan where there are phos-
phate deposits.   Cyprus has iron and other minerals
and cement in the Turkish sector.   In 1978, over
15 per cent of the EEC's visible exports went to
these 14 countries.[27]

h) CONCLUSIONS

     The European Investment Bank has supported the
wish of EEC countries to build up economic links
with Mediterranean countries.   The Bank's investments, particularly in some forms of infrastructure,
have contributed to improvements in living standards and to an easing of work in food production.
Now that Greece has joined the Community, she, too,
is represented on the Bank's Board of Governors
and, as more Mediterranean states join the Community, their views may alter somewhat the policies
laid down for the Bank by northern European member
states.
     The Bank's interventions have not, however, led
unqualifiedly to improvements in living standards
for the peoples of Mediterranean countries.   In
particular, there is as yet little sign of a re-
appraisal on the part of the Bank's Board of
Governors of lending policies following failures,
apparent by 1977[28] in the south of Italy. The economy of the Mezzogiorno is very similar to that of
Greece, Portugal and Spain, and to certain
areas of Turkey. Thus, there has been apparently
little attempt to avoid or diminish mistakes.   It
is to be hoped, in view of the present world
recession, that the EIB may give still more emphasis, in its operations in Mediterranean countries,
to helping independent small and medium-scale
enterprises and to co-operatives, and less to aid
for large industries such as are already in difficulties in the EEC.   It is also desirable that
future EIB investments should be directed to a still

greater extent to the encouragement of new technologies in waste management and control, renewable fuel sources, conservation of energy and to the elimination of pollution.

NOTES

1. EIB, Information, No.25, April 1981, 3.

2. Treaty of Rome, Part Four, Art. 131 and Annex IV of the Treaty, Art. 237 (Applications for membership); Art. 238 (Association with non-member states).

3. EIB 1968 Annual Report, 128. Special Study: 'The Bank and its Associations with Greece, Turkey and the African States and Madagascar'.

4. EIB, 1962 Annual Report, 32-3.

5. EIB, Annual Reports, 1968, 132-33; 1964, 51-2; 1963, 61.

6. EIB, Annual Report 1962, 32.

7. EIB, Information, No.3, November 1975, 5, 7. EIB, 1958-1978, 53, 55; EIB, 1964 Annual Report, 70.

8. Financial Times, 22 September, 1979, 'Athens: city without a face'.

9. EIB, Press Release, 64/81, 14 October, 1981; 1980 Annual Report, 53, 61.

10. Ibid.; Press Release, 60/81, 6 October, 1981.

11. EIB Press Release, 63/81, 13 October, 1981.

12. EIB, 1980 Annual Report, 53, 61.

13. A pipeline, Batman-Iskenderum, was opened on 4 January, 1967.

14. EIB, Annual Reports, 1964, 21; 1965, 70; 1968, 145.

15. Small and medium-sized family farms predominated along the Black Sea and Aegean coasts. But large estates cultivated by tenants predominated in Anatolia on the Mediterranean coast. Most industry was also located in the west of the country. EIB, 1968 Annual Report, 140.

16. EIB Research Department, Activities of the EIB in Turkey, 1965-1974, 23,27:Ann.Reps.:OJ C56/4, 16 March, 1981, Written Question No.1405/80.

17. Ibid., 25; EIB, 1968 Annual Report, 127.

18. EIB, Research Dept., op. cit., 31, 33.

19. EIB, Press Release, 8/80; 27 February, 1980.

20. EIB, Research Dept., op. cit., 31, 33.

21. OJ C160/2-3, 30 June, 1980. Written Question No.1842/79.

22. Financial Times, 25 July, 1979; 13, 16 January, 27 March 1980; also 14 June and 5 September, 1979, changes in patterns of West German-Middle East trade. And 28 March, 1980, Soviet offers of spare parts for oil and gas equipment to Iran. In February, the West Germans were trying to mount a financial rescue operation for Turkey with help from the IMF, the World Bank, private banks and the OECD, see Times, 26 and 29 February, 1980. The Federal Republic regarded massive financial and military aid as its main response to the Soviet invasion of Afghanistan. Times, 'Business News', 8 May, 1981, 'OECD aid for Turkey'.

23. EIB, Annual Report, 1964 - for details.

24. Guardian, 2 October, 1979. C. Stevens, ed., EEC and the Third World: a survey, 70.

25. EIB, Information, No.12, February 1978, 7-8; 1958-1978, 59. Press Release, 27/81, 17 June, 1981, development of eucalyptus forest industry. See also, Financial Times, 20 December, 1979, for the dispute between Plessey and the Portuguese government over telecommunications developments.

26. Ibid, 11 October, 1979; Times, 8 March, 1980. As yet, no EIB loans have gone to Spain, although she is currently negotiating entry into the EEC where she will be welcome not least because of her large mineral deposits which include coal and lignite. See EIB, Information, No.18, July 1979, 4-7. Financial Times, 1 and 22 November, 1979.

27. EIB, Information, No.18, July 1979, 4; No.23, November 1980, 10-11; C. Stevens, ed., op. cit., 68-9.

28. EIB, Information, No.11, November 19, 1977, 2-7.

251

APPENDIX 14A: Financing provided by the EIB in the Mediterranean region from 1963 to 1980 (Countries)

	Operations mounted from EIB own resources			Operations mounted from Special Section resources			TOTAL		
	No.	Amount (m.ua.)	%	No.	Amount (m.ua.)	%	No.	Amount (m.ua.)	%
Northern Mediterranean	66	797.4	80.3	60	561.0	92.9	126	1,358.4	85.0
Greece	37	341.4	34.4	1	10.0	1.7	38	351.4	22.0
Portugal	19	301.0	30.3	-	-	-	19	301.0	18.8
Turkey	8	105.0	10.6	59	551.0	91.2	67	656.0	41.1
Yugoslavia	2	50.0	5.0	-	-	-	2	50.0	3.1
Maghreb	5	75.0	7.5	3	34.0	5.6	8	109.0	6.8
Algeria	1	20.0	2.0	-	-	-	1	20.0	1.2
Morocco	1	26.0	2.6	2	19.0	3.1	3	45.0	2.8
Tunisia	3	29.0	2.9	1	15.0	2.5	4	44.0	2.8
Mashrek	11	118.7	11.9	2	3.8	0.6	13	122.5	7.7
Egypt	3	65.0	6.5	-	-	-	3	65.0	4.1
Jordan	3	15.0	1.5	1	0.3	-	4	15.3	1.0
Lebanon	4	23.0	2.3	-	-	-	4	23.0	1.4
Syria	1	15.7	1.6	1	3.5	0.6	2	19.2	1.2
Other									
Malta	1	3.0	0.3	1	5.0	0.9	2	8.0	0.5
TOTAL	83	994.1	100.0	66	603.8	100.0	149	1,597.9	100.0

SOURCE: EIB, 1980 Annual Report, 54-5.

Chapter 15

THE EUROPEAN INVESTMENT BANK'S FINANCING IN THE REST OF THE WORLD

The European Community's and the European
Investment Bank's financial interventions far beyond the Mediterranean area arise from the fact
that when the six countries joined together to form
the Community in 1957, their overseas interests remained unchanged. They still needed food and raw
materials for their own manufactures from many
countries outside the Mediterranean area. To a
far greater extent than either the United States or
the Comecon countries, the EEC economy rests on
processing raw materials, many of them being
imports from non-industrialised countries, and on
selling the finished products for which non-industrialised countries represent an important market. Hence
EEC states wanted to maintain existing economic and
political links with colonies and former colonies.
This was envisaged in the Treaty of Rome, under
Article 130(a) and (c) to which the original six
member states added a Declaration of Intent on:

1. the association of independent countries
    of the franc area within the EEC.

2. the kingdom of Libya.

They also agreed to take over the Trust Territory of
Somaliland, then administered by the Italian Republic, and the Dutch colonies of Surinam and the
Netherlands Antilles.[1]
    Following the 1962 decision that the EIB has
to play a part in financing outside the Community
(see Ch.14), discussions began about projects which
were to receive loans from the Bank. However, the
form of association originally envisaged was being
overtaken by events as an increasing number of
colonies obtained independence. Thus, they gained,
among other things, the right to choose whether or
not they would continue an association with the EEC.

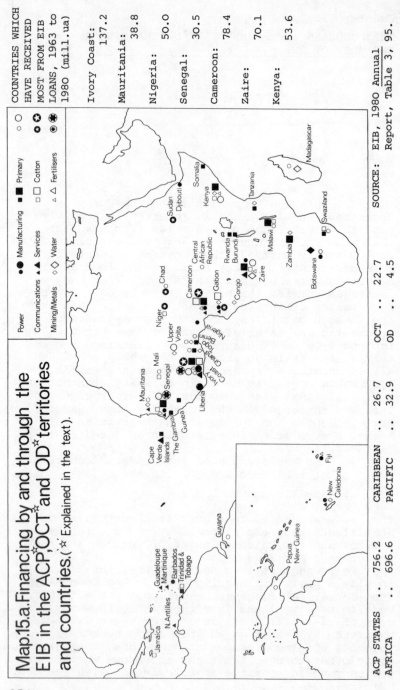

Map 15.a. Financing by and through the EIB in the ACP, OCT and OD territories and countries. (☆ Explained in the text).

COUNTRIES WHICH
HAVE RECEIVED
MOST FROM EIB
LOANS, 1963 to
1980 (mill.ua)

Ivory Coast: 137.2

Mauritania: 38.8

Nigeria: 50.0

Senegal: 30.5

Cameroon: 78.4

Zaire: 70.1

Kenya: 53.6

Power   ●○ Manufacturing ■□ Primary ○
Communications ▲▲ Services   □ Cotton   ✪ ✪
Mining/Metals   ◇ Water   △ Fertilisers ✪ ✪

SOURCE: EIB, 1980 Annual
        Report, Table 3, 95.

| ACP STATES | .. | 756.2 | CARIBBEAN | .. | 26.7 | OCT | .. | 22.7 |
| AFRICA | .. | 696.6 | PACIFIC | .. | 32.9 | OD | .. | 4.5 |

Most of them decided to do so. Since the Treaty of
Rome Declaration no longer covered this new situation, the Community governments followed the pattern
established in the case of independent Greece and
Turkey, by negotiating an Agreement not with each
individual country but with a group. It is known
as the Yaoundé Convention, and was signed on 7 July,
1963, by the EEC countries on the one hand and, on
the other, by 17 African mainland countries, Madagascar and other overseas countries and territories.
Under this Convention, most of the finance to be
provided by the EEC countries was in the form of
outright grants, primarily through the European Development Fund, or through 'soft' (i.e. low
interest) loans, some of them from the EIB.

a) THE EIB'S MANDATE FOR INTERVENTIONS
   IN DEVELOPING COUNTRIES

   The Bank's role in providing finance in support of the Community's interests in these Yaoundé
countries was evolved simultaneously with the legal
framework for its loans to Turkey. On 27 May, 1963
shortly before the signing of the Yaoundé Convention, the EIB's Board of Governors made the necessary authorisations for the Bank's interventions:

1)   It was to grant loans of up to 70 million ua
      over a 5-year period from its own resources
      and at its own risk. Of this amount, 64
      million ua was allocated for the African
      States and Madagascar and 6 million ua for
      other Overseas Countries and Territories.
      These were to be accompanied by interest
      bonuses granted case-by-case by the Commis-
      sion from the European Development Fund's
      resources, up to a limit of 3 per cent, i.e. in
      effect interest subsidies (see pp. 76, 233).

2)   The EIB was also to intervene up to a limit
      of 50 million ua (46 million for the African
      States and Madagascar; 4 million for the Over-
      seas Countries and Territories) in order to cover
      the costs of examining and managing special
      loans granted from the resources of the
      second European Development Fund under very
      flexible conditions 'so as to diversify as
      widely as possible an aid which, until then,
      had consisted exclusively of subsidies'.[2]

   The Yaoundé Convention, Title 11 (see below
p.258) specified that the EEC would participate:

In the measures suitable for promoting the
economic and social development of the
Associated States by an effort supplementary
to those made by these States.

The loans from the EIB's own resources, although
of a lesser total amount than those for Greece and
Turkey, and much less than provided by other EEC
grants and loans, were considered important as in-
dicating a change in the relationship of the
Yaoundé countries with the Bank.[3]   Through the EIB
loans it was intended that these colonial and ex-
colonial countries would more and more become equal
partners in the normal pattern of international
financial transactions.   They would be initiated
into dealings on the international money markets.
However, the Bank found that there was a lack of
applications which satisfied the terms for its
long-term yield financing at market conditions.

b) ECONOMIC CONDITIONS IN THE ASSOCIATED
   OVERSEAS COUNTRIES

There were, of course, considerable differences
in the economic levels and condition of these different associated countries.   Some areas in the
Ivory Coast, Senegal, the Congo and Gabon were not
very different from subsistence farming areas in
Greece and Turkey, and the Italian regions of Calabria and Basilicata.   But there were striking dis-
similarities, in particular the African Associates
had a much lower population density than the EEC
countries and, taken altogether, their populations
at that time amounted to only a third of the whole
population of the six EEC countries.   The Bank remarked that not only was public finance in the
Yaoundé countries often out of balance, but only
three of them were able to allocate as much as 10
per cent of their current receipts for capital expenditure.   Their Gross Domestic Products and
exports were growing only very slowly.   In ten of
these states, 70 per cent of exports consisted of
only two products, the outlets for which were also
growing very slowly and this, in turn, contributed
to their rising foreign debts.   The per capita
income of their populations was generally very low,
the level of local savings was low and their internal trade was not concentrated in central markets
which required a transport network, but was com-
partmentalised into numerous local markets.[4]   The
Bank did not, however, mention in this assessment
the prices which these countries were paid for their

exports.   Nor did it say anything about how far
they were able - given that their expectations were
much lower than in prosperous EEC countries - to
feed, clothe and house themselves without aid from
industrialised countries.   It did not assess how
far their citizens had some kind of economic security, so long as the traditional extended family
system survived, nor how that security might be
preserved under the impact of European economics.

c) DEVELOPMENTS IN EIB FINANCING IN
   ASSOCIATED OVERSEAS COUNTRIES

    The EEC's financial aids under the first
Yaoundé Convention of 1963 were increased by an EEC
Council Decision of 25 February, 1964.   At the
same time, the EIB's Board of Governors decided
that loan operations under special conditions made
from the European Development Fund's resources were
to be dealt with by the Bank through the Special
Section.   In these EDF operations, the Bank and
EEC Commission at first jointly carried out the
preliminary investigations, then the Bank managed
the loan on the basis of mandates from the Community.[5]
    The Community's economic aid, including the
EIB's loans, followed a definite pattern.   First
cash was poured in to build transport and energy
infrastructure and then aid for other aspects of the
economies of the Yaoundé countries followed.   By
1969, when the first Yaoundé Convention ended, the
EIB lent 73 million ua from its own resources for
23 projects:

    31.2 mua (43%)   to energy and road infra-
                      structure

    22.0 mua (29%)   to the development of ex-
                      tractive industries, mainly
                      potash, in Congo-Brazzaville;
                      copper in Mauretania;   nickel
                      in New Caledonia.

    20.5 mua (28%)   to industrial development,
                      mainly of the agricultural
                      and food industries.

    The Bank estimated that its loans would in-
crease the revenues of the states involved by nearly
30 million units of account and lead to annual savings
in foreign exchange of about 40 million ua.[6]   However, the joint total of their external indebted-
ness at the end of the first Yaoundé Convention in

257

1969 amounted to 2000 million ua.

A second Yaoundé Convention was signed in 1971 and the number of Third World signatories rose to 19, with Mauritius joining the group.   When Britain joined the Community in 1973, the Association countries encompassed her former colonies and her main overseas territories, including the Antarctic Territory, the Indian Ocean Territory and a number of Caribbean Islands.   A new arrangement was necessary.   So, on 28 February, 1975, the enlarged EEC signed the Lomé Convention with the increased number of Third World countries, and this came into effect on 1 April, 1976.

This Agreement on economic co-operation now involved 46 countries in Africa, the Caribbean and Pacific.   They were known from then on as the ACP states.   They had between them a population of 281 million, compared with the EEC's then population of 262 million.   On the basis of a Decision of the Council of the European Communities of 29 June, 1976, provisions similar to those under the Lomé Convention, including, of course, financial aid, were applied to Overseas Countries and Territories (OCT) which are dependencies of EEC member countries, so that altogether 53 countries became associated with the EEC.   The first Lomé Convention remained in force until 1 March, 1980.

d) EIB FINANCING UNDER THE YAOUNDE II
AND LOME CONVENTIONS

The EIB's operations under the Yaoundé and Lomé Conventions were a part of overall Community financing programmes, as Table 15a shows.   EDF loans carry a lower rate of interest than those made from the EIB's own resources, or than the Special Operations loans in Mediterranean countries. It is generally about 1-3 per cent a year according to the nature of the project, over a maximum period of 40 years.   The maximum length of the period over which repayment can be deferred is ten years. Special EDF loans cover anything up to the entire cost of a project.   They are paid in the currencies of the Community countries and according to their contributions to the EDF.   In addition, there are outright grants which cover the interest due on loans, so that the EDF aid in effect provides interest rebates.   Under the Lomé I Convention, as the non-European countries were becoming increasingly aware of their economic strength, the amounts of these rebates were raised and the procedure for obtaining them was simplified.

258

TABLE 15a: Methods of financing by the European Investment Bank and European Development Fund in the ACP/OCT/OD Countries

METHODS OF EIB PARTICIPATION					METHODS OF EUROPEAN DEVELOPMENT FUND PARTICIPATION		
Loans, rarely over 40% of the cost of fixed investments	Management of Risk Capital provided by member states; used for pre-investment subsidies OR to enable a recipient government or national development institution to acquire a stake in an enterprise OR to enable the EIB to acquire a stake in a new enterprise in order to facilitate EEC participation in financing projects	Occasional contributions to the formation of risk capital	Management of EEC countries' loans	Organising finance	Loans for investment	Special loans to finance examination of projects	Grants

259

The EIB, in addition to granting loans, organising finance, managing member states' loans and contributions to risk capital, occasionally itself contributes to the formation of risk capital. Also EEC states, from time to time, ask the European Investment bank to use risk capital to buy into a new undertaking, an unusual step, for the purpose of 'bolstering their (i.e. ACP/OCT enterprises) equity by acquiring a stake in their share capital'. The EEC could then contribute 'by means of shareholders' loans, subscription of bonds and aid of a quasi-capital nature'. That is, under normal company practice, a Community country or institution, like any other shareholder, could be approached for a loan, could subscribe to a company bond issue or take up further shares. The Bank could also use risk capital to buy a share in an enterprise,' as it was allowed to do under Article 20.2 of its Statute if 'this is required to safeguard the rights of the Bank in ensuring recovery of funds lent'. The EIB has used the device as infrequently as possible and any share it has taken in an enterprise has always been small. Thus, in 1977, on behalf of one or more member states (unspecified) through its Special Operations section, and again in 1980 using Community budgetary funds, the EIB acquired shares in Zaire's Société Financière de Développement (SOFIDE). A most elaborate network of financing was thus provided by the EEC, with the Bank naturally occupying a central position.

The centrality of the EIB was slightly weakened in 1975 under the Lomé Convention. For whereas under the Yaoundé Convention, the Bank and the Commission together appraised and approved special loans from the European Development Fund, under Lomé this has been done solely by the EEC Commission. The Bank merely acts on the EEC's behalf to ensure recovery of funds[8] so that here, too, there has been a tendency to stress its agency role.

e) A CASE STUDY - CIMENTS DE L'AFRIQUE DE
   L'OUEST (CIMAO)

As can be seen from Table 15b and Map 15a, most of the Bank's loans for the ACP/OCT countries have gone to industrial projects, not least to the cement industry. A West African venture in this field illustrates the role of the European Investment Bank in this kind of operation, although it should be noted that financing for each loan is individually tailored to suit the project and the circumstances of the beneficiary states. The instance in the cement industry, discussed here, involved the governments of Togo, Ghana and the Ivory Coast, who were persuaded to co-operate in a joint venture, the Tabligbo cement plant. EEC loans via the EIB enabled each of these countries to buy one third of 92 per cent of the shares of a company set up for the purpose, Ciments de l'Afrique de l'Ouest, CIMAO. The remaining 8 per cent of the equity was owned by French cement manufacturers, Origny-Desvroise, who provided management and technical services, and two local clinker-grinding companies, Société des Ciments d'Abidjan of the Ivory Coast, and the Ghana Cement Company. The British Associated Portland Cement Manufacturers Ltd.[9] provided the engineering. All the raw materials for the production of Portland cement are to be found 80 km. from Lomé in Togo, at Tabligbo where the plant was built. It was estimated that total production capacity would reach 1.2 million tons per year when the plant came into operation in 1981, rising to 1.8 million tons later. The three African states involved were expected to take all the cement produced. The costs of the scheme at 1976 prices were:

	Million ua	
for industrial development	190	used partly to pay French and British contractors with finance contributed by the EIB, the World Bank, Caisse Centrale de Coopération Economique de France, the Arab Bank for Economic Development and the African Development Bank
for railway, port & energy infrastructure for the plant	35	with finance contributed by the EEC European Development Fund, the Canadian International Development Association (CIDA), the African Development Bank, and the West German Kreditanstalt für Wiederaufbau
	245	

While Togo was to provide the ingredients for the cement, Ghana was to supply power from the Akosombo hydro-electric station on the Volta River, and further supplies were to come from another plant, the Kpong power station, still under con-

struction in 1976.   This power station, too, was
internationally financed by the EIB among other institutions.
    The EIB involvement in the CIMAO cement works
was:

i)   March   1976   5.925 mua loan to CIMAO (15 years)
      December   1976   14.0 mua loan to CIMAO (14½ years)

ii)   Three risk capital operations (i.e. in which member
      states provided the capital and bore the risk) at 6%
      interest p.a. to the three countries to help them
      finance their shares in the CIMAO preference capital
      on the following terms:

            1)   2 mua each for 20 years;
            2)   grace period, 14 years;
            3)   interest initially fixed at 2%.

      These were subordinated loans repayable only after the
      other loans had been paid off.

    The Bank saw the benefits to Togo, Ghana and
the Ivory Coast as:

1.   A certain supply of 70 per cent of their cement
      requirements.

2.   Diversification of Togo's economy away from agricultural
      products.   The country is heavily dependent on three
      exports: cocoa, coffee and phosphates, commodities
      whose prices are subject to considerable fluctuation.

3.   Therefore, considerable improvement in Togo's balance
      of payments could be expected.

4.   The creation of at least 600 permanent jobs, and when
      construction was at its height, 3,000 temporary jobs.

Ghana would be offsetting the purchase costs of
clinker through her supplies of electricity.
    The Bank considered as 'perhaps the most impor-
tant aspect of the project', its contribution to
breaking down the rather strict division between
anglophone and francophone areas in this part of
West Africa.   In this way, the CIMAO project
pointed to wider industrial activity which could result from the closer collaboration of these two
linguistic blocs and lead to the 'pooling of resources and national markets.'
    Although the EIB acts primarily in the interests of
EEC member countries, it also advises the Associated
Countries.   For instance, short of foreign exchange,
they often charge high import tariffs on raw materials
and capital goods required for new industrial pro-

262

jects, including some of those which the Bank and
EEC were encouraging. Because of this, the EIB, in
1968, at the time of the Yaoundé Convention, declared itself 'in favour of lower import charges' in
cases where it was unlikely the Third World signatories of the Yaoundé Convention 'could produce such
goods themselves in the near future'.[10]

In general, the EEC and EIB until the mid-1970s
furthered Western-style industrialisation and economic development in all the usual infrastructure
spheres. Railways, river transport and roads have
been funded in order to bring products from, for
instance, up-country forests to production plants in
Cameroon. They have assisted the construction of
dams to provide hydro-electricity and irrigation,
and the growing of cash crops, such as oil palms,
pineapples and sugar (Appendix 15A). Concentration on cash crops created two problems for the
people of the ACP/OCT countries. Firstly, such
concentration often disrupted, but did not then repair, a traditional subsistence economy to which
women made a major economic contribution. Thus,
they were economically independent and were not regarded as dependants of men. Cash provided by the
EEC and Bank, like other foreign investments, tends
to go to those who can afford to repay it, that is,
to the wealthier farmers, while the poorest may
lose their land. All too often it emphasises and
encourages social inequalities.

Secondly, concentration on cash crop production
has tended to put a stop to subsistence farming in
the same area. People become dependent for an income on external markets, in which, as the EIB admitted in the case of Togo, conditions are often
erratic and on crops, such as sugar, with a low
nutritional value. If prices suddenly drop, small
producers are faced with starvation, so that they
may be no better off than when they farmed primarily
for subsistence and the local market, and were
vulnerable to climatic aberrations such as drought.
But whereas the industrialised North is able to de-
rive no advantage from subsistence farming in these
countries, cash crops provide it with food and raw
materials. Some crops, however, created economic
problems. For example, sugar exports from, say,
the Republic of Upper Volta, financed by the EEC
through the Bank and by the Caisse Centrale de
Coopération Economique de France, competed with
sugar beet production inside the Community, as well
as with Caribbean sugar.

The EEC and EIB have also been involved in
financing mineral extraction, for example, copper in

Mauritania, nickel in the French colony of New Caledonia and copper and cobalt in Zaire. The Bank has lent for aluminium production in Cameroon at Edea, where the transnational Pechiney-Ugine-Kuhlman has interests in aluminium and steel, and the French firm, Imetal (whose main shareholder is Rothschilds) has bauxite mining interests. Because of the current high capital costs of mining, large Western companies have preferred joint enterprises similar to that of the CIMAO cement project. In 1981, the EIB announced its first loan for uranium mining in the ACP countries, granted to the conglomerate, Compagnie Mines d'Uranium de Francville, which includes COGEMA and Imetal-Mokta of France.[11]

In addition, the Bank has given considerable support for textile operations, including cotton production at Garoua and Douala in Cameroon, through Cotonniére Industrielle du Camerun, CICAM, in which French and German firms have interests.

Just as in the Community itself and the Mediterranean countries, recognition of the importance of help to small and medium-scale ventures was slow. The Bank was providing finance for them in some of the ACP/OCT countries only from the late 1970s. However, these loans were much more difficult for the Bank to supervise than those for large projects. As a result, in 1980, it tightened up conditions on which it made its Global Loan allocations.

f) OVERALL EFFECT OF EIB AND EEC FINANCIAL
   INTERVENTIONS IN ASSOCIATED OVERSEAS COUNTRIES

There is only one declared instance of EIB financing of energy conservation in one of the ACP/OCT/OD states, a 1979 Special Operations loan, to a Senegal solar energy enterprise (see Appendix 15A). There is also unfortunately little reference in the EIB's publications to substantiate its claim that it has been able to exact environmental standards above those usual in the Associated Countries, for projects it has assisted. However, some reassurance came as a result of questions from Mr. Hemmo Muntingh, a Dutch Euro-MP, on the environmental impacts of the extension of a coal-fired power station in north-east Botswana for which the EIB announced a loan in December 1980. He was informed that the EIB had ensured:

> that the new boiler, like its predecessors, is equipped
> with dust collectors to filter the smoke so that....
> even when the plant is working at full load over a long
> period of time, the dust content will not exceed 450 mg.
> of dust per cubic metre of smoke, which largely cor-

responds to the standards in force in member countries
of the Community for power plants of this type.

and that....

> In any event, the EIB considers that the equipment or
> measures required to protect the environment must form
> an integral part of any investment project for which its
> aid is requested.   Such equipment is covered by the
> overall financing plan for the project approved by the
> Bank.   The same is true of other Community sources of
> financing.[12]

On the latter point, the EIB, of course, now no longer carries out assessments on behalf of the EDF.
      Mr. Ortoli's reply made clear the crucial role
the Bank can play in protecting the environment.
The Special Operations solar power loan was more important.   For EEC encouragement through the EIB of
an indigenous energy source may one day cut dear
fuel imports and perhaps help towards improving the
Associated countries' balances of payment.   It was
perhaps a token of changed EEC attitudes.

g) CHANGING ATTITUDES TO AID AND INVESTMENTS

      The European Investment Bank saw aid to the
Associated Countries as promoting the interests of
both the Community and the recipient countries, the
development of a 'beneficial interdependence'.[13]
Despite increasing amounts of various forms of aid
from Western countries, including the EEC 'Nine',
by the time the first Lomé Convention came into
operation in April 1976, the recipient countries
were not entirely happy about it.[14]   However, the
industrialised countries had started to re-assess
their interventions in Third World countries as
complexities they had not understood became evident
to them, and they began to emphasise self-
sufficiency in food production as the first priority for ACP states.[15]   Some of the international
banks were increasingly uneasy about the growing
trade deficits of non-industrialised countries.
This re-appraisal was epitomised in the Brandt Commission's Report, North-South: A Programme for
Survival, published in 1979.
      The bitter fact was that some of the EEC/
Associated countries, for instance, Zaire and Niger,
had been self-sufficient in food at the time they
gained independence.[16]   However, part of their
growing food deficits resulted from growth in population
lation and the increasing proportion of their
people who were creating a new class of urban poor.
Some part of their problems arose from an abrupt and

unimaginative attempt in which the Bank played a
role to draw them into the world market economy. The
Organisation of African Unity's special summit
meeting, in April 1980, demonstrated Third World
governments' realisation that increased participation in the world market economy alone was not
necessarily beneficial to their countries.   One of
the OAU's main recommendations in its Plan of
Action, therefore, was self-sufficiency in food production, as the magazine, West Africa, reported:

> Over the last two decades, and at a time (when) the
> African Continent is facing a rapid growth in population
> and urbanisation, the food and agriculture situation in
> Africa has undergone a drastic deterioration;   the
> shortfall in food production, coupled with high levels
> of post-harvest losses and periodic severe shortages,
> have led to rapidly increasing dependence on food im-
> ports, resulting in a drain on foreign exchange resources
> and creating major constraints in financing the develop-
> ment of African economies.17

The second Lomé Convention was signed on 31 October,
1979, and came into force on 1st January, 1981.[18]
It embodied all the new ideas first collated in the
OECD's 1976 Study of Trends in World Supply and
Demand of Major Agricultural Commodities, 1975-1985.
        Whereas recognition of the need for environ-
mental protection and conservation of resources inside the Community was still developing only slowly
and positive support from the EIB for projects of
such a kind is as yet small, they appear as basic
in the second Lomé Agreement.   A second essential
element of the new Agreement is that local, indigenous kinds of work, technologies and the views of the
local people shall be taken into account.   These are
the very methods which the Italian government belatedly
started to apply in the Mezzogiorno in 1977.
In line with the statement of the Organisation of
African Unity, the links between industry and other
economic sectors are to be used 'in order to slow
down the rural exodus'.   In the sphere of energy,
the EEC pledged itself to promote environmentally
positive projects and minimise the negative effects
of energy projects.   For the first time, so far as
is known, the EEC was to co-operate in the preparation of inventories on energy resources and demand,
including non-commercial demand, and in establishing
a rural energy programme to meet basic needs.
Assessment of projects and programmes is to be by
analysis not only of their financial and economic
aspects, but also of their technical and social

aspects and they are to include examination of
variants. When local skills will not suffice, the
Community may contribute to training people to enable them to use applied research in order to adapt
technology to their needs. [19]

h) CONCLUSIONS

The will and ability of governments of EEC and
other industrialised countries to help the Third
World has now, however, been impaired by the development of world recession.[20] Their cut-backs in
construction and manufactures have led to a drop in
demand for Third World products. The EEC as a
whole is thus torn between protectionism and the
policies of interdependence, above all their own
dependence on world trade. The Community has, however, so far opted for greater and more thoughtful
assistance to the Third World in opposition to the
policy of the United States, and two of its own members, West Germany and Britain.[21]

The EIB noted in its 1980 Annual Report that,
except for the oil-producing ACP countries: Nigeria,
Gabon, Cameroon, Congo, Trinidad and Tobago, the
economic situation in the developing countries had
grown 'bleaker'. However, there had been significant price increases in their sugar exports, because
of falling world production, and in cotton exports
because of the increase in prices of man-made
fibres. It could therefore congratulate itself on
its financing of production developments in both
these articles. It looked to Lomé II to make 'a
favourable contribution' to the economic development
of ACP states in the future.[22]

A factor which may inhibit future EEC investment may be the failure of Western finance in Turkey
(shown in Chapter 14). As in the Mezzogiorno, mainly
very large companies have the expertise to provide
capital and know-how for some enterprises which non-
industrial countries want and need. The Bank as a
non-profit-making institution is well placed to
assess how far in the long-term some of the projects
in which these companies are interested and which
EEC governments support, may ultimately be beneficial
to all parties concerned, including the host countries.

The re-examination of policies towards the
Third World, which has now begun in the North, together with collective pressure for changes from
those countries, and growing concern about the consequences of financial interventions by the North,
has led to important modifications in the policies
of overseas financing of the European Economic Com-

munity and its European Investment Bank. Compared
with the amounts of cash channelled through the
Bank to projects within the Community, the amounts
to countries outside has been small. But since
many Third World countries did not have cash economies, the impact of even small amounts of finance
has been considerable and enough to orient the
economies of regions in directions in which the
Community countries want them to go. The European
Investment Bank, therefore, bears some responsibility for future as well as for past economic, social
and environmental developments in the countries
associated with the Community.

NOTES

1. Treaty of Rome, Part Four, Art.131 and Annex IV of the
   Treaty.

2. EIB, 1958-1978, 46.

3. EIB, 1968 Annual Report, 134, 140. A large part of infrastructure development in Associated Countries has been
   funded by bilateral EEC grants.

4. EIB, 1968 Annual Report, 134.

5. Ibid, 87. The EIB continually assesses value added,
   foreign exchange earnings, numbers of jobs created and
   the effects on revenues of governments in recipient countries. See EIB, Information, No.13, June 1978.

6. EIB, Operations in the Associated African and Malagasy
   States and Overseas Countries and Territories, pp.8-10.

7. Ibid, 10.

8. Ibid, 11.

9. See Father Patrick O'Mahony, Multinationals and Human
   Rights, 1981, 1.

10. EIB, Information, No.8, February 1977, 7-8. European
    Environmental Bureau, The Community's Financial Instru-
    ments and their Impact on the Environment, July 1980, 8:
    the ACP countries are responsible for drawing up 5-year
    plans of action in respect of EDF and other EEC grants.

11. EIB, Press Release, 36/81, 10 July, 1981.

12. OJ C140/12, 10 June, 1981, Written Question No.2051/80 by
    Mr. Muntingh of 25 February, 1981 and Mr. Ortoli's reply
    of 6 May, 1981. EIB, Press Release, 75/80, 10 December,
    1980.

13. EIB, 1980 Annual Report, 58-60, 62.

14. Financial Times, 28 June, 16 October, 1979.

15. OECD, Study in Trends in World Supply and Demand of Major Agricultural Commodities, 1975-1985, Paris 1976.

16. O. Matzke, 'Agrarian Strategy for the Third World', Swiss Bank Corporation, Prospects, 1981/1, No.177, 7-12; Africa Research Bull., 15 June-14 July, 1976, 3949; Financial Times, 9 July, 1976.

17. West Africa, 26 May, 1980, 915 ff. Financial Times, 28 May, 1980, p.2.

18. Lomé 11 covers 60 ACP countries: OCT and OD countries are covered by a separate Decision, EIB, 1980 Annual Report, 10.

19. Second Lomé Convention, Articles 66 d), e); 68 d), 76 a), g), h), i); 83 2f), 84 a), h); 93, 2i); 112 b); 145-148.

20. Financial Times, 31 October, 1979, 'The Tokyo Round'; 11 May, 1981, Survey, 'World Banking'. Matzke, op. cit.; Idem, A. Schwietert, 'The Recession Risk - and a Chance of Supply-Side Economics', inside front cover.

21. Times, Annual Financial Review, 2 October, 1981, VII, 'Europe is vulnerable to the unstable south'.

22. EIB, 1980 Annual Report, p.17.

APPENDIX 15A: Financing from and through the EIB for ACP/OCT/OD countries is arranged through governments. However, a number of companies are involved, some of them set up with the Bank's help, in which EEC interests may be concerned

Sector	Company	Years	Amounts (m.ua.)
Mining & Quarrying	Soc. Minière de Mauritania (SOMIMA)	1968	11.0
	Soc. Nationale Industrielle et Minière (SNIM - iron) ..	1969	29.0
	Soc. le Nickel (New Caledonia, French territory)	1969	2.0
	Generale des Carrières et des Mines du Zaire (GECA Mines - copper & cobalt)	1971,1974	32.6
	Soc. des Mines du Rwanda (cassiterite & tungsten)	1977	3.0
	Phosvalor & Industries Chimiques du Sénégal (ICS - phosphates)	1978,1980	9.2
	Mines de Fer du Senegal Oriental (MIFERSO)	1979	1.0
	Ghana Consolidated Diamonds Ltd.	1978	0.25
	Roan Consolidated Mines Ltd. (Zambia - cobalt processing: bituminous sandstone)	1979,1980	9.1
	Soc. Kraomita Malagasy (KRAOMA - chrome)	1979	1.0
	Upper Volta Soc. de Récherches d'exploitation Minières (re-opening gold mines - SOREMIL)	1980	11.5
Metal production & semi-processing	Soc. Camerounaise de Transformation de l'Aluminium ..	1965	1.2
	Compagnie Camerounaise de l'Aluminium (ALUCAM) ..	1969	7.6
	Compagnie des Potasses du Congo (CPC)	1976	9.0
	FRIGUIA (Guinea - aluminium)	1980	4.4
Construction materials	Soc. des Cimenteries du Cameroun (CIMECAM - cement & clinker crushing)	1967,1972 1977,1979	10.8
	Soc. des Ciments de l'Afrique de l'Ouest (CIMAO)	1976	11.9
	Chilanga Cement Co. Ltd. (Zambia)	1978,1980	3.6
	Soc. Financière de Dévelopment (SOFIDE)/Soc. des Ciments et Matériaux du Shaba (Zaire)	1977	1.1
	East African Portland Cement Co. Ltd. (Kenya)	1977	3.0

APPENDIX 15A (cont'd.)

Sector	Company	Year	
Conservation of Environment	Soc. Industrielle des Applications de l'Energie Solaire (Sénegal - solar collectors & insulated tanks	1979	0.5
Textiles	Cotonnière Industrielle du Cameroun(CICAM)/Textile du Cameroun pour le Linge de Maison (terry towelling mill)	1965, 1969	6.5
		1970,1979	1.2
	Soc. Textile du Tchad (STT)	1967	4.5
	Soc. Industrielle du Gabon (printed textiles)	1968	5.4
	Union Industrielle de Côte d'Ivoire (UTEXI)	1972	1.7
	La Cotonnière Ivoirienne (COTIVA)	1974	2.4
	SOFIDE (Zaïre)	1971,1977	6.5
	Soc. Nouvelle Nigérienne du Textile	1978	1.0
	Gezira Managil Textile Co. Ltd. (Sudan)	1978	1.0
Food Production & Processing	Soc. Nationale de Conditionnément (SONACO) - bananas	1965	
	Soc. des Ananas de la Côte d'Ivoire (SALCI)	1968	
	Soc. pour le Dévelopment et l'exploitation du Palmier a l'Huile (SODEPALM)	1967	3.7
	Consortium des Légumes et Plantes à Parfum de Côte d'Ivoire (Consortium CL) - fruitjuice & essential oils factory	1969	0.5
	Soc. Ivoirienne de Cocorapé	1977	1.7
	Palmindustrie	1977	7.5
	Soc. Ivoirienne d'Engrais (fertilisers)	1979	5.2
	Soc. Africaine de plantations d'Hevéas (latex processing)	1979	4.6
	Soc. Moulin du Sud-Ouest	1980	3.0
	Soc. Meunière et Agricole du Gabon	1968	0.5
	Les Grands Moulins Voltaiques (GMV) - flour	1970	0.5
	Soc. Camerounaise de Palmeraies (SOCAPALM)	1976	2.3
	Soc. Sucrière Voltaique (SOSUHV) & Republic of Upper Volta	1976	4.4
	Sucrière du Tchad (SONASUT) - to finance the Chad government's majority shareholding in this Company	1976	7.5

(All Ivory Coast)

APPENDIX 15A (cont'd.)

Sector	Company	Years	Amounts (m.ua.)
Food Production & Processing	Soc. Nationale pour le Dévelopment de la Palmeraie et des Huileries (Togo)	1977	6.5
	Dwangwa Sugar Corp. Ltd. (Malawi) ..	1977	7.5
	South Nyanza Sugar Co. Ltd. (Kenya) ..	1977	12.0
	Furfural Co. Ltd. (furfural, acetic aid & formic acid) ..	1977	7.0
	Palmeraies du Zaire (palm oil)	1978	5.4
	Higatura Processing Party Ltd. (palm oil – Papua New Guinea)	1978	8.9
	Demerara Woods Ltd. (financing stake of Guyana government in this Company)	1978	3.2
	Botswana Vaccine Institute (Proprietary) Ltd.	1980	4.0
	Soc. Nationale de Commercialisation des Oléagineux(Sénegal) ..	1980	3.0
Conservation	Soc. Industrielle des Applications de l'Energie Solaire (plant to produce solar collectors & insulated tanks)	1979	0.5

NOTE: Financing by the Bank and through Special Operations, etc. are added together in totals for each enterprise.

SOURCE: EIB, Annual Reports.

Chapter 16

CONCLUSIONS

a) THE EIB'S TECHNICAL SUCCESS

i) Borrowing

The European Investment Bank's technical performance in the banking world has been highly successful.   Within a short space of time it secured
its Triple A rating and, with the vast security of
the assets of the EEC member states behind it, not
only in the form of guarantees on subscribed capital, but also for all operations entailing special
risks, including all those grouped in its Special
Section, it has been able to channel into the Community and Associated States, increasing amounts of
finance through its borrowings on capital markets,
especially that of the United States of America.

As inflationary pressures built up, the Bank
met the rising demands of EEC member states' governments and enterprises for finance and did not show
signs of strain until 1980.   Moreover, it achieved
success with a very limited staff.   Thus, in respect of both its borrowings, and the management of
its own and other EEC investments, its performance
has been impressive.

ii) Management of Financing on behalf of the EEC

Precisely because of its technical success, the
EIB has been able to fulfil its role as the major
long-term financing instrument of the Community. It
has contributed to the development of the Community,
and if that development has not been as 'steady and
balanced' as was hoped in 1958, it has been partly
due to factors outside the control of the Bank.
However, until the early 1970s, overall, standards
of living rose in the EEC countries and the funds
the EIB raised for investment in Community projects

made a significant contribution to this development.

b) THE BOARD OF GOVERNORS AND LENDING POLICIES

Ultimately the crucial determinant of the EIB's performance as a long-term investment body is the governments of the EEC member countries. For they control the Bank's lending policies through their Finance Ministers, who make up the Bank's Board of Governors. Further, the EIB cannot make any loan without the approval of the government of the member state in which the project is situated. It is they subscribe and guarantee the Bank's capital. The Board of Governors appoints the Bank's Directors whose discretion in deciding on loan projects is limited by the guidelines laid down in the Bank's Statute and by the Governors and, to a more limited extent, by the financial and technical viability of projects.

Up to 1980, on the few occasions on which the Bank disapproved of lending policies demanded by member states, the issue has been financial and the Bank's resistance successful. Thus the EIB opposed the use of its own resources for loans to Turkey and other non-EEC countries where they felt the risk was unacceptable and the Special Operations Section was set up as a result. The Bank insisted that the British government provide exchange risk cover to borrowers when the pound was under pressure in 1977, and the government did so.

Despite changes on the Board of Governors occasioned by national elections, the Bank has consistently preferred making large investments in large public and private enterprises. But since 1968 the EIB has allocated an increasing proportion of its financing to small and medium-scale businesses. It was a response partly to the increased volume of requests for financing from smaller businesses, partly to the realisation of their importance as a stabilising social and economic factor, and partly to the awakening of large firms to the importance of their innovative role. Precisely because of that role, particularly as the need for new environmentally sounder technologies was acknowledged, it was unfortunate that the Bank's policy was not to support them more strongly.

Large private concerns more than small, benefitted indirectly from the EIB's infrastructure loans. While in the Community, as a whole, the onus of providing infrastructure has tended to fall on large public rather than on private undertakings, contracts for the construction work involved have

274

generally gone to large private firms.   Secondly,
large firms might have been more hesitant about
taking advantage of the cheaper production costs and
low-interest loans available in industrially under-
developed areas of the EEC, but for the special provision of essential services, often assisted by the
EIB.   Directly and indirectly, the overall effect of
EIB financing has strengthened the trend towards the
concentration of industry into fewer and larger units.
The Bank's lending to small and medium-sized enterprises has been too small to reverse this development.

c)   THE EIB'S LOANS FOR REGIONAL DEVELOPMENT

The Bank's efforts to assist the poorer regions
of the EEC countries have not been wholly successful,
as the richer regions have gained more in prosperity
than the poor, so that major disparities have not
yet been eliminated.   They have worked better in
the south of France and the Rhône valley than in the
south of Italy and the islands, and in the United
Kingdom.   The EIB's interventions in this connection seem to have been most effective in Ireland,
primarily because it is a small country.

There is some evidence that the Bank's assistance has not helped to reconcile the people of all
areas to membership of the Community.   There is
considerable opposition in the United Kingdom and in
the new member, Greece, despite large proportions of
EIB financing devoted to these areas.   In Greenland,
too, in spite of EIB loans for a satellite link and
for harbour facilities, there have been signs, since
the inauguration of home rule in 1979, that the
majority opposition to EEC membership may still pre-
vail.[1]

d)   CONSTRAINTS ON THE BANK'S LENDING POLICIES

The EIB's choice of loan projects is limited
by the normal requirement that it should lend only
to enterprises likely to show a profit, hence its
support for large firms.   However, sometimes other
factors, such as slowing job losses, have been paramount.   With international competition increasing,
it was inevitable that, for instance, the Fiat company, like steel and chemical enterprises, should
experience difficulties and reduce its workforce.[2]

The EIB's choice of loan projects has also been
limited by its need to borrow on capital markets.
For its success depends partly on the approval of
those to whom it looks for funds for its investments.

e) EIB LENDING POLICIES IN ENVIRONMENTAL
   PROTECTION AND ENERGY CONSERVATION

Whereas, until 1970, environmental matters were barely considered, subsequently they have been forming an increasingly important criterion of the EIB's lending. Indeed, the Bank's loans for the environment, natural resources and employment have exceeded the provisions of its Statute in the sense that it was given no special mandate to pay attention to those things. The EIB's influence has been limited by old-fashioned regulations and the relatively weak policies of member states' governments on improving standards. Many of the big infrastructure projects financed partly by the EIB, such as energy and water supplies, were organised and funded before awareness of the importance of the environment was generally realised. Legislation tends to lay down standards for new enterprises, but there is less regulation for those already in existence. The EIB's loans for the development of oil and gas supplies, the fission process in nuclear power, the encouragement of motor traffic and of chemical industries, were made when environmental standards had yet to be modernised. Thus, they helped to create environmental problems of different sorts, as well as improving living standards. The Bank's loans in these cases were double-edged.

Despite the EEC's State of the Environment Reports, there is as yet apparently little recognition, on the part of EEC member governments, of the need for a fundamental change in economic imperatives.[3] The arguments for environmental protection and conservation were cogently stated in 1972 by the Club of Rome. They were endorsed by the US Senate when it agreed to Senator Pell's Amendment which lays a responsibility on the US government to conclude a treaty in international environmental impact assessments.[4] Yet there seems to have been little response from the EEC in practice. Hence the Bank has continued to be bound by old economic categories.

One heartening sign of moves towards the adoption of more modern standards has been the upgrading, in 1981, of the Commission's Environment and Consumer Protection Service to the status of a Directorate General covering the Environment, Consumer Protection and Nuclear Safety (DG XI). The agreement to the Directive on compulsory Environmental Impact Assessments will also help when it becomes effective in 1982. The restiveness displayed towards it in some quarters, and the question of permitted derogations from its requirements, should by then have been largely resolved, and member states should have created the necessary legal measures to ensure its observance. As they do this, in line with Article 20 (6) of its Statute, the EIB can use its Technical Assessment procedure to back the Directive.

While the Bank is now being more explicit in its Annual Reports and other publications about environmental aspects of its loans, this is an area in which more information would be useful. It may well be that it has been more exigent in its requirements from borrowers than appears, and has been doing itself a disservice by its reticence on such matters.

f) RELATIONS BETWEEN THE EIB AND THE COMMISSION OF THE EUROPEAN COMMUNITIES

The relationships between the EIB and the Commission have been becoming closer since 1977, as the Bank has been managing new Commission funding instruments. The present recession has tended in the same direction, as the Bank's President, M. Yves Le Portz, indicated in his 1981 statement to the annual meeting of the Bank's Board of Governors. Adversity is rendering co-operation more necessary.

The result has been more emphasis on the Bank's agency role. Originating in its handling of risk capital operations on behalf of member states' governments, the Bank itself institutionalised this aspect of its operations when it set up its Special Section to deal with financing in Turkey in 1963. When, as a result of the deepening recession, member states' governments sought to raise more finance on the world's capital markets, by empowering the Commission to act on their behalf, the Bank's expertise in carrying out these operations was invoked through this apparatus.

The large amounts which the Commission was to lend for nuclear and other energy provision, and for various infrastructural schemes, raised the prospect of its almost rivalling the EIB as a lending institution in the Community. However, precisely because of the recession, the possibility of raising these additional large amounts on top of the Bank's own borrowings has receded.

It is important that the EIB's autonomy should not be eroded. For it is one of many EEC anomalies, that while the Commission and the Community, as a whole, may be in advance of member governments on the need for structural changes and environmen-

tal protection, it seems that the Bank is, if anything, even more sensitive to public concern, since,
like any other bank, it sees social stability as a
prerequisite of secure financing. The very slim-
ness of the Bank's staffing makes it theoretically
more easily accessible than the labyrinthine Departments of the Commission, witness the fact that
in the matter of environmental policy and parameters
it now makes available more information than is
obtainable in its reports. In this respect, it
compares favourably with many large firms and private banks.

g) THE BANK'S REACTIONS TO STRUCTURAL CHANGES IN MEMBER STATES' ECONOMIES

One of the most disturbing features of the
EIB's operations, and one which is highly relevant
to environmental protection and energy conservation,
is that, although it is primarily a long-term lending institution, the policies pursued by EEC member
governments (and those, therefore, to which the expertise of the Bank has been to, some extent,
directed) have been short-term. As the Commission
of the European Communities pointed out in the
autumn of 1981, since their terms of office are
limited, member states' governments tend to pay more
attention to immediate issues which bring immediate
political benefits. Thus, in the Commission's view,
they lack objectivity. There has been a tendency
for member states' governments, especially when
faced with economic difficulties, to rush into projects that are dubious environmentally, economically
and socially, and to use the EIB to support such
projects. Thus, in the later 1960s, some of them
were looking to large chemical undertakings in reaction to the crisis of 1964-67; when the oil
prices rose, they rushed into nuclear energy; when
the steel industry was patently under threat from
overseas competition, the Bank was enlisted to pour
funds into modernisation and conversion of units
that subsequently had to be abandoned. With the result that, in such cases, there is little sense of
sober medium- or long-term planning.

The Commission itself, however, is to some
extent culpable. Its demands for a medium and
long-term planning body, in 1981, are inexplicable
since such bodies were set up in 1964.[5]

Perhaps the most crucial failure of the Community and of the Bank, as its main long-term
financing instrument, has been the delay in promoting diversification of the industrial structures of

the EEC countries when the effects of the destruction of work by automation and other technological means, and of cheaper goods from the Newly Industrialising countries of Asia, the 'NICs', were first acknowledged in the mid-1960s. These aspects of the current economic crisis in the West are more significant than the raising of oil prices by Arab states.

The Bank's increased support for small and medium-sized enterprises from 1968 onwards was the first indication of reaction to changing economic attitudes. But it continued to concentrate on the modernisation and conversion of enterprises in the face of severe competition from overseas, when its funding could have been used to build up sectors more likely to survive, and so to provide more long-term jobs for those bound to be made redundant in industries under threat. It would seem that there is still an inability to make use of the EIB as an instrument in effecting structural changes, partly because of vested interests in the present economic structure.

In 1974, the EIB claimed:

> perhaps the main lesson from the experience of the severe economic and financial pressures to which the European Community was subjected in 1974 is the importance of the role of confidence in the field of investment.[6]

Yet, by 1981, the economic and social concepts that dominated the Community's development and the choice of projects financed by the EIB were the subject of agonising reappraisals within the Community. There was an acknowledgment of shortcomings in huge motorways, linking one vast conurbation to another, of the unlimited consumption of natural resources and a disregard for the consequences of large-scale development of various energy sources and chemicals.

As a Council of Europe seminar concluded in April 1981:

> the background to the urban crisis lay not only in the crisis of the Western economic system but also in the crisis affecting urban models successively put forward in this century as ultimate, universal solutions.[7]

The 'prospect of continuous, unlimited urban development' had to be reviewed. M. Le Portz, President of the Bank, himself spoke at the 1981

Annual Meeting of the Board of Governors, of 'disquieting levels of underemployment.' His belief was that they were growing particularly in areas faced with the most acute structural weaknesses, because of the inadequacy in investments in energy and the importance of more rational utilisation of energy if long-term economic revival was not to be compromised. By 1981, the situation on the capital markets was so bad that he bluntly told the Board of Governors that the demand for loans could not be met. He explained that:

> Member States' measures to curb inflation, defend national currencies and maintain external trade balances in equilibrium have led to very high short-term interest rates which in turn have caused pressure on long-term interest rates and extremely irregular trends on capital markets....It has rarely been as difficult as it is today to reconcile the need for short-term equilibrium with the objectives of long-term re-organisation and growth, and the target of curbing inflation or achieving a balance of payments equilibrium with concern for industrial activity and employment,[8]

h) THE EIB AND THE NON-EEC RECIPIENTS OF LOANS

The failure to diversify and the mistake of trying to export infrastructure and industrialism on the northern EEC model has caused problems in peasant and even pre-peasant economies outside the Community. The social costs of projects involving large multi-national companies, whether in chemicals or in nuclear power, oil and gas developments, have to be reckoned internationally, if only because the major firms concerned are international.

The EIB's role in assisting the imposition on non-industrial countries of technological and social developments now acknowledged to be seriously flawed is, therefore, also in question. Here, too, both the types of project supported and the concepts of development applied are under review as the monied North is realising that the problems of the development of Third World countries are far more complex than they had realised.

The Bank has helped to improve living standards through infrastructure loans and has played a part in developing indigenous industrial enterprises. Its importance has lain in its ability to arrange financing rather than its own loans, in its management of European Development Fund grants, which have been much larger than its own investments, and risk

capital operations on behalf of EEC member states,
and in arranging joint investments with other
public and private financing bodies.   It has helped
to add to the widening gap between 'North-South'
because the bulk of the funds it has gathered on the
world's markets have gone not to the poor countries
of the 'South', but to the relatively well off EEC
countries.   Of these, only the south of Italy had
living standards roughly on a par with those of
some ACP/OCT/OD countries.   It has thus played a
part in increasing the growing disparity between the
wealthy and poor nations.

But notwithstanding economic recession, the
Community as a whole has not abandoned the aim
expressed in the Treaty of Rome, of furthering 'the
interests and prosperity of the inhabitants of
these countries'.   It is too dependent on them.
Despite the hard line adopted by two of its member
states, the Federal Republic of Germany and, particularly, the United Kingdom, it produced in 1981
a plan of action to tackle world hunger and poverty.[9]   Proposed measures, which the Bank, as a Community financing instrument, would have a role in
financing, include the reduction of waste, the pre-
vention of the destruction of forests and of the
spread of deserts into arable land.   Meanwhile, as
a result of yet another agonising reappraisal and,
perhaps, at the instance of the governments of some
of the recipient countries, the emphasis in EIB
lending has showed signs of changing in favour of
small and medium-scale enterprises, and a few co-
operative ventures.

i) PUBLIC RESPONSIBILITY FOR EIB POLICIES

However, if the policies upheld and developed
through EIB interventions have created problems,
the fault does not lie solely with the Bank, or its
Board of Governors.   The consensus on the kind of
economic development pursued in the Community was
not merely governmental;   it was broadly supported
by the majority of EEC citizens.   For the Community countries are, at any rate, constitutionally
democracies.   The populations have some freedom of
speech and of assembly, and they have been using
them to some purpose, as witness the changing attitudes to the environment, to waste, to conservation.
The questioning of the possibility of 'safe' nuclear
power has slowed down, even halted, programmes in
the Federal Republic of Germany.   Public opposition
does not make for secure investments, as the EIB
well knows.   It is disquieting, therefore, that

there have been signs that public opinion is being
muffled in France and it has been mooted in Britain.
For instance, in 1979, a working party was set up:

> ....because of increasing unease about the effects
> of public participation and the number of contro-
> versial public enquiries on motorways and energy
> developments.

Mr. Michael Heseltine, Secretary of State for the
Environment, therefore proposed that it should
take place only '.....within a structured framework.'10

M. Le Portz, in 1980, referred to the possible
necessity in the future of more stringent choices
of loan projects, thus confirming that the Bank has
a choice.   By its selection of projects, it can
assist a redefinition of goals and strategies.
It is up to the citizens of the Community to bring
pressure to bear insofaras they wish to ensure
that the direction of loans should be towards improving the quality of life.   However, in 1981,
M. Le Portz pointed out that the immediate future
for the EIB had become 'rather unclear' because of
difficulties in raising finance.   Hence, he pointed
out that the Bank could not resolve difficulties
solely by its operations and ability to adapt.
Yet, in spite of his gloomy review of the
world's capital markets, in some ways the outlook
for EIB lending is more hopeful than in the past.
Firstly, there is the re-orientation of the Community's aid policies towards countries outside the
Community in favour of a greater environmental concern.   Then there are tangible proofs of change in
the Bank's policies.   Finally, M. Le Portz himself
added in his 1981 review, that the Bank would

> make as positive a contribution as possible by
> drawing on its borrowing capacity, experience and
> imagination (author's italics).....

An unexpected word from a banker, yet one that
augurs some attention to conservation, waste recycling, environmental protection, intermediate
technologies and other initiatives lagging for want
of financial commitment.   These are areas where,
according to the EEC Commission, there is some hope
of increasing employment.

NOTES

1. _Times_, 21 August, 1981.

2. Ibid.

3. See R.E.Stein and B. Johnson, _Banking on the Biosphere_, Lexington, Mass., and Toronto, 1979, for impacts of various developmental Banks and Funds.

4. USA 95th Congress, Second Session, S. Res. 49 (Report No.95-990), 21 July, 1978.

5. _Times_, 14 October, 1981.

6. EIB, _Investment in the Community and its financing_, 1974, 43.

7. Council of Europe, _Forum_, No.2, 1981, 6-7.

8. EIB, _Information_, No.26, July 1981, 4-5.

9. _Times_, 2 October, 1981, Special Suppl., 'Rich Man, Poor Man....', viii; 5 October, 1981.

10. _Times_, 29 February, 1980.

11. EIB, _Information_, No. 26, July 1981, 5

I N D E X

285